Wilhelm Geiger, Friedrich Heinrich Hugo Windischmann, Darab dastur Peshotan Sanjana

Zarathushtra in the Gathas, and in the Greek and Roman classics

Wilhelm Geiger, Friedrich Heinrich Hugo Windischmann, Darab dastur Peshotan Sanjana

Zarathushtra in the Gathas, and in the Greek and Roman classics

ISBN/EAN: 9783743373167

Manufactured in Europe, USA, Canada, Australia, Japa

Cover: Foto ©Thomas Meinert / pixelio.de

Manufactured and distributed by brebook publishing software (www.brebook.com)

Wilhelm Geiger, Friedrich Heinrich Hugo Windischmann, Darab dastur Peshotan Sanjana

Zarathushtra in the Gathas, and in the Greek and Roman classics

ZARATHUSHTRA IN THE GATHAS.

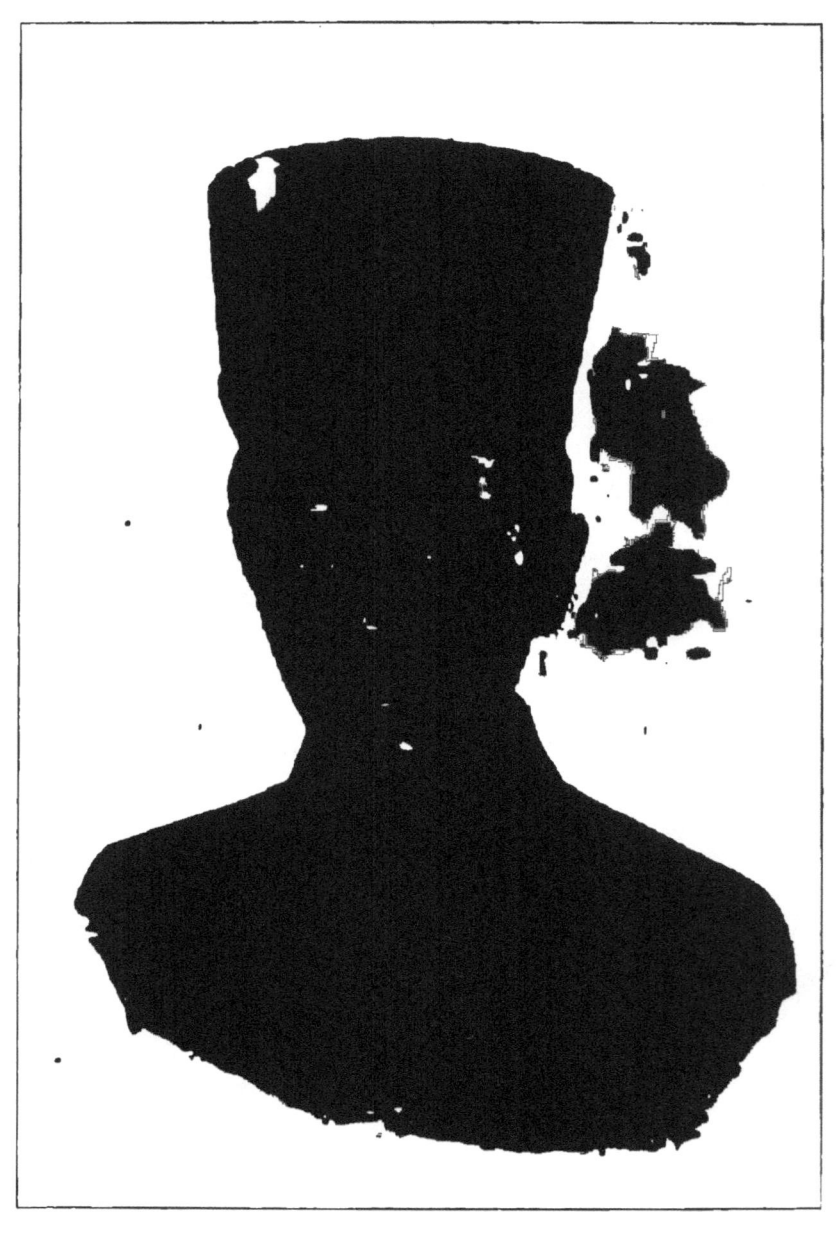

Yours ffS
C. M. Cursetjee

ZARATHUSHTRA IN THE GATHAS.

AND IN

THE GREEK AND ROMAN CLASSICS,

Translated from the German

OF

DRS. GEIGER AND WINDISCHMANN,

WITH NOTES ON M. DARMESTETER'S THEORY REGARDING
THE DATE OF THE AVESTA,

AND

AN APPENDIX,

BY

DARAB DASTUR PESHOTAN SANJANA, B.A.

LEIPZIG: OTTO HARRASSOWITZ.

1897.

LOAN STACK

ALL RIGHTS RESERVED.

BL1570
G4
1897

Dedication.

Inscribed

TO

THE PIOUS MEMORY

OF THE LATE

Mr. KHARSHEDJI MANECKJI KHARSHEDJI.[1]

"When Faith and Love, which parted from thee never,
   Ripened thy youthful soul to dwell with God,
   Meekly thou didst resign this earthy load
Of death, called life, which us from life doth sever.

Thy works, and alms, and all thy good endeavour,
   Stayed not behind, nor in the *kate* were trod;
   But, as Faith pointed with her golden rod,
Followed thee up to joy and bliss for ever.

Love led them on, and Faith, who knew them best
   Thy handmaids,[2] clad them o'er with purple beams
   And azure wings, that up they flew so drest,

And spake the truth of thee on glorious themes
   Before the Judge; who thenceforth bid thee rest,
   And drink thy fill of pure immortal[3] streams."[4]

---

[1] The son of Sir Jamshedji Jijibhai, Bart., C. S. I., who, if he had survived, would have become the Fourth Baronet of the Sir Jamshedji family.

[2] *Cfr.* Hâdôkht Nask II, 22, *seq* :—

[3] *Ibid*, II, 38.

[4] *Cfr.* Milton's Sonnet XIV.

CONTENTS.

ZARATHUSHTRA IN THE GATHAS.

	PAGE
Introduction	1
I.—The Authorship of the Gâthâs	9
II.—The Religious and Social Reform of Zarathushtra	18
III.—Zarathushtra's Monotheism	28
IV.—The Theology of the Gâthâs	38
V.—Zoroastrianism is not a Dualistic Religion	50

VIEWS OF THE CLASSICAL WRITERS REGARDING ZOROASTER AND HIS DOCTRINE.

Pythagoras	65
Democritus	73
Xanthus the Lydian	74
Herodotus	81
Plato	83
Diogenes of Laërte	85
Eudoxus	86
Dino	86
Aristotle	91
Theopompus	92
Plutarch	93
Hermodorus	102
Sotion	104
Hermippus	106
Strabo	115
Agathias	120
Plinius	121
Berosus	125
Moses of Chorene	128
Cephalion	129
Syncellus	131
Clementinian Recognitions	132
Clementinian Homilies	134

Dio Chrysostom 135
THE ALLEGED PAHLAVI LETTER OF TANSAR
   TO THE KING OF TABARISTAN 143
OBSERVATIONS ON DARMESTETER'S THEORY. 153

THE GERMAN TEXT OF "ZARATHUSHTRA IN DEN GATHAS."

Einleitung 159
I.—Die Autorschaft des Gâthâs 164
II.—Die religiöse und soziale Reform Zarathushtra's ... 170
III.—Zarathushtra's Monotheismus 177
IV.—Die Theologie der Gâthâs 184
V.—Ist die zoroastrische Religion eine dualistische ? ... 192

APPENDIX 205-256
   THE ALLEGED PRACTICE OF CONSANGUINEOUS
    MARRIAGES IN ANCIENT IRAN

OPINIONS 257

PREFACE.

It is now fully ten years since the Oxford Clarendon Press issued in two volumes my English translation of the German of Dr. Wilhelm Geiger's *Ostirânische Kultur im Altertum*. This volume on *Zarathushtra in the Gâthâs and in the Western Classics* was then intended to have been the third of that series. But owing to the precedence of publication which I have given to my editions of some of the important Pahlavi Texts, this volume had to be put off for several years.—The essay on "Zarathushtra in the Gâthâs" is the rendering of the German MS. text of Dr. Geiger, which is for the first time printed in this volume (*vide* pp. 159 *seq*). It may be regarded as the first concise and lucid discourse upon the authorship, theology, and monotheism of the Avestic Gâthâs, the oldest and most sacred hymns of the Zoroastrians. Herein Dr. Geiger is able to draw from his close research the following inferences :—(1) The Irânians had in very olden time, and without any foreign influence, independently acquired through the Zoroastrian Reform, the possession of a monotheistic religion, and its founders had attained to that stage in ethics to which only the best parts of the Old Testament rise. (2) The Irânians display an inclination towards that depth of moral intuition which is perceptible in Christianity ; at a very early period the Gâthâs knew about the ethical triad of the righteous thought, the righteous word, and the righteous deed.

The second essay on Zoroaster in the Classical Writers is selected and translated from the late Dr. F. Windischmann's posthumous work, *Zororastrische Studien*. The German heading under which this essay is given, is *Stellen der Alten über Zoroastrisches*, "References in Ancient Writings to Zoroaster and his Doctrine." It is highly interesting, giving as it does a comprehensive collection of the foreign views of classical authors regarding the Persian Zoroaster and his Revelation.

As a supplement or appendix to the latter I have inserted in this volume my refutatory discourse on the Alleged Practice of Consanguineous Marriages in Ancient Irân to which the classical writers allude, as will be noticed from my translation of Windischmann's German.

As to the theory of the age of the Avesta, which I have here briefly touched upon, it is a pleasure to observe that those who imagine, like Darmesteter, a later origin for the Avesta, are compelled to assume that they were written in a dead language with all the older forms of the names. But this explanation presupposes that Avesta scholars in the time of Vologeses were already acquainted with the philological arguments developed in the nineteenth century A. D., which is absurd.

I must take this opportunity of acknowledging my deep gratitude to the learned friends who have kindly rendered me very prompt assistance in the course of my work. I have also to thank the Trustees of the Sir Jamshedjee Jeejeebhai Translation Fund for their kind patronage to this volume.

DARAB DASTUR PESHOTAN SANJANA.

15th December 1897.

ZARATHUSHTRA IN THE GATHAS.[1]

GENERAL REMARKS.

Every religion, wheresoever and whensoever it may have sprung up, has its history and its development. No religion appears of a sudden as something perfectly novel and unexpected. The eye of the historical investigator who seeks to prove and understand every event in the history of mankind according to causes and effects, will perceive that every new form of religion is preceded by a period of time which we may call the period of preparation. At such a period there appear certain phenomena in the intellectual, moral, and economical life of the people which point to an imminent revolution of ideas. As these phenomena become more numerous and more powerful the desire for a reformation of the whole system of life will become more and more powerful and vigorous, until, one might say, with a certain natural necessity, the personage appears who will be able to give an expression to the wishes and hopes of all the people, and thus turn out to be the founder of a new doctrine. To the contemporary this doctrine may in sooth appear as something quite unexpected and unheard of; because he cannot yet grasp the causes and effects of the events which he himself lives to behold. But the historical inquirer who is capable of doing it, will trace the phenomena which prepare such an important event,

---

[1] *Vide* the German text.

and he will discover them everywhere and at all times, whether he turns his attention to the history of Christianity or Islamism, of Buddhism or Zoroastrianism.

As every religion has, however, its pre-history, so it has also its development. Not only do the natural religions of the wild Africans, Americans, and Australians contain a continuous transformation and variation, such is also the case, although in a smaller measure, with the so-called book-religions, *i. e.*, with the religions which depend upon sacred documents as compendia of their doctrines, as the rule and standard for the life of their adherents.[1] Even in the Jewish religion, so far as it is known to us in the Old Testament, we discover traces of development and decay. It has not entered on its existence as something finished and complete from the beginning; but it has also undergone decay as well as development and improvement.

Now the investigator who has made the contents and the history of any of the religious systems the theme of his discourse, will have to face the task of never losing sight of the idea of development and of tracing the course of this development. He will have to give himself the trouble of establishing, if possible, the original or primitive form of the religion, and of distinguishing the oldest form from what has been added to it in the course of time, and from what must indispensably have been added to it. I say "indispensably," because as the religion of a nation must be reckoned as one of its most important social advantages, so it will experience, like all other social endowments, certain changes in the course of centuries. The general social standard

---

[1] 1 Comp. Prof. Max-Müller's "Lectures on the Origin and Development of Religion," pp. 149-150.

of the people becomes altered, their economical conditions are changed, even their dwellings may be transplanted; therewith also ideas and views, thoughts and learning, undergo their changes, and even what man preserves as his highest and holiest good, his religion, will adapt itself to such transformations. The substance, the nature, and the kernel of the thing remain the same, unless a people breaks entirely with customs and tradition, and endeavours to search out entirely new ways; but the old contents are embodied into new forms, and this must be so if religion is not to lose that power in the social life of the people by which it moves and always animates afresh the intellect and the heart. It is self-evident that it is only then possible to find out or establish the original substance of any religious doctrine, when literary materials are extant which either proceed from the founder of the doctrine itself or at least are traceable to his time, and which thereby bear the stamp of truth and authenticity.

If we make an attempt in the following pages to trace back to its oldest and most primitive form the Zoroastrian doctrine which, after a duration of certainly twenty-five centuries, and after an eventful history of battles and triumphs, persecutions and successes, is professed even now-a-days by about 100,000 persons, the question arises whether this is altogether still possible. Do we possess documents, the composition of which may be ascribed to the founder, or which had at least their origin in his time and perhaps belonged to the circle of his first adherents and friends? We can answer this question in the affirmative; for we are in fact still in the possession of such documents, and *such documents are the Gâthâs, i..e., the holy hymns, which constitute the oldest portion of the Avesta, the Religious Book of the Zoroastrians.*

It is here superfluous to characterize in detail the form and contents of the Gâthâs. They form, as is well known, a part of the *Yasna, i.e*, of the holy manual which is prescribed for recitation at the sacrificial ceremonies. However, they stand in no intimate connection with the Yasna; but they are inserted quite irregularly, and without coherence with the rest of the text, in that part of the Yasna where their recitation, corresponding to the ritual, has to be performed during the divine service. Consequently, the Gâthâs form for themselves an independent whole, just as the sacred law-book, the Vendidâd, the chapters of which are in a quite analogous manner inserted between the different sections of the Yasna in the manuscripts of the so-called *Vendidâd-Sâde*. From the rest of the Avesta, *viz.*, the *Yasna*, together with the *Visperad*, the *Vendidâd*, and the *Yashts*, the Gâthâs are already distinguished externally by the metrical form in which they are composed—which reminds us often of the metre of the hymns of the Rig-veda—as well as by their language which differs materially from the ordinary Avesta dialect.

The extent of the Gâthâs is unfortunately scanty. From my calculations the following figures are given which might not be without interest:—

1. Gâthâ *Ahunavaiti*, 300 lines; about 2,100 words. (*Yasna*, chaps. XXVIII-XXXIV).

2. Gâthâ *Ushtavaiti*, 330 lines; about 1,850 words. (*Yasna*, chaps. XLIII-XLVI).

3. Gâthâ *Spentâ-mainyû*, 164 lines; about 900 words. (*Yasna*, chaps. XLVII-L).

4. Gâthâ *Vohû-khshathra*, 66 lines; about 450 words. (*Yasna*, chap. LI).
5. Gâthâ *Vahishtô-ishti*, 36 lines; about 260 words. (*Yasna*, chap. LIII).

Hence these Gâthâs contain in all 896 lines and about 5,660 words. Now this is in itself scanty enough. But the matter is rendered even more discouraging by the considerable difficulties which the interpretation of the Gâthâs offers in many passages. Several lines and strophes are so obscure that it is difficult to settle a definite translation. Very often we are compelled to admit that the one as well as the other rendering is possible; however, none can be regarded as absolutely right, and none as absolutely false. But such obscure strophes and lines are either not at all, or only with the greatest reserve and caution, to be admitted as proofs for any essential exposition of the subject to be treated. Often enough, too, a translator will regard as certain and doubtless what others will dispute. *Under all circumstances the utmost precaution is urgently required in making use of the Gáthâs for any material explanation of the Zoroastrian doctrine.*[*]

While writing this discourse we have been well aware of all these difficulties. Nevertheless, we are able to assert that the original form of Zoroastrianism, the philosophical and religious ideas of its founder and of its first professors can be represented, at least in their general features, upon the basis of the Gâthâ texts, and that such a glimpse into the earliest ages of *one of the purest and most sublime religions which have ever existed,*[*] must be considered as exceedingly instructive.

---

[*] The *Italics* are marked by an asterisk when they are mine.— Trans. note.

Regarding the Gâthâs, we directly meet with an objection in the beginning of our research, which must be refuted before we can enter into the subject before us. The points in question may be summed up as follows: Whether the Gâthâs proceed from Zarathushtra or his first adherents or disciples; whether they actually reach back to the primitive age of Zoroastrianism; nay, whether they are in general older than the rest of the Avesta. Among the Avesta scholars in Europe there are many who dispute all these points, who want to make Zarathushtra a "mythical" person, and who take the differences between the Gâthâs and the rest of the Avesta to be not of a temporal but of a local nature. Thus they assume that the Gâthâs were composed in other parts of Irân than, for example, the Yashts and the Vendidâd, and especially that the difference of the dialects is sufficiently explained from this circumstance. However, this idea seems to lose more and more ground in modern times, and the latest translator of the Gâthâs, the Rev. Dr. L. H. Mills, maintains their antiquity with great resoluteness.

The metrical form of the Gâthâs can scarcely be adduced as proof for their higher antiquity,* because in the rest of the Avesta we also find numerous pieces which were orginally composed in metre. In many passages the metre is still preserved intact. In other passages no doubt the text must first be cleared from the additions and interpolations made in the first redaction of the Avesta. Already of greater importance would be the circumstance that the majority of the verses in the Gâthâs is so well preserved, incomparably better than in the metrical fragments of the remaining Avesta. This certainly proves that in the redaction mentioned, above the Gâthâs are looked upon as something holier and more inviolable [*lit.*, " untouchable "] than the texts otherwise transmitted to us.

The anomalous dialect of the Gâthâs, too, does not prove to us that they are older than the rest of the Avesta.* The dialect of the former indeed shows many forms which are more antiquated, but also many which seem to be more polished and changed. All this is far better explained by a local than by a temporal difference of the two dialects.

But what undoubtedly distinguishes the Gâthâs from all the other parts of the Avesta and *marks them as far older, is their contents,** which evidently carry us into the period of the foundation of the new doctrine, into the time when Zarathushtra and his first adherents still lived and worked, while in the younger Avesta they are no doubt personalities of a remote past.

This has already been set forth by me most decidedly on a former occasion in my "Ostirânische Kultur im Alterthûm,"[1] and our exposition is yet in no way confuted. Lately Dr. Mills[2] has expressed the same ideas :—" In the Gâthâs all is sober and real. The Kine-soul is indeed poetically described as wailing aloud, and the Deity with His Immortals is reported as speaking, hearing, and seeing; but with these rhetorical exceptions everything which occupies the attention is practical in the extreme. Grehma and Bendva, the Karpans, the Kavis, and the Usijs (-ks) are no mythical monsters. No dragon threa-

---

[1] Compare the " Civilization of the Eastern Iranians in Ancient Times," by Darab Dastur Peshotan Sanjana, Oxford Edition, Vol. II., p. 116 *seq.*

[2] The Zend Avesta, Part III, The Yasna, etc., translated by L. H. Mills (The Sacred Books of the East, Vol. XXXI., Introduction, p. xxvi.).

tens the settlements, and no fabulous beings defend them. Zarathushtra, Jâmâspa, Frashaoshtra, and Maidhyô-mâh, the Spitâmas, Hvôgvas, the Haêchat-aspas, are as real, and are alluded to with a simplicity as unconscious as any characters in history. Except inspiration, there are also no miracles."

We shall still often have occasion to refer to this, I might say, realistic character of the Gâthâs, and the truth of the thesis established by us above, that *the Gâthâs belong to the epoch of the foundation of Zoroastrianism,** will then in due course appear to the reader himself. It will occur above all when we fix our eyes upon the parts played by Zarathushtra and the other characters in the Gâthâs, who in the traditional history of the Parsees are regarded as his contemporaries.

The later legend regarding Zarathushtra, his life, and his works, furnishes us with the following details from which we have excluded all embellishments which can easily be recognised as such.[1] Zarathushtra is descended from a kingly family. His pedigree can be traced back to Minucheher. Among his forefathers are Spitama and Haêchat-aspa. Pourushaspa is his father. The holy religion is revealed to Zarathushtra by Ahura Mazda; and by Zarathushtra first of all to Maidyô-mâh, the son of Zarathushtra's uncle Arâsti. At the command of God Zarathushtra goes to the court of King Gushtâsp of Baktria, in order to promulgate his doctrine there. The wise Jâmâspa is the King's minister. The prophet succeeds in winning him over to himself, as well as his brother Frashaoshtra, next the King himself and his

---

[1] *Cfr.* Spiegel, *Eránische Altertumskunde*, Vol. I, p. 684 *seq* :—
"Gushtâsp and Zoroaster," translated from the German of Spiegel, by Darab Dastur Peshotan Sanjana, *vide* Vol. II of the "Civilization of the Eastern Iránians," pp. 189—192.

consort, and therewith he puts the new faith on a firm footing. Zarathushtra married Hvôvi, a daughter of Jâmâspa. He died at a mature age, having been destined to live long enough to witness the first fruits of his announcement of the religion.

CHAPTER I.

THE AUTHORSHIP OF THE GÂTHÂS.

Now we cast a glance at the names of persons occurring in the Gâthâs. It is very remarkable that they all relate to the legend about Zarathushtra as we have already abridged it by excluding from it all exaggerations. We find mentioned the names of Zarathushtra, Vîshtâspa, Jâmâspa, Pourushaspa, besides Maidhyô-mâogh; the family names of Hvôgva, Spitâma, and Haêchat-aspa; and the families of Jâmâspa and Zarathushtra themselves. Lastly, the daughter of the prophet is mentioned. But, with a single exception, we find none of the names very often occurring in the well-known heroic legends of Irân and also in the remaining parts of the Avesta—neither Thraêtaona nor Keresâspa, neither Haoshyagha nor Kavî Husrava nor Arjat-aspa. Yima only is named in a single passage.

Is this a mere accident? Or, rather, is not the assumption more probable that the Gâthâs are descended from Zarathushtra himself and his companions, and delineate the experience, hopes, wishes, and fears of that narrow circle from which they have emanated? It will be easy to ascertain the truth of this assumption, if we undertake to examine the passages where these names occur.

Zarathushtra is, to my knowledge, named altogether sixteen times in the entire Gâthâs; in the Gâthâ Ahunavaiti three times, in the Gâthâ Ushtavaiti five times, in the Gâthâ Speutâ-mainyu twice, in the Gâthâ Vohu-khshathra twice, and lastly, more often in proportion to its extent, four times in the Gâthâ Vahishtô-ishti. Nevertheless, this last Gâthâ plainly appears to me to be the youngest of all. The introductory strophes in which Zarathushtra, Kavî Vîshtâspa, Pouru-chishta, the daughter of Zarathushtra, and Frashaoshtra are mentioned, seem to me to comprehend a retrospective view of the Zoroastrian epoch. I do not believe that these strophes have originated directly from any of these persons.

Of greater importance are the passages wherein Zarathushtra speaks of himself in the first person. As for instance, *Yasna* XLVI, 19, says:—" He who in righteousness seeks to evince goodness to me — to me Zarathushtra—for him the heavenly spirits will grant as a reward that which is most fit to strive for, namely, the eternal beatitude." I mean, it is evident, that we have here before us words uttered by Zarathushtra himself. Such a passage is perfectly distinguished from the passages of the later Avesta, wherein the prophet does not speak himself, but is made to speak by the composer of the texts; as for example, the beginning of *Yasna* IX (which undoubtedly contains an old hymn, but which at the first glance seems to have originated long after Zarathushtra) when it says:—"At the time of morning Haoma came to Zarathushtra as he was consecrating the fire and reciting aloud the Gâthâs. And Zarathushtra asked Haoma:—'Who art thou then, O man! Who art of all the incarnate world the most beautiful in thine own body of those whom I have seen, O glorious one ?' "

We are certainly authorized from the entirely distinct manner in which Zarathushtra is mentioned in the former and the latter passage, to draw a conclusion as to their relative age. In an analogous way Prof. Oldenberg has recently proved a remarkable distinction between the older and the younger hymns of the Rig-veda, according as the manner of the poet's expression is such and such, which may or may not demonstrate the fact of his having been synchronous with certain historical events. Thus Rigveda VII, 18, is distinguished from the rest of the hymns of the same book as far older, because its author speaks of the great battle which King Sudâs fought as of something which had but just happened, while in other hymns mention is made of the same battle as an event of the past time.

But if we accept the strophe, *Yasna* XLVI, 19, as the words of Zarathushtra, we might just as well assert the same undoubtedly for all the hymns contained in the same chapter. It is, however, uncommonly rich in personal allusions. In the 14th strophe Zarathushtra is accosted with the words : " O Zarathushtra, who is thy friend ?" This, nevertheless, does not at all controvert our opinion that all these hymns originate from Zarathushtra himself. The poet in a purely poetical liveliness lets this question be put to himself, upon which he himself gives the answer : " It is he himself, Kavî Vîshtâspa." Expressed in other words, the passage simply means : " I have found no better friend and adherent than Kavî Vîshtâspa. "

Further on, the poet, *i. e.*, Zarathushtra, alludes to his own family, the Spitâmidæ, and makes mention of Frashaoshtra and Dê Jâmâspa, and, at the end, in the words quoted above, speaks of himself in the first person. And he promises all those that joined him, paradise as the reward of the faithful.

If we next refer to the Gâthâ Ushtavaiti, we find in it another hymn, *viz.*, *Yasna* XLIII, which vividly reminds us of what is described above. Here, too, the poet asks himself the question :—Who art thou then, and whose son ? And again he gives the answer himself : " I am Zarathushtra, an open enemy of all evil ; but to the pious I will be a powerful helper as long as I am able to do so." And the poet concludes this time with a reference to himself in the third person : "Now Zarathushtra and with him all those who adhere to Ahura Mazda, declare themselves for the world of the Good Spirit."

This use of the third person, when the poet speaks of himself, should not surprise us. It is found exactly so in the Rig-veda. Here it is said :— " So has the Vasishtha, *i. e.*, I, the singer, who is descended from the race of the Vasishtha, praised the powerful Agni " (VII, 42, 6) ; and then again :—" We, the Vasishthas, wish to be thy adorers" (VII, 37, 4) ; and so on expressed in one form or another. Evidently, it was thus quite usual in the ancient hymnology that the composer mentioned himself in the third person, and this use is also not quite unknown in our modern poetry.

From the Gâthâ Ushtavaiti we pass on again to the Gâthâ Ahunavaiti. Here we light on a striking change. In *Yasna* XXVIII, 7-9, the poet speaks of himself in the first person; so there exists also no doubt that he lived in the period of the foundation of the new doctrine; however, I am inclined to think that Zarathushtra is not the author, but one of his friends and contemporaries. In the three strophes mentioned above (*Yasna* XXVIII, 7-9), the same poet prays to God in the following manner:— " Bestow (Thy) powerful spiritual help upon Zarathushtra and upon all of us;" in the next strophe :—" Grant power unto Vîshtâspa and to me ; " and in the following verse :—" I beseech Thee, grant the best good to the hero Frashaoshtra and to me." The parallelism is so clear in these three stanzas that we can only assume that the poet here represents himself as somebody distinct from Zarathushtra, Vîshtâspa, and Frashaoshtra. Hence he was not Zarathushtra himself.

Just as the Gâthic *Yasna* XXVIII does not originate in my opinion from Zarathushtra, but from one of his disciples or adherents, so also does the Gâthic *Yasna* XXIX. In the latter hymn the composer or the bard makes *geush-urvan,* " the kine-soul," implore the heavenly spirits for help and for salvation from the misery and embarrassment in this world, which befall her from evil people. The heavenly spirits make her look for the mission of Zarathushtra as a prophet, by whose teaching or doctrine the remedy against that evil shall be procured. *Geush-urvan,* however, is not satisfied with this promise, since she does not wish to have a powerless mortal as helper and saviour. Now, according to my interpretation, this Gâthâ XXIX concludes with a strophe, wherein Ahura Mazda promises that He would help on the weak ones and replenish Zarathushtra with His grace and power, so that

He might be capable of thereby carrying out His difficult commandment. But whatever may be the case, whether this Gâthâ concludes actually in the somewhat uncertain manner in which it does in its present surviving shape, or whether the strophe which formerly formed the end is lost, it seems very probable that the original composer of these hymns was not Zarathushtra himself but one of his friends, who refers to the prophet as the man that was chosen and sent into this world by God for the purpose of annihilating the work of the evil people.

The remaining chapters or hymns of the Gâthâ Ahunavaiti present no sure clue to its authorship. In *Yasna* XXXIII, 14, Zarathushtra is only once mentioned in the third person: " Thus, as an offering Zarathushtra gives the life of his very body," which does not enable us to form any opinion. But it is certain that all these hymns belong to the life-time of Zarathushtra. They presuppose all the relations and conditions of life which, as we shall see further on, are characteristic of that period. But whether the prophet himself is their author, appears to be uncertain. Several times their tone and character are doctrinal, and the dogmas of the Zoroastrian religion are explained at large, which seems to speak more for the assumption that a disciple of the prophet had composed them, who had now clothed in a compact and definite form and transmitted to the people of the world whatever he had heard directly from the prophet's mouth.

In the Gâthâ Spentâ-mainyu (*Yasna* XLIX, 8) the poet mentions himself along with Frashaoshtra without even specifying his own name. In the following stanza Jâmâspa is mentioned in connection with another professor of the new doctrine, who, might perhaps be understood to be Vîshtâspa. (*Vide* Dr. Mills, S. B. E., Vol XXXI, p. 166).[1] Nothing prevents us from believing that Zarathushtra is the great speaker. It is, however, certain that the poet lived in the age of the prophet. The forty-ninth hymn ends with the words :—" What hast Thou as a help for Zarathushtra who invokes Thee ? " which does not speak quite against the authorship of the prophet.

Of still greater importance is the hymn that follows, *Yasna* L, 5-6, a passage the right sense of which has first been explained by Dr. Mills.[2] Here mention is made of Zarathushtra in the third person, as of one who declares the songs and sayings or the *mâthras* to Ahura Mazda and the heavenly beings, and then prays : " In good mind may he announce my laws." The author here evidently stands next to Zarathushtra, just as we have already observed him

---

[1] Yasna XLIX, 9 :—
"Laws let the zealous hear to help us fitted ;
Let no true saint hold rule with the faithless,
Souls should unite in blest rewardings only ;
With Jâmâsp thus united is the brave (hero) ! "

[2] [*Vide* "The Sacred Books of the East," p. 167 *seq.* : —
"The most striking circumstance here, after the rhetorical and moral religious peculiarities have been observed, is the sixth verse ; and as to the question of Zarathushtrian authorship, it is the most striking in the Gâthâs or the Avestâ. In that verse we have Zarathushtra, not named alone, which might easily be harmonized with his personal authorship, nor have we only such expressions as ' to Zarathushtra and to us' (Yasna, XXVIII, 7); but we have Zarathushtra named as *mahiyâ râzeng sâhit*, ' may he declare my regulations,' which could only be said without figure of speech, by some superior, if not by the prime mover himself. Were these verses then written by the prime mover ? And was he other than Zarathushtra ? . . . . Zarathushtra was mentally and personally the superior of all of them. In fact, he was the power behind both throne and home, and yet without a name ! " *Trans. note*].

in *Yasna* XXVIII. Perhaps it is Vîshtâspa who here speaks, perhaps Jâmâspa. At all events he appears to be less a priest than a prince or a grandee in the land, who makes use of the important authority of Zarathushtra in order to introduce in league with him all kinds of reforms in the political and social order of affairs. We will observe that Zarathushtra is in fact a great reformer in social as well as religious matters, therefore, such an idea is not absolutely impossible.

That the Gâthâ Vahishtô-i-hti belongs in my opinion to a later, perhaps even a post-Zarathustrian period, I have briefly stated beforehand. As to the still surviving hymn, Yasna LI., *i. e.*, the Gâthâ Vohu-khshathrem, I would again be inclined to ascribe it to Zarathushtra himself. This assumption is already confirmed by the fact that this hymn bears unmistakeable resemblances to *Yasna* XLVI, which we likewise assume to be Zarathushtra's own. Dr. Mills has referred to it in the thirty-first volume of "The Sacred Books of the East," p. 182.

Just as in *Yasna* XLVI, 14,[1] so in *Yasna* LI, 11, the poet puts himself the question: "Who, O Ahura! is a loyal friend to the Spitâma, to Zarathushtra?" He answers then for the first time in the negative:—"Vicious heretics and false priests have never gained the approval of Zarathushtra" (see § 12).[2] These are exposed to perdition, while Zarathushtra

---

[1] [§ 14. "Whom hast thou Zarathushtra! thus a holy friend for the great cause? Who is it who thus desires to speak it forth?" (Zarathushtra answers.) "It is our Kavi Vîshtâspa, the heroic." *Trans. note*].

[2] "Paederast never gained his ear, nor kavi-follower," (Mills, S. B. E.)

grants to his followers the prospect of paradise as their reward (see §§ 13-15). And now he enumerates all his friends :—In the first place he names Kavi Vîshtâspa, then the Hvôgvid Frashaoshtra and Jâmâspa, and, lastly, the Spitâmid Maidhyô-mâoğh. Characteristic are the words at the conclusion of strophe 18, which, however, seem to be suitable only in the mouth of Zarathushtra : " And grant me also, O Mazda! that they, that is Vîshtâspa and Frashaoshtra and Jamâspa, may adhere firmly to Thee." Accordingly, God is solicited to fortify and strengthen the belief of the first adherents, so that they would truly adhere to the doctrine of Zarathushtra, which they have already recognized as true and right.

The results of our investigations upon the personal names occurring in the Gâthâs, and specially upon the references to Zarathushtra in them, are as follows :—

1. The Gâthâs were all composed in the age of Zarathushtra with the single exception of *Yasna* LIII, and they are distinguished, therefore, essentially from the rest of the Avesta in which Zarathushtra is a personage of the past period.

2. Some of the Gâthic hymns, particularly *Yasna* XLVI, XLIX, and LI, were very probably composed by Zarathushtra himself.

3. Other hymns do not directly proceed from Zarathushtra, but from one of his friends and followers or disciples, which may be proved with some certainty from *Yasna* XXVIII, XXIX, and L.

4. Under all circumstances we have here a collection of hymns wherein the same spirit prevails throughout, and all of which give expression to the same wishes and hopes, sorrows and fears, to the same

joyfulness of the faith, and to the same trust in God. Our theme " Zarathushtra in the Gâthâs " is, therefore, now to be treated more concisely as: THE REFORM OF ZARATHUSHTRA ACCORDING TO THE CONTEMPORARY DELINEATIONS OF THE GÂTHÂS.

CHAPTER II.
THE RELIGIOUS AND SOCIAL REFORM OF ZARATHUSHTRA.

As we have stated above, Zarathushtra was a reformer as much in the social as in the religious sphere. A glance at the contents of the Gâthâs, provides us with sufficient information as to this. No great reform can be achieved without the waging of battles, and in point of fact it is a period of embittered fighting which unfolds itself before our eyes, when we look at the scenes portrayed in the Gâthâs.

We may represent the matter in the following manner. The Arian people, that is, the still united Indo-Irânians, in their migrations from the Oxus, had descended southward and settled themselves in the river valleys situated to the North and South of the Hirdukush. But here the habitable soil which was available, was insufficient for the accommodation of so great a number of tribes and races. New masses pressed after them from the North, and so it happened that the tribes that had moved forward farthest to the South, had stretched far to the East and entered the valleys of the Indus. A remarkable schism had thereby taken place. Those of the Arians who remained behind in the earlier settlement on the Hindukush, formed the subsequent Irânian nation ; while those who emigrated towards the East, the subsequent Indian people. The latter were then passing through the Rig-veda epoch of civilization, whilst conquering the modern Panjâb in their fight with *Dâsa* and *Dasyu*. Now for the Irânians, too, an important period of their history began. The land which they had in their occupation, did not prove quite sufficient to maintain a larger number of nomadic races with their herds; for such were the Irânians of that period. The land also was favourable to nomadic life in many parts where the mountains run towards the steppes and gradually subside into lower and broader ridges; but in other parts where the ground is rough, rugged, and mountainous, it hindered the free and unlimited wandering of the nomads. Thus, naturally, one portion of the Irânian tribes was very soon compelled to take to a settled life and to practise agriculture. The Irânian people of the Gâthic period were, in fact, sub-divided into husbandmen and nomads, and in the sharp opposition, which obtained between the two, the prophet Zarathushtra played a prominent part. In a number of Gâthic passages we see him standing as an advocate of the settled husbandmen. He admonishes them not to be tired of their good work, to cultivate diligently the fields, and to devote to the cattle that fostering care which they deserved. And far and wide spreads the dominion of husbandmen and "the settlements of the pious people increase," in spite of all molestations, all persecutions, and violence, which they have to suffer from the nomads who attack their settlements in order to desolate their sown-fields and to deprive them of their herds.

It may be sufficient to hint at this primitive condition here in a few words, since this social revolution, which the Avesta-people passed through in the Gâthic period, has already been described at length (in my *Ostirân-ische Kultur im Alterthum*),[1] and we may avoid repeating the same in this place. What is here of special interest to us is *the spirit and the religious sentiments of Zarathushtra*, and of his friends and first adherents as they appear in the great conflict, and as far as it can be understood from the Gâthâs.

The conflict between the nomads and the agriculturists, between the followers of the prophet and his enemies, was bitter and of varying fortune. There were times of despair and extreme embarrassment, so that the prophet disparagingly utters the words :—"To what land shall I turn; aye, wherein shall I enter." And he laments that even his friends and relations leave him beset with difficulties, and the rulers of the land refuse to give him their protection and support (*Yasna* XLVI, 1). Yet such outbursts are proportionately rare in the Gâthâs. Zarathushtra and his friends, indeed, know about a helper out of all difficulties. It is Ahura Mazda, Who has sent them, and Who guides them in all their ways; unto Him they turn in times of distress, and on Him they look with a firm trust in God.

The poet Zarathushtra, therefore, continues after the opening words of the hymn, which are cited above :—

"Yea, I know that I am poor, that I possess scanty herds or flocks, and scanty followers; I cry to Thee, behold on me, O Ahura! and bestow on me help even as a friend bestows help on his friend." (*Yasna* XLVI, 2.)

---
[1] Darab Dastur Peshotan Sanjana, B. A., "Civilization of the Eastern Irânians in Ancient Times," Vol. II., pp. 119 *seq.*

The consciousness that Ahura Mazda Himself has sent Zarathushtra into this world for the purpose of announcing the new doctrine to mankind, and that God stands always by his side as his adviser or guide, comes out prominently in the Gâthâs. The prophet directly expresses it (*Yasna* XLV, 5), when he says that God communicated to him the Word which is the best for man. From the beginning he was chosen for that Revelation (*Yasna* XLIV, 11). He declares himself prepared to undertake the functions and duties of a prophet:—
"I will profess myself as Your adorer, and will continue so as long as I may be able through the support of *Asha*;" and he prays only that Ahura Mazda may bestow success on his work (*Yasna* L, 1). With pride he styles himself the "friend" of Ahura (*Yasna* XLIV, 1)[1], who truly and firmly adheres to Him, and who on his part can rely on His help. In another passage (*Yasna* XXXII, 1) Zarathushtra and his disciples call themselves "the messengers" of Ahura Mazda, through whose mouth God revealed to the world His *mysteries*, that is, His Revelation that was unknown and unheard of till then. Here we are vividly reminded of the same expression (*malâk*) occurring in the Old Testament, which denotes principally angels who serve as "the messengers of God," and who act as intermediaries between Jehovah and man. Then again it denotes the prophets and priests who serve as representatives of Jehovah on earth, and exercise his will; and, lastly, even the whole Israelite nation which is sent by God among the heathens in order to convert them. Here as well as there, namely, among

---

[1] Compare analogous passages in the Rigveda 2-38-10; 5-85-8; 7-29-8; *etc.*

the Israelites as well as among the Irânians, the consciousness is clearly manifest that the new religion is not the work of a man, but that God Himself speaks through His prophets, and that the latter are sent on their mission by Him, and that they are His servants, His heralds or His messengers.

This confidence in God has its highest and surest support or confirmation in the belief that, earlier or later, every man has at least to share in, or submit himself to, the lot which is assigned to him by the divine justice, and which he deserves in consequence of his good or bad actions. If in this life the evil person seems oft enough to enjoy an undeserved happiness, the punishment which is his due will, however, befall him directly in the next world. A life in darkness and torment and torture of the soul awaits him yonder. But, on the other hand, the prophet is able to console and strengthen his faithful adherents in all their miseries, struggles, and persecutions, by alluding to the joys of paradise which God will bestow on them in the next life. (*Cfr. Yasna* XXX, 4; XXXI, 20; XXXII, 15; XLV, 7; XLVI, 11; and XLIX, 11).

In point of fact such a firm confidence in the divine dispensation, and in an adjustment between reward and punishment in the next world, is always indispensable when enemies abound, when the good cause is found in the highest danger and numbers only a few followers who adhere to it faithfully.

The enemies of the new religion, in the first place, the nomadic tribes that feel disdain for settled life, the establishment of agriculture and careful tending of cattle, still pray to the old nature-gods, the *daevas*, the *dēvas* of the Indians. In the eyes of the adherents of Zarathushtra, or the Gâthic Zarathushtrians, these *daevas* become distinctly evil existences, deceitful idols, and demons. Those men or women who follow these *daevas* or demons, and offer to them sacrifices and reverence, are called friends of the *daevas* (*daevâzushtâ* "dear to the *daevas*," in *Yasna* XXXII, 4), just as Zarathushtra and his followers are designated the friends of Ahura. And still more in a strophe of the Gâthâs the authors say :—"Among the unfaithful to Ahura are seen the demons themselves in bodily forms, and the name of *daeva* shall, likewise, be applicable to such men." (*Yasna* XXXII, 5, *etc.*)

Another denomination for the unfaithful enemies is the word *khrafstra* (*Yasna* XXXIV, 9), which may mean perhaps "vipers." In another passage they are called *khrafstrâ-hizvâ* " having viperous tongues," (*Yasna* XXVIII, 6), and in a third strophe (*Yasna* XXXIV, 5) the *khrafstra-*men are named immediately and synonymously with the *daevas* themselves. The unfaithful have also their priests, the *Usij,* the *Kavis,* and the *Karapans* (compare *Yasna* XLIV, 20). The unfaithful are generally designated by the word *dregvantô* ; the pious on the contrary are called *saoshyantô* in certain passages (*Yasna* XXXIV, 13 ; XLVIII, 9 ; and especially in XLVIII, 12). They (*viz.,* these priests) are naturally the most inveterate enemies of the new doctrine through which their gods are dethroned, and they themselves lose all their influence on the people. The false priests, the *Usij*, the *Kavis,* and the *Karapans,* often succeeded in bringing the rulers over to their side. " With the princes have the Kavis and the Karapans united," so complains the holy singer in *Yasna* XLVI, 11, in order to corrupt man by their evil deeds. Self-evidently it was of the highest importance that the rulers should come to a determination as to the side they should take in such a matter; for if the prince professed the new religion or stood opposed to it, his subject as a rule very likely followed him. Hence it is that Zarathushtra now and then praises the religious fidelity of Vîshtâspa, and hence the reason why the poet prays to God:—"May good princes reign over us, but not wicked princes!"

Among the princes that stood against Zarathushtra as his enemies, the mighty *Bendva* might be included, who is mentioned in *Yasna* XLIX, 1-2. From the context of the passages we can of course conclude that he stood on the side of the infidels. A family or a race of princely blood were probably the *Gréhma* (*Yasna* XXXII, 12-14). Regarding them it is said that they, having allied with the Kavis and the Karapans, have established their power in order to overpower the prophet and his partisans; but sneeringly it is said of them that they will attain in hell the sovereignty for which they are striving. With all their adherents, the idolaters and false priests, they will go to eternal perdition. But the prophet, who is here in this world so much abused and distressed, will enter with his family, relations, and followers, into the joys of paradise.

Now, it is interesting to observe how the composers of the Gâthâs place themselves in contrast with these their enemies, and what sorts of ideas and sentiments they set forth against them. First, it is regarded as a sacred obligation to convert the infidels by means of words and doctrine (*Yasna* XXVIII, 5). The religion of Zarathushtra is a religion of culture, of spiritual and moral progress and proficiency. It penetrates through all conditions of human life, and it considers every action of life, as for instance, the clearing of the soil, the careful tending of herds, and the cultivation of the fields, from the standpoint of religious duty. Such a religion, or such a philosophy, cannot be confined to a narrow circle; the propagation of it and the conversion of all men to it, are ideas which are at the basis of its very essence. We, accordingly, find complete hymns, as *Yasna* XXX and XLV, which were evidently intended to be delivered before a numerous audience, and in which Zarathushtra, or one of his friends, expounds the essential points of the new doctrine for the approval of the hearers. Such a position follows clearly from the beginning strophe of the forty-fifth Gâthic hymn:—

> "I will announce it, now hear and understand,
> Ye who have come from near and from afar!
> Now hast Thou made evident all, O Mazda!
> In order that no false teacher shall again destroy the life (of our mind)
> Through false beliefs, a wicked person who speaks forth evil texts."

Evidently has Vîshtâspa, or else another provincial ruler, permitted his people to meet in a large assembly. In this assembly the Kavis and the Karapans may have delivered their songs in which they revered the *daevas*, the gods of storm and thunder, of the sun and stars. Probably they, too, brought offerings to their gods to gain their assistance in any enterprise, or to propitiate their wrath. But now Zarathushtra steps forward and addresses the assembly. To his triumphant eloquence the priests of the nature-religion had to give way, and his doctrine or religion, " until then unheard," which declared Ahura Mazda as the sublime Creator of the world and expounded the sacred duty of all men to fight strongly against the infernal power of evil, was re-echoed and applauded by the attentive audience. Not bloody offerings or senseless customs constitute the true worship of God; but the moral purity of the mind, an ardent fulfilment of the duties to which man is invited in this life, as well as piety and industry.

Whenever the prophet meets with an open opposition, and all preachings and expositions prove fruitless, then he denounces upon his opponents the full burden of divine wrath. The good shall hate the evil. There is no reconciliation, no forbearance, no connivance. Every act of forbearance in such a case would be a sin, because it encourages evil rather than destroys it.

This spirit of intense hatred against the wicked stands, I believe, parallel to the ideas of the Old Testament. In the latter scriptures Moses, too, summonses the Levites to draw their swords and to kill the apostates who instead of holding firmly to the worship of Jehovah made a golden image and adored it (2 *Moses* 32, 25 *seq.*). Jehovah is a "jealous god," a god of wrath, who commands to destroy the idols of the pagans and to throw down their altars :—" God of vengeance, Jehovah, God of vengeance, show thyself." So the psalmodist invokes him (*Psalms* 94). " Lift up thyself, thou judge of the earth : render reward to the overbearing! How long shall the wicked triumph, Jehovah ? . . . . . They congregate to threaten the life of the righteous, and condemn the innocent blood. But Jehovah is my citadel, and my God is the rock of refuge. He shall repay them their injustice, and shall annihilate them on account of their malice. Jehovah our God shall extirpate them."

"Jehovah saves all who love him; but he destroys the wicked" (*Psalms* 145, 20.) Through perverseness Jehovah's indignation will be excited; now he grows angry and pays with the sword those who revolted from him (*Psalms* 78, 56 *seq.*). When the sons of Korah rebelled against Moses, Jehovah split the earth, and Korah with his relations, family, and property, was swallowed by it (4 *Moses* 16, 1 *seq.*).

These passages from the Old Testament are culled at random. It would be easy to multiply them tenfold. The hatred which does not tolerate connivance with the sinner; but demands and expects his immediate punishment, yea, even his total annihilation by the divine justice, is even a trait of the old Israelitish spirit. We cannot refuse it our admiration. There is vigour and energy free from all feeble wavering, rising to violence and fanaticism. And now when Zarathushtra proclaims in the Gâthâs:— "Would that I could be a tormentor for the wicked, but a friend and helper for the pious" (*Yasna* XLIII, 8); or when he admonishes the people:—"None of you shall mind the doctrine and precepts of the wicked; because thereby he will bring grief and death in his house and village, in his land and people! No, grip your sword and cut them down!" (*Yasna* XXXI, 18); or when he denounces death and ruin upon those who did not adhere to him. All this vividly puts us in mind of the spirit of the Old Testament.

In fact, the opposition between the pious and the impious, the believers and the unbelievers, seems very often to have led to open combat. The prophet prays to Ahura that He may grant victory to his own when both the armies rush together in combat, whereby they can cause defeat among the wicked, and procure for them grief and trouble (*Yasna* XLIV, 14, 15). Whosoever deprives the liar and the false teacher of his power or of his life, can count upon Ahura's favour or grace (*Yasna* XLVI, 4). In any case, however, the wicked will not escape the eternal judgment, and if not already in this world, certainly in the next world, Ahura will inflict punishment upon them and dash them into the torments of hell and damnation (*Yasna* XXXI, 20; XLV, 7; XLVI, 6, 11; XLIX, 11).

CHAPTER III.
Zarathushtra's Monotheism.

That the Reform of Zarathushtra called forth a lively agitation of the mind, that it even gave occasion to bloody combats and wars, is easily understood from the contents of the Gâthâs. It broke away almost entirely from all ideas extant before the Gâthic period, and offered in fact something quite new. It placed itself in a conscious opposition to the religion of nature which had been handed down from the old Arian times, and was still cherished by the people; and whatever it took over from the nature-worship and retained in itself, was exalted into a far higher moral sphere and penetrated with its spirit; and thus the form acquired a new substance.

Here we speak of the Gâthâs and their contents, not of the entire Avesta, because it seems to me – and the surviving chapters will prove it – that the Gâthâs plainly preserve Zoroastrianism in its purest and most original form, as the founder of this sublime religion had thought out and imparted it. If the present Parsees, the modern professors of the Zoroastrian religion, would learn to be familiar with its contents and spirit, as it originated directly from the prophet, they would always have to refer to the Gâthâs; and they ought to endeavour to penetrate deep into the meaning which is indeed often obscure and difficult. I believe that it will also have an important practical effect in increasing their love and esteem, and in preserving in a pure state this religion as a rare and valuable possession.

The prophet, too, qualifies his religion as "unheard of words" (*Yasna* XXXI, 1), or as a "mystery" (*Yasna* XLVIII, 3), because he himself regards it as a religion quite distinct from the belief of the people hitherto. The revelation he announces, is to him no longer a mere matter of sentiments, no longer a merely undefined presentiment and conception of the Godhead, but *a matter of intellect, of spiritual perception and knowledge.** This is of great importance; for there are probably not many religions of so high an antiquity in which this fundamental doctrine, that *religion is a knowledge or learning, a science of what is true,* * is so precisely declared as in the tenets of the Gâthâs. It is the unbelieving that are unknowing; on the contrary, the believing are learned, because they have penetrated into this knowledge (*Yasna* XXX, 3). Every one that is able to distinguish even spiritually between what is true and what is untrue, will enlist himself on the side of the prophet (*Yasna* XLVI, 15). Between the truthful (*adrujyantô*, "not speaking lies") and the liars there is strictly the same antithesis as between the believers and the unbelievers, the adherents and the opponents of the new religion (*Yasna* XXXI, 15, *etc.*). It is thereby expected from every individual that he or she should take a place in the great question, and come to a decision on the one or the other side. "Man for man" shall the people examine or test whatever the prophet has announced to them (*Yasna* XXX, 2), and learn thereof the truth. Clearly enough it is an open breach with the old national religion. To the follower of Zarathushtra the religion is no longer a "reliance" on unknown and more or less unintelligible higher powers; it is to him rather *a "freedom" of the spirit, an exempton from all superstitions and false notions, an independent penetration into the perception of the divine truth which was to him a mystery before then.** That the religion should develope from a feeling of dependence into that of freedom, is the most important step that could be taken generally in the sphere of religious life.

We will again mention the Old Testament where belief and perception, unbelief and folly, are likewise regarded as identical ideas. I need only refer to the famous passage of *Psalms* 14, : —"The *fool* speaketh in his heart. There is no God. Corrupt and abominable are their works; there is none among them, that doeth good. But Jehovah looks down from heaven upon the children of men, to see if there were any that did understand, that seek God; but all are apostatized, all are corrupted; none is there that doeth good, no, not one." (Cfr. *Psalms* 53, 2.)

But wherein consists the new doctrine "unknown till then" of the Zoroastrian religion, as it clearly emanates from the Gâthâs? It exists in the *preponderating monotheistic character of this religion*. Its founder has got rid of the plurality in which the Godhead had been split up by the popular belief and naturalism, and elevated himself to *the preception of the divine unity* which pervades nature in manifold ways.

It is sufficiently known that in the Zoroastrian religious system *Ahura Mazda* is conceived as the Ruler and Commander in heaven and on earth, and as the Highest and the First of the Genii. This double name, in the given consecutive order, occurs in the later Avesta as the constant and established designation of God. Exceptions to this use are not found in it, or are certainly met with very seldom only. The case is different in the Gâthâs, and I come thereby to a most highly significant distinction between the old hymns and the younger fragments of the Zoroastrian religious documents Such a name as became afterwards stereotyped for the Godhead, does not yet exist in the Gâthâs. We find sometimes *Ahura*, sometimes *Mazda*, sometimes *Ahura Mazda*, and sometimes *Mazda Ahura* applied to the Deity. God can be designated by " Lord " (*Ahura*) as well as by " All-wisdom or Omniscience " (*Mazdâo*). It seems even that in the Gâthâs the appellative signification of the two names had been felt still more than in the later writings. This is proved by the passages wherein *Ahura Mazda* (*Yasna* XXX, 9 ; XXXI, 4), or *Mazda* alone (*Yasna* XXXIII, 1; XLV, 1), is used in the plural number. The *Mazdâonghô* then evidently form the totality of the heavenly spirits. If we further consider the fact that in the old Persian Cuneiform Inscriptions of the Achæmenian dynasty occurs the name of God, *Auramazdâ*, as a single word which is only inflected at the end, it certainly follows hence that we have to deal here with the results of development in different historical epochs. Generally speaking, Zarathushtra had not found out originally any exact proper name for the Godhead. He designated Him sometimes by one, sometimes by another name, but we can translate most of the different names, which are used in the Gâthâs, simply by "God." Later on the name Ahura Mazda was strictly adhered to exactly in the same relation and succession of the two words, and therewith was now for the first time created a real or definite name of the Deity, the use of which corresponds to the name of Jehovah in the Old Testament. In a still later period the two names blended into one, because they were continually used in the same succession as though they formed a compound. Nevertheless, both the component parts are still discernible from the name *Auramazdâ*, since they are both declined in one passage only of an Inscription of Xerxes. The last phase of development is represented by the forms of the name used in middle and modern Irânian dialects: Pahlavi *Auharmazd*, and modern Persian *Ormazd*. The blending of the two words is here so complete that they do no longer bear an independent meaning in the final form.

Now the essence of polytheism consists in the religion in which man exalts the different powers of nature separately to individual godheads, and fixes the limit of their sphere of activity against each other. Generally speaking, we can, therefore, call the religion of the Rigveda a polytheistic doctrine. *Indra* is the god of weathers; *Agni* rules over the fire; the *Maruts* are the genii of storms. However, there exist already in the Vedic hymns ideas which lead us gradually upwards from polytheism to monotheism. We can observe how the virtue or efficiency of one or more gods is here and there transferred to an individual god. This is especially the case in many of the hymns dedicated to *Varuna*. In those hymns Varuna is represented as the creator of the universe, as the giver of all good things, as the warden of truth, and the avenger of sins. (*Vide* Rigveda I, 25,20 ; II, 27,10 ; VII, 86, 1 *seq.*) In other sacred songs the same qualities and powers are transferred to other gods: thus Indra, Soma, and Agni may be occasionally regarded as the highest gods. Of the last mentioned god, Agni, it is said directly in Rigveda V., 3, that he is the same as *Indra*, *Vishnu*, *Savitri*, *Pûshan*, *Rudra* and *Âditi* ; accordingly he is identified with the whole body of the gods.

Thus we can observe in the Rigveda how the singers and priests search after the conception of the divine unity, and how they are kept away from it for this reason only that they have not the moral courage to break with the notions, conceptions, and names, which are handed down since ages. In the Gâthâs the position is different. The important step which the Vedic singers lingered to take, was adopted by the Gâthic Irânians. The plurality of the nature-gods is set aside, and *one* God is selected in their place, who comprehends all, and is as great and as powerful as the Jehovah of the Old Testament, and at any rate not more anthropomorphous than the latter.

In the 104th *Psalm*, Jehovah is extolled as the creator and regent of the world. "Light is the garment which he puts on. He stretcheth out the heaven like a tent. He vaulteth his chamber with water. He maketh the clouds his chariot and ascendeth upon the wings of the wind. He maketh the winds his messengers and the fire-flame his ministers. He propeth the earth upon its foundations so that it quaketh not for ever. He created the moon to regulate the seasons, the sun knoweth his going down. Thou makest darkness that there will be night, wherein all the beasts of the forest stir about. The young lions roar after their prey and seek their meat from God. The sun riseth: these beasts run away and couch themselves in their dens, when the man goeth out to his work and keepeth himself to his daily labour until the evening."

I would put side by side with this Psalm some stanzas from the Gâthâ XLIV, where Ahura Mazda appears as the almighty God, Who created the universe, Who maintains it, and rules over it. The resemblances between the 44th Gâthâ and the 104th Psalm strike us at once, and we must concede without any hesitation that the author of the 44th Gâthâ has penetrated into the perception of God, the Creator of the world, not less profoundly than the poet of the Psalms. In *Yasna* XLIV, 3-5 and 7, it is said:—

(3) "This I ask Thee, give me the right answer, O Ahura!
Who was the Generator and the first Father of the world-system?
Who showed the sun and stars their way?
Who established it, that the moon thereby waxes and wanes,
if Thou doest not?
These things all, O Mazda! and others still I should like to know."
(4) "This I ask Thee, give me the right answer, O Ahura!
Who hath firmly sustained from beneath the earth and the
atmosphere,
That they do not fall down? Who created the waters and the
plants?
Who hath given their swiftness to the winds and the clouds?
Who hath created, O Mazda! the pious thoughts (within our
souls)?"
(5) "This I ask Thee, give me the right answer, O Ahura!
Who hath created skilfully the light and the darkness?
Who hath made skilfully sleep and activity?
Who hath made the auroras, the midday, and the evening,
Which remind the discerning man of his duties?"
(7) "This I ask Thee, give me the right answer, O Ahura!
Who hath created the blessed earth together with the sky?

Who hath through His wisdom made the son in the exact image of the father?
I will call Thee, O Mazda! the judicious,
As the Creator of the universe, the most Bountiful Spirit."

The correspondence of the religious ideas mentioned above in the Gâthic hymns and the Psalms, is in point of fact unique. The conformity to law in nature, such as the course of the stars, the waxing and the waning of the moon, and the succession of the day-time during which man's activity is fixed, attracted the attention of both the poets. *In the Gâthâs Ahura Mazda, in the Psalms Jehovah, is the Creator of the Order of the World.* As such Mazda is freely and frequently mentioned in the Gâthâs. He is "the essential Creator of the Order of the World."

Haithyô ashahyá dãmish,
in *Yasna* XXXI, 8, an appellation which we must emphasize, as it will hereafter be of importance for considering the relation in which Ahura Mazda stands to the Amesha-spentas.

If Ahura Mazda is the Creator of the world, He, too, deserves all those attributes which are ascribed to Jehovah in the Old Testament. As we have already remarked Ahura Mazda is the *Holy* and *All-just;* He hates the evil or wicked, and punishes them in this world as well as in the next according to their due; but He takes the pious under His protection, and bestows eternal life upon them. He is the *Immutable,* Who is "also now the same" (*Yasna* XXXI, 7) as He has been from eternity: He is the *Almighty,* Who does what He wills (*Vasô-khshayãs, Yasna* XLIII, 1); He is the *All-knowing,* Who looks down upon man from heaven (*cfr.*

Psalms 14 quoted above), and watches all their projects and designs which are open or secret (*Yasna* XXXI, 13). Ahura Mazda is a *Spirit*; He is a Being, Who cannot be invested with human traits of character; He is the *Spenishtâ Mainyû*,[1] "Most Bountiful Spirit" (*Yasna* XLIII, 2), the Absolute Goodness or Bounty. In fact, anthropomorphistic ideas or representations are very rare in the Gâthâs. Where such ideas occur, they are to be interpreted as the simple result of poetical usage or license. To Zarathushtra Ahura Mazda was doubtless as much a spiritual, supersensible, incomprehensible and indescribable Being, as Jehovah was to the poets of the Psalms.

Ahura Mazda is certainly called in *Yasna* XXXI, 8; XLV, 4; XLVII, 2, the Father of Vohu-manô, Asha, and Ârmaiti; but it is to be remembered that Vohu-manô, Asha, and Ârmaiti are only abstract ideas: "the pious mind, holiness, humility and devotion." Hence it positively follows that we have here not to deal with human ideas or conceptions such as are current in the Greek and Roman mythology; but simply with a poetical mode of expression. It means nothing more than saying: God is the Father of all goodness, yea, He is "our Father."

In *Yasna* XLIII, 4, mention is also made of the "hands" of Ahura Mazda. It would be ridiculous if we were to trace therein any anthropomorphism whatever. Such phrases Zarathushtra could use as naturally as the Christian does, when in his prayers he lays all his cares and wishes in the fatherly hands of God. It is neither

---

[1] In other Gâthic passages *Spentâ-mainyû* seems to be a being distinct from Ahura Mazda; it is perhaps a particular trait of His nature by which he becomes the giver of bounty in the creation (*Yasna* XLV, 6; XLVII, 1; *etc.*)

heathenish nor Muhammedan nor Zoroastrian nor Christian, but a common mode of human expression.

However, any traits which would allow us to infer that Ahura Mazda had been represented in a certain figurative form in the oldest period of Zoroastrianism, are certainly not to be derived from the Gâthâs. If we find in later times, as for example, in the monuments of the Achæmenian kings a figurative representation of Ahura Mazda, I think we ought not to lay much stress upon it. In the first place it is to be observed that the Persians of the Achæmenian period had obtained Zoroastrianism as something foreign from without; thus they may have added or changed many religious notions. Secondly, has not also Michael Angelo drawn an image of the God Father and therewith given to the ecclesiastical art of the West a type for the representation of the Godhead?

We have seen that Zarathushtra has arrived at the idea of an Almighty, All-wise, and All-just God, of a Creator and Preserver of the world; and he has thereby provided his people with the monotheism in the place of a polytheistic nature-worship. Further, we have seen that the manner in which this sole Godhead is conceived, vividly reminds us of the representations of Jehovah in the Old Testament, and indeed so well in the general as in the many particular characteristic features. Nevertheless, I declare it as an *entirely mistaken assumption* that Zarathushtra borrowed the Jehovah idea directly or indirectly from the Israelites. We find nowhere else in the entire Avesta any traces of actual contact between the Irânians and the Semites, which would justify a theory of a borrowing of religious notions or conceptions from one another. Again the cult of Ahura Mazda has yet its genuine national stamp in spite of all resemblances with the Jehovah-worship. Let us only consider the close connection of the religious and economical life, which plays so prominent a part already in the Gâthâs, and forms a characteristic feature of the entire Avesta. Generally I regard it as most hazardous to assume a borrowing on the basis of simple resemblances of religious ideas. If Ahura Mazda and Jehovah bear a certain affinity in idea and comprehension, that is plainly owing to the reason that we have to deal with a monotheism among the Irânians as well as among the Jews. But when monotheism is once firmly established, then certain similar ideas are sure to be forthcoming, which are peculiar to monotheism and form part of its essence. He who does not altogether deny that a people or a pre-eminent genius at any time among a people, can attain independently to the idea of the unity of God—he who does not dogmatically adjudge the monopoly of monotheism to the Jews—will surely agree with me in the assertion that the Irânians had in a very olden time, and without any influence from without, *independently acquired through the Zoroastrian Reform the possession of a monotheistic religion.*

CHAPTER IV.

THE THEOLOGY OF THE GÂTHÂS.

We now approach an objection which might possibly be raised against our comprehension of Zarathushtra's doctrine. It might be asked:—Is then Zoroastrianism, indeed, a positive monotheism? Does not the Avesta extol and profess the existence of a complete list of good spirits such as the *Amesha-spentas, Mithra, Sraosha, Verethraghna, Haoma, Ardvi-sûra,* and others? Have not several of these good spirits, as for example

Mithra, forms which are derived from the pre-Zoroastrian times and are also met with in the Indian Vedic hymns, and which consequently belong, no doubt, to the Arian nature-worship?

We do not wish to misapprehend the importance of these objections. We are willing to concede to them even a certain justification and truth. *But here is the point where we have surely to distinguish between the Gâthâs and the rest of the Avesta, between the doctrine as it comes directly from Zarathushtra himself and as it developed among the people later in the course of time.* If, indeed, we consider the Gâthâs alone, we light on a far purer monotheism. In the later Avesta the doctrine appears confused and restricted in different ways. Even to-day the Parsee will have to prefer the Gâthâs, if he wishes to understand his religion not only in the oldest, but also in the purest form.

How sharp and definite the representation of the genius *Mithra* appears in the later Avesta, especially in the *Mihir Yasht* dedicated to him. He is the genius of the morning-sun, who brings hither the light. As such he is the enemy and vanquisher of the demons of night. But he is also the *yazata* of truth, of rights and contracts. The sphere of his might ranges still further. He is prince and king of the earth, the helper in battles whom the warriors invoke at the commencement of fighting, and who helps them on to victory. Lastly, he takes vengeance on the wicked. He especially inflicts punishment on liars and violators of promise.[1]

In a similar manner we can describe *Tishtrya*[2] from the later Avesta. He is the *yazata* of stars, in parti-

---

[1] Compare Spiegel, Erânische Alterthumskunde, Vol. II., pp. 77; seq.
[2] Comp. *ibid*, pp. 70; seq.

cular he presides over the star Sirius. To him is attributed the power of distributing rain on dry fields. He fights against the demon of aridity and barrenness. That he has generally in his hands the dominion of the stars cannot be surprising. Also the *Fravashis*,[3] the manes, allot the fertilizing water over the earth; they distribute in general all sorts of good things, cause trees and plants to thrive, and are like Mithra, helpers in war and fighting. In short, we have in the later Avesta to deal with genii who vividly remind us of the gods of the Rigveda, of *Varuna, Indra, Mitra,* and others.

If we now turn again to the Gâthâs, the subject appears to us in quite a different light. Here the names of a Mithra or Tishtrya are not mentioned even once. The Fravashis, too, are never directly alluded to; so also Haoma, or Verethraghna the angel of victorious battles, or Anâhita the angel of the waters. In the Gâthâs we fail to find the names of all those good spirits who in the later Avesta are especially drawn as plastic representations, and who mostly appear exhibited with individual attributes.

Are we to explain this as a simple accident? I would regard such a supposition, of course, as an error, although I am convinced on the other side, however doubtful or critical every *documentum e silentio* is. There are sometimes circumstances under which we arrive at nothing by the assumption of an accident, and by which much obscurity and confusion is caused. If in the Gâthâs we could nowhere find a convenient occasion for mentioning Mithra or Tishtrya or the Fravashis generally, it might be explained as an accident when their names do not occur. But such opportunities of

---

[3] Comp. Spiegel *,Erânische Alterthumskunde,* Vol. II., pp. 91 *seq.*

mentioning these good spirits, occur sufficiently often in the Gâthâs. Why is Mithra, for example, not alluded to in the passages where the conflict against the unbelievers is mentioned? It is said of Mithra in *Yasht* X, 36:—

"Mithra opens the battle,
He takes his place in the battle;
And standing in the midst of battle
He breaks asunder the lines arrayed (for the battle)."

Or, the Fravashis, too, would have been here fitly invoked; for

"They bring the greatest help in fearful battles." (*Yasht* XIII, 37).

Besides, the Gâthâs speak very often of fields and herds; but even with such an opportunity Tishtrya is never referred to, although he renders the fields blessed and the herds thriving.

Similar is the case with regard to the other good spirits of whom, too, the Gâthâs make no mention. One cannot say that in general no occasion is found to name them; but *their non-mention is evidently the result of an object aimed at.*

The entire character of the Gâthâs is so philosophical, abstract, and transcendental, that such yazats or angels as are mentioned above would be quite unsuitable in their theology. I do not say that Zarathushtra and the other poets of the Gâthâs knew altogether nothing about Mithra or Tishtrya or Anâhita. These yazats were, no doubt, much revered by the people; but the prophet did not approve of such a cult. He wished to substitute higher and more philosophical ideas in the place of these good spirits, who in their entirety too much resembled the gods of the old Arian nature-worship. All those genii that are named in the Gâthâs along with Ahura Mazda, are in point of fact such abstract conceptions; their position with reference to the monotheistic doctrine of the Gâthâs as is set forth by me, will be indicated later on.

Mithra, Tishtrya, and other yazats, who are not mentioned in the Gâthâs, are in the later Avesta pretty strongly anthropomorphized. They are conceived and described quite in the same way as the godheads of the Rigveda. They are represented in human form, as man or woman (like Anâhita), wearing armour and clothing, bearing weapons, driving in chariots, and dwelling in palaces. Sometimes they appear even in the shape of animals. But, as we have observed, such anthropomorphous conceptions are quite foreign to the Gâthâs.

Those genii, on the contrary, who with Ahura Mazda are mentioned in the Gâthâs, especially the Ameshaspentas, are very little, or properly speaking not at all, anthropomorphized even in the later Avesta. Sraosha perhaps forms only an exception. In the Gâthâs he is wholly an abstract figure; but in the later Avesta he is described as a genius whose attributes exhibit many resemblances to those of Mithra.

Hence, we are able to establish an authoritative distinction between the theology of the Gâthâs and that of the later Avesta. In the former only such genii have their place near God as are principally nothing more than abstract ideas; in the latter, on the contrary, are also mentioned such genii as appear in more plastic forms and may be compared with the gods of the Indians who were originally of the same tribe as the Irânians. If from amongst the names of the genii who belong to the latter category, only one or two did not occur in the Gâthâs, we should be inclined to call it perhaps an accident; but where the distinction is one so continuous and almost without an exception, certainly we ought to recognize therein a system and purpose.

Now, the question is: How did those genii who are more and more anthropomorphized like Mithra, *etc.*, get into the Zoroastrian system in later times? I believe that it is not at all difficult to explain this. The Zoroastrian Reform is an energetic opposition against the ancient Arian nature-worship. Consequently, not a single one of the genii that belong to the latter cult, occurs in the Gâthâs. Every opposition naturally goes to the extreme point and seeks its success in the absolute annihilation of the existing system. In a passage of the Gâthâs (*Yasna* XLVIII, 10) the cult of Haoma, at least in the form in which it was at that time practised, is even put down as something despicable and abominable.[1] But on such a practice must follow a reaction in due time. The results to which this reaction led, are placed before us in the theological system of the later Avesta. Here we light on a compromise with the older national religion. The gods, who were revered in the latter, are, notwithstanding their altered and spiritualized form, taken back into the new religious system, in order to form to a certain extent the holy retinue and court of Ahura Mazda. However, as we have said, the ideas undergo many transformations; they are adapted to the new circumstances, and this is effected particularly by placing more in the foreground the moral side in the nature of an individual genius than the physical side. This corresponds with the essence of the Zoroastrian system in general, which is principally founded on an ethical basis.

The modern Parsiism, according to the whole tendency of our age, will have again to embrace the form of his religion, as it is given in the Gâthâs. It will place the philosophical element of his faith in the front just in the

---
[1] [Doubtful. The Pahlavi seems to have understood "magic." Comp. S. B. E., Vol. XXXI. *Eng. Trans*.]

same way as the Christian will more emphasize the moral power of his religion than its dogmatic doctrines. By giving prominence to what is common to the different religions, the connecting bridge between them is directly found.

To the development of the Zoroastrian religion, as I have described it, similar analogies are also found amongst us in the West. In Germany, too, the first proclaimers of Christianity proceeded with the object of extirpating heathenish beliefs. Nevertheless, at this day every intelligent and unprejudiced investigator concedes the fact that many a heathen element is still found hidden in our national ideas and customs. It is well-known that in the saints as they are worshipped in many countries of Germany, particularly by the country-people, are revived old heathen gods, or rather they are preserved in altered forms and designations. Thus *Thor*, the god of tempest, the constant attendant of *Wotan*, has become Saint Peter ; and we can no longer be astonished if Peter has also taken upon himself, according to popular belief, other functions too, which had belonged to his heathen predecessor, as for example, the causing of rainy weather. The old conception of a god bringing down the rain has even been retained, but connected with the person of Peter, as Thor's name had no longer a place in the new church. As regards Parsiism the case was different. Herein the old appellation also came into use with the religious idea itself. We must here remark that Parsiism is, however, an outcome of the old Iranian nature-religion, while the old German national belief was something foreign to Christianity. Thus a compromise was entered into between Christendom and Heathendom by the former accepting many popular ideas which are deeply rooted in the heathenish belief, but impregnating them with the Christian spirit.

Now, the celestial beings whom the Gâthâs mention along with Ahura Mazda, are, as I have already stated, principally the six Amesha-spentas: Vahu-manô, Asha, Khshathra, Ârmaiti, Haurvatât and Ameretât, to whom I add Sraosha and Ashi. It is not my intention to explain in detail the conceptions that are connected with these Amesha-spentas. It would be an idle repetition.[1] For our purpose it may only briefly be said that *Asha* is the genius of the cosmic and moral order as well as the warden of fire; his name signifies "piety." *Vohu-manô* is the good and pious mind; he protects the herds, with the breeding of which is also united the nursing of the pious mind or feeling. *Khshathra* denotes the "kingdom," the dominion of the pious and faithful here on earth, and the kingdom of heaven in the next world. *Ârmaiti* is the "humility" and "devotion," the preserver of the earth. *Haurvatât* and *Ameratât* denote "welfare" and "immortality;" they rule over water and plants. *Sraosha* is "obedience," especially to the will of God and the precepts of the holy religion. Also *Ashi* appears to bear a similar meaning in the later Avesta.

Now the question which here interests us is: In what relation do these Amesha-spentas stand to Ahura Mazda? Will the monotheism, admitted by us in the theology of the Gâthâs, be not impaired and restricted through them, or perhaps even be abandoned? If we take an external view of the matter, we must concede that the Amesha-spentas scarcely seem to play a part inferior to Ahura Mazda. The word *Asha*, for example, occurs in

---

[1] Cfr. "Civilization of the Eastern Irânians in Ancient Times," Vol. I., pp. XXXII; seq.

the Gâthâs about 180 times ; the name *Mazda* about 200 times ; *Vohu-manô* (also *Vahishtem-manô*) perhaps 130 times; and the rest of the names, of course, not so often. It is not the number of times that a name is mentioned, which enables us to conclude from external evidences as to the varied value of the different ideas ; and still there exists such a distinct difference, that it is quite impossible to place Mazda and Asha in one and the same grade, nay, even to compare them with one another.

Mazda has become, indeed, a proper name to designate the Highest and only One God, no less than Jehovah in the Old Testament, or Allah in the Muhammedan religion. Asha, on the contrary, and even the other Ameshaspentas named above, *can* only occasionally attain to a sort of personification, the original abstract signification being still clearly perceived. In the majority of passages the abstract idea is the only right meaning; in others we would hesitate to fix the correct import of the word, nay very often the double meaning is perhaps aimed at by the poets of the Gâthâs. Similar personifications of abstract ideas are occasionally noticed also in the *Psalms* (*vide* 85,11-14) :—"Near lieth Jehovah's help unto His adorers, so that glory will stay in the land. Mercy and truth have met together ; and righteousness and peace do kiss one another. Truth shall spring out of the earth ; and righteousness shall look down from heaven. Jehovah, too, shall grant happiness, and our land shall yield her produce. Justice shall go before his sight and stalk forward upon her path. "[1]

Strictly speaking, Asha and Vohu-manô, Khshathra and Ârmaiti, when they designate abstract conceptions,

---

[1] [Here I have followed the authorized English Version of the Bible. *Eng. Trans.*]

are, in the first place, no special genii who stand in a line with Mazda; but they represent certain powers and qualities of the Godhead, which are included in Mazda and in His Essence. Such is at all events the original idea; but we do not wish to argue that these Amesha-spentas never and nowhere arrived at a certain independence. This is particularly the case in those passages where the Amesha-spentas are named together with Mazda, and stand perfectly parallel to Him. In that case I might compare them with the angels of the Old Testament. The latter were, likewise originally, only phenomenal forms of Jehovah Himself, and later on they constituted to a certain extent His followers and companions or His court. Thus, for example, Mazda's name appears amongst those of the first Amesha-spentas (*Yasna* XXVIII, 3):—

"You, O Asha! will I praise and the Vohu-manô, the incomparable,
And the Mazda Ahura, with whom the eternal Khshathra is united,
And the blessing dispensing Ârmaiti: come hither to my call to help me!"

And quite similarly *Yasna* XXXIII, 11 (cfr. also 12 and 13).

"Thou Who art the most beneficent Ahura Mazda, and Armaiti,
And Asha who furthers on the settlements, and Vohu-manô and Khshathra,
Hear me, have mercy upon me, have always kind regard for me for ever."

That Asha and the other Amesha-spentas are, nevertheless, only an emanation from the Essence of Mazda, is poetically expressed in His designation as their Father and Progenitor as well as their Creator. Where God is regarded as the Creator of the spirits existing by and outside of Himself, there can be no reference to any kind of polytheism. The question then—Whether there are any spiritual existences outside of God, who stand to a certain extent as intermediaries between Him and man—has nothing to do with the definition of the idea of monotheism. In reference to the theology of the Gâthâs it is still to be fully maintained that the names of the Amesha-spentas are chiefly abstract conceptions. When Mazda is called the Father of Asha, it only signifies that He has created the moral and the cosmic order. Hence He is also designated *Ashâ hazaosh* " of one will with Asha;" since what He does is in accord with the world ordained by Him. Or when He is called the Father of Vohu-manô and Ârmaiti, it signifies that all good intentions and all humble devotion, that is, every life which is agreeable to God, depends upon Him or emanates from Him.

Consequently, the belief in the Amesha-spentas does not interfere with the monotheism of the Gâthic theology. In spite of all, Ahura Mazda stands out as the Almighty Being (*Yasna* XXIX, 3). It is He Who gives decision upon all, since everything happens according to His will (*Yasna* XXIX, 4). He is of one nature with them all, or, as the poet puts it: He dwells together with Ahsa and Vohu-manô (*Yasna* XXXII, 2 ; XLIV, 9), that is, He has these powers at His disposal; they stand at His command. They issue from Him, and go back unto Him. Ahura Mazda existed first of all. Khshathra and Ârmaiti, Vohu-manô and Asha are associated with Him as natural evolutions from His Being. Such powers only emanate from Him. He allots them unto men (*Yasna* XXXI, 21). He stands far above them:—

" This I ask thee, give me the right answer, O Ahura !
Who hath created the blessed Ârmaiti together with Khshathra?
Who, through his wisdom, hath made the son in the image of the father ?

> I will designate thee, O Mazda ! to the intelligent, as
> The Creator of all, Thou Most Bountiful Spirit!"

(*Yasna* XLIV, 7)

Lastly, I have still to add a few words with reference to *Ashi* and *Sraosha*. How much the theology of the Gâthâs differs from that of the later Avesta is plainly manifested by these yazats. In the former *Ashi* can scarcely be considered the name of a genius as in the latter. The word has in the Gâthâs rather its original abstract signification : *reward*, or *recompense* ; then *blessing*, or *success* (*Yasna* XXVIII, 4; XLIII, 1, 5, *etc.*). I cannot specify any Gâthic passage where *ashi* may be conceived with some probability as a proper name. The progress of the development of an abstract idea into the name of a *yazata* is clearly perceptible as regards the word *ashi* in the period which intervenes between the epoch of the Gâthâs and the age of the later Avesta.

Similar is the case with *Sraosha*. In the later Avesta the word denotes throughout a genius of a pretty fixed and permanent nature with distinct individual characteristics. In a still later time he is described as the messenger of God, who has to convey His orders unto man. However, no such traits are observable in the Gâthâs. Here we discover only the first beginnings of the personification of the word in such passages as *Yasna* XXXIII, 5 where the poet invokes the "mighty Sraosha," and *Yasna* XLIV, 16 where the author implores the bestowal of a commander for protection against enemies, and wishes that "Sraosha with Vohu-manô" may accompany him, in other words obedience to the holy religion and pious mind. In the latter passage, I believe, a double sense is implied ; but in other passages where *Sraosha* occurs it has the etymological abstract meaning of "obedience," "devotion"; or the concrete meaning of "the obedient," "the devoted," "the pious." The contrary expression *asrushti* hence signifies "the disobedient" in *Yasna* XXXIII, 4 and XLIV, 13.

We can now sum up the results of this chapter in a series of propositions as follows :—

(1) The theology of the Gâthâs is more abstract and philosophical than that of the later Avesta. It represents the oldest and most primitive form of the Mazdayasnian religion.

(2) The veneration of the more popular divinities such as *Mithra* and *Tishtrya*, is unknown to the poets of the Gâthâs. The cult of these *yazatas* was first adopted in a later epoch by a sort of compromise with the popular religion.

(3) The theology of the Gâthâs is monotheistic. Mazda Ahura is the Godhead *per se*.

(4) This monotheism is in no way interfered with by the genii alluded to in the Gâthâs, since these Ameshaspentas and yazatas are only hypostases of abstract conceptions, they are everywhere comprehended in their original import, and stand, moreover, in conformity with their nature under Mazda, being themselves regarded as His creatures.

CHAPTER V.

Zoroastrianism is not a Dualistic Religion.

The Zoroastrian religion has often been called a dualistic religion. This term we are, however, only then authorized to apply to it, when we understand under dualism a religious system wherein the existence of a power working in opposition to the good-creating and good-wishing Godhead, is also assumed besides

Him. In this sense the Old Testament religion may, likewise, be denoted a dualistic system. Strictly speaking, we could only then point to a religion as a dualism when both the good and evil principles stand one against the other with equal rights, and are equally mighty; when both influence the world to an equal extent; and when man feels himself equally dependent upon and acted on by both of them. But where man can, by the power of his moral freedom of choice, decide upon goodness, and turn himself away from evil or vice, as is conspicuously often manifest in the Gâthâs, the term " dualism " is no longer justified in my opinion. The existence of a dualism would, as I believe, require, among other things, that man should persevere in evincing the same veneration to the evil spirits as to the good spirits, that he should offer to the former sacrifices and prayers in order to propitiate them and to avert all sorts of mischief caused by them, as in (their) turn he offers them to the good spirits in order to share in their blessings. I need scarcely here emphasize that no traces of such ideas are found in the Avesta.

The Avesta, of course even in its oldest parts, recognizes an evil spirit, who in every point stands opposed to the good spirit. The assumption of his existence should be the solution of the question, which every philosophic mind will naturally dwell upon, as to how evil comes into the world, if the Deity is essentially good and can, accordingly, produce only good things. Whence originate crimes and sins; whence all the misery and imperfections, which cling unto man as well as to the whole creation ? Zarathushtra and the other poets of the Gâthâs have endeavoured to solve that question in a philosophical way, and I will make an attempt, in the following pages, to expound briefly their system as it seems to unfold itself from the Gâthâs. I say "seems," because the Gâthâs have not at all in view the object of developing a system of philosophy. Their composers do not mean to address individuals from amongst the people, but the whole community; because they chiefly take into their consideration the practical side of religion, *viz.*, ethics, and not the philosophical form of its doctrine. We must, therefore, assay to construe from the brief indications and isolated passages of the hymns the ideas which may have presented themselves before the minds of these poets upon the question of evil. Naturally, these are distinct passages wherein the prophet is led by the context to speak of the nature of evil. But (in regard to this) we must at once renounce all claims to be able to represent clearly all the individual traits of the philosophical system which Zarathushtra may have established for himself. In reference also to the principal points, such as I shall attempt to describe, opinions might frequently differ. Others will very easily find out certain passages, of which the meaning has not been sufficiently established by me, or which appear to be not quite consistent with my own views.

In the later Avesta, the opposition between the spirits of the good and the evil world is also carried through formally and most precisely. As Ahura Mazda stands at the head of the former, so Angra Mainyu stands at the head of the latter. As opponents of the six Amesha-spentas or arch-angels stand the six arch-demons: *Akem-manô* is opposed to Vohu-manô; *Indra* or *Andra* to Asha; *Sauru* to Khshathra; the demon of arrogance, *Nâoghaithya*, to Spenta-ârmaiti; *Tauru* and

Zairicha to Haurvatât and Ameretât. Then follows the army of the good spirits of light against the band of the *daeva* and *druj*.

In the Gâthâs the system, as it appears to me, is not so thoroughly developed. Aɣra Mainyu occurs here only once as the name of the evil spirit, and of course in a single passage (*Yasna* XLV, 2) where *spanydo mainyush* and not, as one would expect, Ahura Mazda, is mentioned as his opponent. Likewise, *akô mainyush* occurs only in one passage (*Yasna* XXXII, 5); *ahem manô* is found twice named (*Yasna* XLVII, 5; XXXII, 3), which, however, has in other passages the original abstract sense of " evil mind," and *achishtem manô* also twice (*Yasna* XXX, 6; XXXII, 13), which is employed as an appellative of the evil principle.

Now at the first glance it might seem as though *aɣra mainyush* and *akô mainyush* were formally the adversaries of *spenta mainyush*, and *akem manô* and *achishtem manô* of *vohu manô* and *vahishtem manô*. However, such is not the case in the Gâthâs. All these names evidently denote, without any distinction, the evil spirit who is called simply Aɣra Mainyu in the later Avesta. Thus, for example, in *Yasna* XXXII, 3, the *daeva* are designated as the brood (*cithra*) of Akem-manô who must be, in such a context, manifestly the highest and the head of the world of evil spirits. The same is probably the value of Achishtem-manô, when it is said in *Yasna* XXX, 6, that the demons flock together around him, while the good spirits are associated with, or collect around, Spenta Mainyu (*Yasna* XXX, 7, and comp. 5). Nay, it even appears that in the same passage Aeshma, too, which is otherwise the name of a particular demon, serves only as the appellative of Aɣra Mainyu.

Now as regards the exposition of the relations in which the good spirits stand to the evil spirits, it is important to note that there is no regular counterpart principally of the name Ahura Mazda. The names which serve as designations of the evil spirit, stand rather as counterparts of the name Spenta-mainyu or Vohu-manô. But where both the good and evil spirits are named together (*Yasna* XXX, 4-7; XLV, 2), the good spirit is not denoted by Mazda, but Spenta- (*spanyâo, spenishta*) mainyu. The essential function of Spenta-mainyu himself does not even seem fully clear in the Gâthâs. He is sometimes identified with Ahura Mazda (*Yasna* XLIII, 2), sometimes he is distinguished from Him (*Yasna* XLV, 6; XLVII, 1); he must hence be a divine being who sometimes rises to the level of the Highest Godhead; sometimes he is distinct from Him, and leads a separate existence.

If we were to compare all these data we should be able to characterize the philosophy of Zarathushtra approxitmately as follows:—The Highest Being, the Godhead, is plainly Ahura Mazda. He is by nature good, and only goodness emanates from Him. Evil is the negation of goodness; it exists only in relation to the latter, just as darkness is only the negation of light. Now so far as Ahura Mazda is the positive, to whom evil forms the negative, He is called Spenta-mainyu, while evil or its personification is Agra-mainyu or Akô-mainyu. Both Spenta-mainyu and Akô-mainyu are hence represented as twins (*Yasna* XXX, 3); they do not exist alone for themselves, but each in relation to the other; both are absorbed in the higher Unity, Ahura Mazda. They existed before the beginning of the world; their opposition is exhibited in the visible world. Ahura

Mazda is the Creator of the universe, but as He, in the form of Spenta-mainyu, creates anything, the negative counterpart of Him is given, *i.e.*, as the poet expresses it in a popular form, Aġra-mainyu, the evil spirit, who produces evil in opposition to goodness (*Yasna* XXX, 4 *seq.*). The first thing which the twins produced, is life or death, or, as it may perhaps be philosophically expressed, the being and not being, wherein the double side of their nature is marked. Thus, if Spenta-mainyu creates light, the darkness, or the not being, or the absence of light, is the contrary creation of Aġra-mainyu; if the former gives warmth, the negation of warmth, *viz.*, cold, originates from the latter. All evil is, consequently, to the Zoroastrian not something properly realistic, existing in and for itself, but only the failure of goodness. Therefore, it is self-evident that good and evil throughout are not parallel ideas of equal value, but the latter has a purely relative existence. If we admit this, we must also assert that Zoroastrianism cannot be called a dualism in the proper sense of the term.

Now, as soon as we ask the question: How does man stand in relation to these two opposite principles? we thereby directly touch upon the sphere of ethics. But when we interrogate: What is the final end (at the last judgment) of this opposition between good and evil? we come therewith to the subject of eschatology, the doctrine of the last things, the end of the world and the last judgment. Both ethics and eschatology are specially weighty points of the Zoroastrian religion. Both naturally stand in a close reciprocal relation. So early as in the Gâthâs we discover numerous and important hints upon ethics and eschatology.

It is a well-known fact that the entire system of Zoroastrian ethics is based upon the triad of "good thoughts, good words, and good actions," the *humata, hûkhta,* and *hvarshta.* This, indeed, presupposes a high standard of moral culture, when the sin in thought is placed on the same level with the sin in action, and, therefore, the root of all actions as well as the measure of every moral discernment is perceived in the mind. *We must hence aver that the founders of the Avesta religion at least attain to that stage in ethics to which only the best parts of the Old Testament rise, and that they display an inclination towards that depth of moral intuition which is perceptible in Christianity.*

Now, we must emphasize this fact that at a very early period the Gâthâs knew about this ethical triad which also sways over the entire later Avesta. There is no doubt, therefore, that the foundation of this ethical system had been laid by Zarathushtra himself. The character of these ethics is thus in fact so personal and individual that we are involuntarily forced to assume that it is the product of an individual supereminent spirit which, endowed with special moral gifts of nature, has attained to such a keenness and preciseness in the conception of the moral laws. That this doctrine developed out of a whole nation, so that it was to a certain extent the property of a community, and gradually took the form in which it is represented in the extant Avesta, seems to me quite incredible.

The poet says in *Yasna* XXX, 3, that the two spirits that had existed from the beginning, the twins, had announced to him in a vision what is good and what is evil in thoughts, words, and actions. In like manner, *Yasna* LI, 21 designates piety as the fruit of the thoughts, words, and deeds of an humble mind. On the contrary, evil thoughts, evil words, and evil works, emanate from the wicked spirit (*Yasna* XXXII, 5). In the service of God this ethical tripartition is manifested in the devout feeling which the adorer shall foster, in the good speech which he utters, and in the offering ceremony which he performs. But it would be only a limitation which is not vindicated by the Avesta texts, were we to regard this triple moral idea exclusively as ritual expressions. That the mind or thought settles the fundamental tone of this moral triad, so that speech and actions must be dependent upon it, and judged according to it, is clearly enough declared by the prophet when he speaks of the words and deeds of a good mind (*Yasna* XLV, 8).

Now as to the position of man in relation to good and evil, the most conspicuous point in the ethics of the Gâthâs is the complete free choice which belongs to every individual. According to the Zoroastrian standpoint, no man stands under any ban whatever of destiny, of a destiny originating from eternity, which binds him and oppresses his will. There is here no original sin for which he has to suffer as the result of the faults of his parents, and which cripples his strength in struggling against evil. The evil lies not in him but out of him. He can let evil approach him and admit it in himself, but at the same time he can keep it off from himself, and struggle with it.

This is certainly a sound moral standpoint which places all responsibility upon man himself, and deprives him of the possibility of making any excuse for his laxity by saying that the matter did not lie in his power (or was a result of destiny).

That the determination in favour of good or evil is a matter of free choice, is typically signified by the fact that the demons, too, place themselves, out of a peculiar motive, on the side of the Evil Spirit. They are, therefore, not evil by nature, but they become so by foolishly declaring themselves in opposition to Ahura Mazda (*Yasna* XXX, 6). Nay, it is even a free voluntary act of the Evil Spirit himself that he chose sin as his sphere of action, while Spenta-mainyu made the choice of piety and truth for himself (*Yasna* XXX, 5). And, likewise, it is only the pious and faithful who make the right choice of the good thoughts, good words, and good deeds; but not the impious (*Yasna* XXX, 3).

This doctrine of the free volition of man conforms with the opinion already expressed by me above that religion is a matter of understanding or judgment, and that righteousness and truth on the one hand, and impiety and falsehood on the other hand, naturally stand in the closest connection. According to the Zoroastrian idea, moreover, man is not fettered with a blind fate, nor prejudiced in his judgment by hereditary sins. God has given him his power of judgment, and he who has ears may hear, and he who has intellect may choose, what is right and true. The sinner is a fool, and the fool a sinner.

The Zoroastrian well understands how great the danger is for each individual, and in how many different ways evil manifests itself in the visible world and threatens to cause the downfall of the pious. His life is, therefore, a constant and indefatigable struggle or combat against evil. It would be superfluous here to cite all the Gâthic passages which touch upon this earnest conception of life as an everlasting combat in the fulfilment of the true obligations. The exhortation that every one shall persevere in righteousness and devotion, and shall not get tired of it, forms rightly and precisely the fundamental tone of most of the Gâthic hymns.

Piety is the most ardent wish of the poet (*Yasna* XXXII, 9). He implores Ârmaiti that she may let him firmly adhere to the faith (*asha*), and that she may grant him the blessing of a pious mind (*Yasna* XLIII, 1). The faith is the highest goodness (*vahishtem*) which he can acquire from God. He implores the Deity to obtain this highest good for himself as well as for his adherent Frashaoshtra (*Yasna* XXVIII, 9). The highest goodness is the property of Mazda. From Him it reaches unto men when the Holy Word is announced to them (*Yasna* XXXI, 6; XLV, 4). In this respect the Gâthic hymns stand far higher than those of the Rigveda. In the Gâthâs the gifts or possessions which the poet longs for, are almost exclusively spiritual and moral ones; it is only in isolated cases that material gifts form the object of his wish. The Vedic singers, on the contrary, pray for horses and cattle and splendid riches.

The absence of cult and ceremonies is a conspicuous feature of the Gâthâs when contrasted with the later Avesta. In the latter, regularly recurring prayers, offerings, recitations, and purifications, which are undergone daily or at certain occasions, play an important part; they form the very contents of the *Vendidâd*, the religious code of the Zoroastrians. The guardians of these numerous precepts are the priests, who have to watch over their fulfilment, and to impose the due penance upon the negligent and tardy people who transgress them. The whole life of the Zoroastrian is governed by these precepts of purification and their minute observances. But if we glance at the Gâthâs, we discover no trace of all these precepts and customs. The reason of the absence of any such trace may be explained in two ways. Either we may assume that the context in the Gâthâs, the tendency and object which their authors pursued, generally offered no occasion to speak of any ritual and ceremony; or we may account for this phenomenon by supposing that in the epoch wherein the Gâthâs were composed, generally speaking no such detail of precepts had existed; but that the whole system gradually developed to perfection when the community became more and more established, and the new doctrine found wider and wider extension. I believe that we should feel no hesitation in following the latter explanation. The Gâthâs are, indeed, not completely silent as regards the external forms of the divine worship. They allude to the hymns of praise whereby the Deity is adored by man (*Yasna* XXXIV, 6; XLV, 6, 8; L, 4). According to *Yasna* XLV, 10, Ahura Mazda is exalted by offerings; and they are the deeds of the good mind whereby one approaches God (*Yasna* L, 9), and propitiates the holy spirits (*Yasna* XXXIV, 1). But these are quite general ideas. The ethics of the Gâthâs are in such a high degree internal or mental; they recognize so decidedly or precisely the piety in a holy course of life and in an energetic struggle against evil, that the idea seems to be hardly compatible with the belief that a reward can be gained by the conscientious observance of external ceremonies at any time. The expression which denotes in the later Avesta the fulfilment of the precepts of purification, is *yaozhdâo*, which occurs only once in the Gâthâs (*Yasna* XLVIII, 5). The Gâthâs do not mention even once a common name for the priesthood. They, of course, refer to the whole community of the believers, and particularly, as it seems, to the teachers and proclaimers of the new religion, by a distinct word *saoshyantô*. This word, however, bears quite a different meaning in the later Avesta, in which the priest is denoted by *âthravan*, an expression which is entirely wanting in the Gâthâs. Without the existence of a priestly institution, however, the observance and management of a ritual entering so much into minute details, just as the Vendidâd teaches, is inconceivable. The absence of any reference to the priesthood as well as to a well-organized system of ritual and ceremonies can be quite easily explained by the general condition of civilization such as is described in the Gâthâs. Herein the Zoroastrian community is represented as a rising generation, the doctrine is still a new one, not long known to the people, nor spread among them. However, those two phenomena, *viz.*, priesthood formed as a separate institution, and a developed system of religious usages and precepts, come into existence only under settled circumstances. They presuppose a certain tradition, a longer period of development in which it became possible to place the system on a firm footing not merely as regards its general characteristic principles, but also its finish in details. The principal traits of Zoroastrianism are, nevertheless, presented in the Gâthâs, its detailed outward structure being found in the later Avesta. There seems to be no doubt that this outward structure certainly corresponds in all points to the spirit which permeates the Gâthâs.

As we have already observed, the Gâthâs did originate in an epoch of ardent conflict. Very often we find the believers in need and distress, while the godless and disbelievers in the doctrine rejoice and seem to claim the victory in the fight. When the thought naturally occurs:—How are the righteous indemnified for the wrong which they endure here on earth, and how are the impious who appear to enjoy good luck and success, punished for their crimes? Hence, in the earliest period of Zoroastrianism the conception of a compensating justice meted out in the next world, was already strong. It formed one of the ground-pillars of the entire system ; for without this hope the faithful adherents of the doctrine would scarcely have overcome triumphantly all the persecutions which they must have suffered at the beginning. Like the Christian martyrs of the first century, they forbore all the afflictions of this world in the hope of the joy and happiness which awaited them in the next world (*Yasna* XLV, 7) :—

"When they will receive the reward of their deeds,
Those who are living now, those who have lived, and those who will live;
Then the soul of the pious will be happy in eternity,
But never will end the torments of the disbeliever;
Thus Mazda hath established according to His power."

Thus merit and fate are adjusted in a divine court of justice. This judgment is twofold, one individual, and the other general. The individual judgment is administered to every individual soul after its separation from the body; the general judgment, on the contrary, to the whole body of the souls at the end of the world, *viz.*, the doom's day. With the latter follow, as it would seem, the perfect separation of the wicked from the good, and the abolition of the negative after which the positive, realistic, and the good alone will survive.

So far as we can conclude from the indications in the Gâthâs regarding the fate of the souls after their separation from the body, the ideas of this epoch correspond to those of the later Avesta. The judgment takes place at the Chinvat Bridge which connects this world with the next. The pious soul crosses this bridge in communion with the souls of all those who have zealously striven for the good on earth (*Yasna* XLVI, 10). It now enters into the "spiritual world" which in the Gâthâs is often contrasted with the visible and corporeal world (*Yasna* XXVIII, 3). Yonder it shares in the highest beatitude, which consists principally in the soul beholding Mazda and the heavenly spirits face to face, and dwelling with them together in Eternal Light. " O Asha, when shall I see Thee," asks the poet in *Yasna* XXVIII, " and Vohu-manô, the possessor of knowledge, and the abode which belongs to Ahura in particular?" To the great discomfort of the evil souls, the righteous souls will be conducted in the future to the abode of the Blissful Spirit, according to *Yasna* XXXII, 15. Whosoever has overcome lying and deceit by dint of truth, will receive from Mazda the heavenly kingdom and the eternal bliss (*Yasna* XXX, 8); and whosoever has adhered firmly to the *Vêh-Dîn* "Good Religion," will enter unhindered the dwelling of Vohumanô, Asha, and Mazda (*Yasna* XXX, 10). God will bestow eternal life upon those who follow Zarathushtra (*Yasna* XLVI, 13), and this life is a life of bliss, for the *Garôdemâna*, "the Abode of Hymns," is called in *Yasna* XLV, 8 the paradise in which the pious dwell.

Further, we observe that the Gâthâs, consistently with their entire character, consider the blissfulness in the next world as an essentially spiritual one, just as in the Christian religion it rests in the "beholding of God" (*schauen Gottes*), in the close communion with the

Godhead. We hardly find any such traces among the Indians. Here Zoroastrianism exhibits a strong opposition to the natural religions, which conceive the life after death as a continuation of the future life with all its joys, advantages, and habits; but without its sufferings and painfulness.

While the soul of the righteous joyfully crosses the Chinvat Bridge, which leads him to the Kingdom of Heaven, the soul of the sinful is stricken with fear and terror, in the presentiment of the penal retribution awaiting him (*Yasna* LI, 13). The Divine Judgment exiles the soul into Hell. Just as the Kingdom of Heaven is pure light, so is darkness the abode of the demons (*Yasna* XXXII, 10, *achishtahyâ demânê mananghô* "in the abode of the evil spirit," is the formal and real antithesis to the *vanghêush â demânê mananghô* in strophe 15). It is in the abode of the demons that the sinful soul is received by the evil spirits with scoffing and disgrace, and entertained with loathsome food (*Yasna* XLIX, 11). But as pure spiritual joys make up the essential constituent of Paradise, so there are, likewise, essential spiritual torments under which the soul of the wicked has to pine after his death. Such a soul is severed from Mazda and the blessed spirits; it dwells with the demons in eternity; it is particularly tormented by its own conscience which accuses it and condemns it (*Yasna* XLVI, 11). Thus tranquillity and serene joyfulness are for the blessed on the one side, and trouble and remorse and repentance for the damned on the other. Such is the compensation in the next world for the disproportion between reward and punishment which we so often perceive in the life of man here on earth.

Such a recompense or retribution is allotted to each individual immediately after death. The material work, however, is not destined to last for ever. It will in the future be annihilated. Thus the final judgment is united with the end of the world. Already in the Gâthâs this idea (of the next world) is clearly observable. The general judgment does not stand in contradiction to the individual judgment. The latter finds its solemn confirmation in the former, and we may probably assume that at the final judgment evil will be annihilated and banished from the world. The Gâthâs, nevertheless, do not speak definitely upon this subject, but the later Avesta contains this doctrine, and we dare say that without it the notion of a judgment at the end of the world would be almost without any object. In the hymns the final judgment is apparently not quite distinguished from the individual judgment. Mazda Who existed from the beginning of the world has laid it down that in His power evil shall be the retribution of the evil, and good the reward of the good at the end of the world. The pious will enter the heavenly kingdom of Mazda at the end of the world (*Yasn.ı* XLIII, 5-6 ; LI, 6), that is, he will outlast the destruction which evil and the evil people will be subject to.

Conclusion.

I now come to the end of my survey. It appeared to me indeed adapted to the spirit of the age, and worth my while to point at once to the Gâthâs as the oldest parts of the Avesta, and to treat the contents of their doctrine separately. The task itself may furnish us with the proof that such a treatment of the subject is practicable. It may prove at the same time to be a contribution to the argument that a deep cleft separates the Gâthâs from the other books of the Avesta, and that the Parsees have been led rightly and by important grounds to ascribe already in an early period a special sanctity to these old hymns. My task appeared to me the more useful as in the Gâthâs a particularly original and antique form of the Zoroastrian doctrine can be discovered; and this form is the purest and sublimest that we know of. It is still free from many later additions, and permits us to observe in a favourable light the personality of Zarathushtra, his moral earnest and yet human intentions, and his philosophical system which ventures to solve the highest and most important problem in religious philosophy. We recognize in Zarathushtra a man who was far in advance of his times, who proclaimed already in a remote antiquity a monotheistic religion to the people, who conceived from a philosophical standpoint the Being of the Godhead, the relation in which man stands to Him, and the origin of evil; and who perceived the chief point not in offerings and external ceremonies, but in a pious mind, and in a life conforming to such a pious mind.

This discourse is addressed to the Parsees of India on the one hand, and to those amongst Europeans on the other who take a warm interest in India and its inhabitants. It will bring before them the oldest and to a certain extent the ideal form of the doctrine, as it was thought out and conceived principally by its founder and author himself. It will at the same time enable also the European who is himself not in a position to study the original texts of the Sacred Writings of the Parsees, to form a correct estimate and to give an unbiased criticism of the Parsee religion and its moral standard. *May it prove a foundation stone in the Bridge which will unite the West and the East with one another.*

VIEWS OF THE CLASSICAL WRITERS REGARDING ZOROASTER AND HIS DOCTRINE.*

The earliest contact between Græcism and Magism that we are informed of, is an intercourse between Pythagoras and the Magi, which lasted for several years. Whilst ancient and modern writers vary as to the year of the birth of this sage, and place it at one time in 608 or 605, at another in 570 B. C. ; so much is, however, certain that the years of his active life fall under the reign of Cyrus, and that he left his native country before the death of the founder of the Persian Monarchy, in order to make scientific travels. If the statements of the chroniclers[1] were true, according to which Pythagoras is said to have served in the army of Assarhaddon, he might have had, already in his earliest youth, an opportunity of conversing with the Magi ; but that is evidently an anachronism. Others,[2] on the contrary, relate that the campaign of Cambyses in Egypt took place during his sojourn in that country ;

---

* *Vide* Fr. Windischmann's *Zoroastrische Studien*, a posthumous German work edited by F. von Spiegel, Berlin, 1863, pp. 263—313 :—*Stellen der Alten über Zoroastrisches.* " References in Ancient Writings to Zoroaster and his Doctrine."

[1] *Chronic Eusebii*, edited by Aucher of Abydenus, p. 26. Comp. M. Niebuhr, *Assur*, p. 497 and 501 ; B. G. Niebuhr, *Kl. Schriften*, p. 206.

[2] *Theolog. Arithmet*, ed., Ast. p. 40 :—"He is said to have been made prisoner by Cambyses, when he went to Egypt, and to have had intercourse with the priest; he came into Babylon and learnt the rites of the barbarians." Jamblichus, in his " Life of Pythagoras," p. 19, narrates the same facts, and adds :—" There he liked to converse with the Magi, and learned their signs and the most perfect mode of serving the gods, and became accomplished in a high degree in the numbers, music, and other sciences. He stayed there for another 12 years and went afterwards to Samos, when he was about 56 years of age."

Pythagoras may have there been taken prisoner and brought with the Persian army to Babylon, where he may have had intercourse with the Chaldæans and the Magi for twelve years; hence he may have returned at the age of 56 to Samos. The campaign of Cambyses in Egypt falls in the Olympiad 63,4 (525 B. C.), and his death in Olympiad 64,4 (521 B. C.). During this interval, therefore, Pythagoras must have come to Babylon, where he remained until B. C. 513. That Pythagoras had been in Egypt is affirmed by Herodotus and Isocrates; but that a man so curious in religious matters should visit also Babylon, the metropolis of Asiatic knowledge, and should make acquaintance with the Chaldæans and the Magi, is a fact so very evident in itself, that I cannot conceive how the very numerous statements of antiquity could be rejected for no other reason than their being found in writers of a later period.[1]

But in making use of these statements it is very important to observe that the majority of the authors

---

[1] Cicero *de fin.*, V, 29:—"Pythagoras had visited Egypt and conversed with the Persian Magi." Valerius Maximus VIII, 7 extern. 2:—"Thence he went to the Persians and was taught the very exact wisdom of the Magi." Plinius, *Hist. Naturalis*, XXX, 12:—"At least Pythagoras, Empedocles, Democritus and Plato sailed off to learn this art (of magic), really undertaking rather exile than travel." Apuleius, *Floridus*, p. 19 ed. Altib.:—"There are writers who say that Pythagoras had been taught by the Persian Magi" (*comp. infra* the whole passage). Clemens Alexandrinus, *Stromata*, I., p. 355:—" He conversed with the best of the Chaldæans and Magi." Diogenes Laertes, VIII, 13:—"Having been still young and curious, he left his native country, and learnt all the rites of the Greeks and barbarians. He was in Egypt when Polycrates recommended him by letters to Amasis. He learned their language, as is stated by Antiphion in his book on those men who excelled in virtue, and afterwards he went to the Magi and Chaldæans." That Pythagoras himself had been in Persia or even in India, must be an exaggeration—a mistake resulting from his intercourse with the Magi.

distinguish between the Chaldæans and the Magi. Porphyrius[1] says in his Life of Pythagoras:—" He has inculcated truth before all things; this alone can render man God-like, since also in God (called by the Magi Oromazes) the body, as he learnt from them, resembles light, whilst the soul is like unto truth." And further on:—" He heard and accepted from the Magi the worship of the divinities and the other precepts of life." What is related here by Porphyrius about the Magi, is taken from pre-eminent sources. If we do not regard the high veneration of the Persians and the Magi for truth, a fact often confirmed elsewhere, the distinction of a body and a soul in God is truly Zarathushtrian. In the *Farvardin Yasht*, §§ 80 to 81, it is said of Ahura Mazda:—" His genius is the most intelligent and the best-bodied; His soul is *Mâthra-Spenta* (the Holy Word), the bright, the shining, the foreseeing, and the bodies which He assumes, are the fine bodies of the *Amesha-Spentas* ('the Blissful Immortal'), the solid ones of the Amesha-Spentas, let us venerate the strong-horsed Sun."

The Holy Word is the very truth, and the Amesha-Spentas are the luminous creations, wherefore it is significant that the Sun is invoked immediately after them. Moreover, we are justified in thinking of Mithra as morally truth and physically light, and as a being who may be regarded as a likeness of Ahura. In the

---

[1] *Vita Pyth.* "Life of Pythagoras," 41:—"He gave these precepts; but before all he taught to speak the truth. For this alone can render man like unto God, since, as he learnt from the Magi, in God too, Who is called by them Oromazes, the body is like unto light, and the soul unto truth." And in chapter 7:—"As to the divine ceremonies and other things referring to the affairs of life, he is said to have been taught and instructed by the Magi."

Hormazd Yasht, § 21 (see *Yasht Fr.* II, § 38) are mentioned the spirit, the intellect and the tongue of Ahura as bearing, remembering and uttering the Holy Word, and in several passages the body of Ahura is mentioned along with His intellectual spirit (*comp. Yasna* I, § 1) *khrathwishtahê hukereptemahê. Yasna* LXXI, § 4, speaks of *vîspem kerefsh Ahurahê*, "the whole body of Ahura." The beginning of the Bundahish, too, completely harmonizes with the passage of Porphyrius.

On the other hand, the same authority[1] relates other facts about the intercourse of Pythagoras and the Chaldæans:—"He had intercourse not only with the other Chaldæans, but also with Zabratas, by whom he was purified from the sins of his earlier life, and was taught how zealous people must keep themselves pure; there he had also heard the doctrine of the nature and the first principles of the universe." What Porphyrius here states, seems to have been taken from Aristoxenus (about 320 B. C.), of whose writings a very large fragment has been preserved by Hippolytus (*Refut. Hæret.* "Refutation of the Heretics," p. 8, Oxford edition. Cfr. Origenes, edition of Lammazsch, volume XXV, page 296 *seq.*; Diodorus the Eretrian is also named as an authority). Aristoxenus narrates that Zaratas set forth his doctrine to Pythagoras:—"There have been from the beginning two causes (or principles) of things, father and mother. The light is the father, the darkness is the mother; the parts of light are the warm,

---

[1] "Life of Pythagoras," 12:—"But in Babylon he had intercourse with other Chaldæans as well as with Zabratas, by whom he was purified from the transgressions of his former life, and instructed as to what the zealous must chiefly abstain from. He learnt there also his (Zabratas's) doctrine about nature and the first principles of the universe."

the dry, the light and the swift; but the parts of darkness are the cold, the wet, the heavy and the slow; of all these is composed the world of male and female. But the world is a musical harmony, wherefore the sun has a harmonical circulation." Yet concerning the things that originate from the earth and the world, Zaratas gave an explanation, says Aristoxenus, in the following manner:—" There are two demons, a celestial and a terrestrial one; the latter takes his origin from the earth, and is water; but the celestial one is fire coupled with air, warm and cold." Then follows the reason why beans[1] should not be eaten on account of the bean having some reference to sexuality. In another passage, too, Hippolytus mentions Zaratas (B. 178) where he says:—" Zaratas, the teacher of Pythagoras, has called the first one father, the second one mother. Thus Plutarch also relates.[2]

It is clear that this doctrine of Zabratas or Zaratas, the Chaldæan, as described by Aristoxenus and Porphyrius,[3] does not contain anything that is specifically Zarathushtrian; but that, on the contrary, it is directly opposed to the system of the Magi in very important points. It is, therefore, not without meaning that Porphyrius distinguishes the doctrine of the Magi from

---

[1] It is very remarkable that the prohibition of bean-eating, which Pythagoras is said to have learnt from the Chaldæan Zaratas, is found in the Old Babylonian or Chaldæan documents. *Comp.* Chwolson, "The Remains of the Old Babylonian Literature," p. 93 *seq.*

[2] *De animæ procreatione*, in Timaeo, chapter II, 2, " Zaratas, the teacher of Pythagoras, calls this (*i.e.*, the *dudda* " the Two") the mother of numbers, and the One he calls father."

[3] Of course we must not imagine that the later writers have authentically made out the contents of the doctrine of Pythagoras. It is sufficient to state that they knew the difference between the Magian and the Chaldæan.

that of the Chaldæans, and explicitly calls Zabratas, a Chaldæan, whilst Jamblichus evidently confounds the two doctrines in the passage cited above ("Life of Pythagoras," 19). The same correct distinction between the Magi and the Chaldæans, Zoroaster and Zaratas, is found also in Clemens of Alexandria, as well as in the passage already referred to, and also in *Stromata*, I, page 357, Potter's edition,[1] where he explicitly calls Zaratas, an Assyrian, whilst he says a few lines above[2]:—" Pythagoras emulated Zoroaster, the Magian and Persian, whose secret writings the followers of the gnostic Prodikos boasted to possess," by which must be understood the later gnostic productions under the name of Zoroaster. It is self-evident that "emulating" does not express any personal intercourse between Pythagoras and Zoroaster.

It is consequently to be ascribed to want of accuracy, if Suidas[3] speaks of some Magian Zaras, who was the

---

[1] " But Alexander, in his work on the Pythagorean creed, narrates that Pythagoras learnt from the Assyrian Nazaratas. Some fancy that this was Ezekiel (a prophet of the Old Testament): yet it is not so, as will soon be demonstrated." The commentators of Clemens have long since observed that we must read Zaratas instead of Nazaratas. The above-mentioned Alexander is Alexander Polyhistor, as *Cyrillus adv. Julianum* asserts :—" Alexander, surnamed Polyhistor, (*lit.* "a man of great learning") in his book on the Pythagorean creed, states that Pythagoras learnt from one Zaras, a native of Babylonia."

[2] " Pythagoras emulated Zoroaster, the Magian and Persian, whose apocryphal writings those who followed the doctrine of Prodikas, boast that they possess." That we must read *ezêlôsen* " he emulated" instead of *edêlôsen* "he announced," is confirmed by an imitation in *Cyrillus adv. Jul.*, III, p. 87, where Pythagoras is called " the best emulator" of Zoroaster. It is true that *zêlôtês* is also employed in the sense of "a true disciple;" comp. *Hermippus* in Diogenes Laertes, VIII, 56. On the contrary, in Strabo, XVI, p. 762, Lycurgus is called *zêlôtês* of Minos.

[3] *Sub voce* Pythagoras :—" This man heard . . . . Zaratas the Magian." *Scholia* to Plato's Republic, X, p. 600 B, have the reading *Zaratas*.

teacher of Pythagoras, or if Plinius[1] names some Median Zaratas. On the contrary, we must assume that Zaratas, the Chaldæan or the Assyrian, is a person quite different from Zoroaster, and that his name is Semitic, perhaps similar to *Zaret* (or *Zereth*) in I. *Chronicles*, IV., 7. Nothing is proved by the fact that some later writers, *e. g.*, Agathias and Photius (see below), call Zoroaster also *Zarades* or *Zarasdes*; for, firstly, this form of the name is not identical with Zaratas, and, secondly, some confusion of the different personalities may have taken place.[2]

So the disagreeable eulogist Apuleius[3] stands quite alone in calling Zoroaster, the teacher of Pythagoras. Better informed writers knew too well that such a personal intercourse between Zoroaster and Pythagoras was impossible.

---

[1] *Historia Naturalis*, XXX, 1, 2 :—" How many are there who know the very names of the Medians, Apusorus and Zaratas, and the Babylonians, Marmarus and Arabantiphocus, or the Assyrian Tarmoenda, of whom there remain no documents ?"

[2] *See* Cotelier, *ad Recogn. Clems.*, IV, 27, and the anathema pronounced there against the Manichæans, wherein it is said :—" I anathematize Zarades, who, Mani says, had flourished before him among the Indians and Persians, and whom he called Helios, the Sun ; with him I anathematize the prayers which are called Zaradian prayers; and further below they are cursed who identify themselves with Zarades, Buddha, Christ, Manes and the Sun."

[3] *Floridus*, p. 19, ed. Altib.:—"There are authors who say that when Pythagoras was brought among the prisoners of King Cambyses into Egypt, he had at that time as teachers Persian Magi and specially Zoroaster, who was initiated into all divine mysteries. A more reliable statement, on the contrary, is that he had sought voluntarily to learn the Egyptian mysteries, and that he had learnt in Egypt from the priest the incredible powers of ceremonies, the admirable sets of numbers, the ingenious formulæ of geometry; but he had not been satisfied with these arts ; so he had soon turned to the Chaldæans and thence to the Brahmans (they are wise men, a tribe of India) and to the gymnosophists (*i.e.*, the sages that lived naked in India)."

This is, therefore, the result of my investigation. It is very probable that Pythagoras came to Babylon, and that he had there come in contact not only with Chaldæans and their sage Zaratas, but also with the Magi properly so called, and became acquainted with the Zarathushtrian doctrine; but no documental authority asserts that he had formed a personal acquaintance with Zoroaster, and it is a mere mistake of the moderns to confound Zaratas with Zoroaster. If Pythagoras came to Babylon at the latest under Cambyses (for those who antedate the year of his birth must likewise antedate his travels back to the beginning of the Persian Empire under Cyrus), it follows, hence, that the Zarathushtrian Reform was not an institution which had just originated, for the authorities do not say a word about it, but only place the wisdom of the Magi, emulated by Pythagoras, directly on a level with the Egyptian and Chaldæan sciences renowned in antiquity. And if we might concede that the whole account of the acquaintance of Pythagoras with the Zarathushtrian system is a later amplification of his travels (though indeed it is already met with in Aristoxenus), still these amplificators have supposed it as historically certain, that the Zarathushtrian Magism had existed long before the period when Pythagoras was still in his prime of life, and thus they consequently bear indirect testimony to the existence of Zarathushtra long before the father of Darius.

The fact that Pythagoras became acquainted with the Magi at Babylon, and that there existed, no doubt, Zarathushtrian schools in this capital in consequence of the Persian conquest, induced the later writers to directly call Zoroaster and Ostanes, Baby-

Ionians. Thus the author of *Theologumena Arithmetica* (page 43, ed. Ast.), says that Ostanes and Zoroaster, the most highly esteemed Babylonians, called the starry spheres *agélas* (herds), or in their holy sayings *àgélous*, or, corrupted by the interpolation of a *g*, *àggélous* "angels," for which reason they called also the stars and demons reigning over these *aggeloi*, angels and archangels, who were seven in number. This may be some transference from the Chaldæan to Zoroaster; yet similar conceptions concerning the chief stars are also met with in the Bundahish, Chapter V.

It is almost impracticable to determine whether there is anything Zarathushtrian, and, if so, what in the doctrines of Pythagoras, since what Pythagoras had taught himself and what his later disciples added, is quite obscure. Among the Pythagorean "beliefs" there are some which remind us of the Zarathushtrian doctrine, for instance: "Not to make water towards the Sun" (which is known also to Hesiod); "not to make water towards, nor to stand upon cut-off finger nails." However, we need not attach any particular importance to it.

Here I may add what is related about the travels of Democritus (who was born about 460 B. C. and died 104 years old, in B. C. 357). He wandered about, according to his own testimony, until his eightieth year, and saw the greatest portion of the known world, and had intercourse with a large number of men (*vide* his *Fragmenta* in Clemens Alexandrinus, *Stromata* I., p. 304). So there cannot be the least doubt as to the truth of what Ælianus[1] affirms:—"He had got to the Chaldæans and to Babylon, and to the Magi and to the sages of India." The time in which Democritus had intercourse with the Magi, falls under the reign of Artaxerxes I. Tatianus[2] says that he praised Ostanes the Magus. It might be supposed that the travels of Pythagoras were fabricated in imitation of the indisputable migrations of Democritus; but with equal right we may also assume that Democritus had been induced by that very example of Pythagoras to search after the wisdom of all nations at its source. In general we have very little idea of the closeness of intercourse existing in earlier times between the Orient and the Occident, and, therefore, we can calculate little upon the active intermediaries between both, *i.e.*, the Greeks of Asia Minor. But when, in consequence of the Persian wars, and still more of the conquests of Alexander the Great, more abundant and more faithful news referring to Persian affairs came across to Europe, the attention of learned Greeks was more and more drawn also to Zarathushtra and his system.

The earliest Greek writer who mentions Zoroaster, is Xanthus the Lydian, granting that the latter's age and authorship are accepted as fully established. For there are well-founded reasons to doubt especially the time in

---

[1] *Var. Hist.* IV, 20:—"Then he came to the Chaldæans and to Babylon, and to the Magi and to the sages, of India," Suidas *s.v. Democritus*:—"According to some writers (he was) a disciple of Anaxagoras and Lencippus; according to others also of the Magi, Chaldæans, and Persians. Clem. Alex., *Stromata*. I, p. 357, ed. by Potter;—"He came to Babylon, Persia, and Egypt, learning from the Magi and priests." This has been quoted by Eusebius in *Preparatio Evangel.*, X. 4.

[2] *Orat. ad. Graec.*, p. 47 ed. by Otto:—"Boasting the Magian Ostanes."

which Xanthus is said to have lived. As in his book a fact which happened under Artaxerxes I. is recounted,[1] we are to believe that he must have written it at least after Olympiad 78, 4 or 79, 1 (B. C. 465). If he was, as Suidas relates, *gegonòs epi tes haloseos Sardeon* " born at the time when Sardis was conquered," and if the conquest of Sardis took place under Crœsus, B. C. 546, and if by the word *gegonòs* is meant his " birth" (Olympiad 58, 3),[2] he must have been 80 years old just twenty Olympiads after, which is not at all impossible. But as Sardis was also taken under Darius Hystaspes in Olympiad 70, 2 (B. C. 499) by the Ionians and Athenians, we have from that time to Olympiad 70, 2 only an interval of 35 years. Here we have to choose whether we should take *gegonòs* in the sense of " born," in which case Xanthus at the beginning of the reign of Artaxerxes might not yet have attained 40 years; or in the sense of " flourishing," in which case he must have been about 30 years old at the time of the said conquest of Sardis, his birth in which city should be placed in B. C. 529, so that he must have been 64 years old during the reign of Artaxerxes, which is not improbable. The testimony of Dionysius of Halicarnassus[3] respecting Xanthus, that " he is one of those historians who were born some time before the Peloponnesian wars and lived to the

---

[1] Strabo I, p. 49, cites a passage from Eratosthenes (flourished about 250 B. C.), who mentions Xanthus :—" So saying he praised the doctrine of Straton the naturalist, and also of Xanthus the Lydian. According to Xanthus there was a great drought under Artaxerxes."

[2] Niebuhr, *Assur*, p. 64, places this conquest of Sardis in Olymp. 58, 1, *i.e.*, in 548 B. C. On account of similarity I follow the *Fasti* of Clinton.

[3] *De Thucyd. Ind. Th.*, VI, p. 817, ed. Reiske.

era of Thucydides," might render it possible to regard the conquest of Sardis (Olympiad 70, 2) as having taken place in the year of his birth; in this case he was at the beginning of the Peloponnesian war (Olympiad 87, 2) not yet 70 years, and was 28 years old at the birth of Thucydides. But if Xanthus was born about B. C. 529, he might have been 98 years of age at the commencement of the Peloponnesian war (an age he might have attained), and 58 years older than Thucydides. But we are not compelled to believe that Xanthus was still living at the beginning of the said war, since it is not implied in those words. It is at all events certain that he did not finish his work before Olympiad 79, and that he was an older contemporary of Herodotus, and influenced, according to Ephorus,[1] in no small degree the Father of History.

As to the authenticity of the works of Xanthus a later critic, Artemon of Cassandra, advanced some doubts and believed that they were by Dionysius Skytobrachion. Yet so early a writer as Athenæus, who is named in the above passage, directs our attention to the fact that Xanthus is mentioned as early as in Ephorus (B. C. 333), and the use unhesitatingly made of Xanthus by authors like Eratosthenes, Dionysius of Halicarnassus, and Strabo, as well as the opinion which they had as to his age, is of by far greater importance than the single assertion of Artemon regarding whose critical capacity we have no information whatever.

We know as little about the time of this Dionysius. Suetonius in his book *De Grammaticis*, chapter 7, says of

---

[1] In *Athen.*, XII. p. 515 :—" Ephorus the historian recounts that he was older than Herodotus and had much influence upon him."

M. Antonius Gnipho :—(He was) "in Alexandria, as some relate, and taught together with Dionysius Scytobrachion; but I can hardly believe this, for their times do not agree." Since Gnipho attained only an age of 50 years, and Cicero, being already prætor, is said to have heard his lectures, we must place his birth about B.C. 100; and if in order to take into consideration the doubts set forth by Suetonius as to the possibility of Gnipho having been educated together with Dionysius, we add still 50 years more for Dionysius, we only reach for the latter the middle of the second century before Christ. If, therefore, Dionysius had really forged the *Ludiaká* ('Lydian Matters') under the name of Xanthus, we are compelled to assume that the genuine *Ludiaká* lay before Ephorus and Eratosthenes, and that later authors, such as Dionysius of Halicarnassus and Strabo, either drew from that *genuine* work, or that they were deceived by a book which had been fabricated a few ages before them, during which time, moreover, the *Ludiaká* of Xanthus, still known to Eratosthenes, must have been supplemented by the spurious *Ludiaká* of Dionysius in such a manner that everything that was quoted from Xanthus by later writers, belonged to the fabricators.

The attempt of my venerable teacher, F. G. Welcker,[1] to prove the falsification from the fragments of Xanthus, is not at all cogent, nay he must even confess that several of them transmit to us popular and very antique legends. This distinguished investigator is chiefly

[1] In Seebode's "New Archives for Philology and Pedagogics," 1830, p. 65—80. With him agree Müller in his extensive "Collection of the Fragments of Greek Historians," and Schwegler in his "Roman History", I, p. 262.

shocked by those very statements which are ascribed to Xanthus concerning Zoroaster and his times, and by the fact that Xanthus is said to have written the *Magikà* ("Matters referring to the Magi,") from which book Clemens of Alexandria[1] draws information about the incestuous marriages among the Magi. But why should a man who has spent his whole life under the Persian sway, and consequently in daily intercourse with Magianism, have been unable to write such a book, whilst Herodotus, soon after him, treats the Persian religion in a very detailed manner?

Welcker, and after him Müller, hold it to be a characteristic of the Alexandrine period, that Xanthus speaks of the *Diadochi* ("successors" or "disciples") of Zoroaster; however, in the Zarathushtrian system this very tradition is proved by the original documents (yet they seem to be the words of Hermodorus, and not of Xanthus). It is self-evident that the conclusion of the fragment in Diogenes: "until the destruction of the Persian Empire by Alexander the Great," could as little be found in a book falsely ascribed to Xanthus the Lydian, as in a genuine work (no forger could be so stupid); and Creuzer has already observed (in his 'History of Greek Fragments,' p. 224), that this conclusion indeed originates from Hermodorus.

---

[1] *Stromata*, III, p. 515 ed. by Potter:—"Xanthus in his book entitled *Magikà*, relates that the Magi have sexual intercourse with . . . ." [This false allegation is refuted by me in my Papers on "The Alleged Practice of Next-of-kin-Marriages in Old Irân," read in 1887 before the B. B. of the Royal Asiatic Society. *Eng. Trans.*] Clemens does not give to Xanthus the surname of "the Lydian." Diogenes Laertius (Introduction 2), on the contrary, expressly calls the Xanthus, whose statement regarding the age of Zoroaster he mentions, the Lydian, with whom the identity of the Xanthus alluded to by Clemens and Diogenes, is not yet strictly proved, though it is rendered probable.

But as to the statements of Xanthus with regard to kindred marriages and to the time of Zoroaster, the former undoubtedly exists in the Avesta texts,[1] and below we shall perceive that Xanthus (he may have written "six thousand" or "six hundred") has drawn his information about the time of Zoroaster from good sources, though he did not perhaps correctly understand them.

But even if we admit hypothetically that the *Ludiaká* of Xanthus was written by Dionysius Scytobrachion, what is proved by it against the *Magiká?* The doubt of Artemon exclusively refers to the former book.

Creuzer, it is true, has adduced a proof for the authenticity of the *Magiká* from the fact that in the narrative of Cyrus and Crœsus (as it is apparently borrowed from the *Ludiaká* of Xanthus), Zoroaster, too, and likewise his *logiá* "sayings" are mentioned. But even without this help we are justified in believing that Xanthus the Lydian had treated of matters relating to the Magi, as long as the contrary opinion has not been proved. Welcker's objections to that narrative are, indeed, exaggerated; even they ascribe to the text an error that is evidently not contained in it. It is of course evident that the dramatical embellishment of the story of the cremation of Crœsus is not the work of Xanthus, but of the vain-glorious rhetorician Nicolaus. Nevertheless, there does not exist the contradiction found therein by Welcker, that on the one hand the Persians, at the rising storm, remember *logiá* or prophetic sayings of Zoroaster; while, on the other hand, Zoroaster is supposed to be still living to forbid the

---

[1] *Comp.* for instance *Visperad* III, § 3 W. (III, § 18 in Spiegel's Translation of the Avesta).

burning of the dead body, and that Crœsus is regarded as contemporary with Zoroaster, while he is said by Xanthus in his *Magiká* to have lived 600 or 6,000 years before the campaign of Xerxes. For the *logia* or sayings of Zoroaster, which occur to the minds of Persians, are designated by this very circumstance as something very old and forgotten, and in the next passage the author says, "as for Zoroaster, the Persians learned from him not to burn dead bodies, not to sully fire on any account, thus confirming the practice that had been established from ancient times." It is evidently the Persians, not Zoroaster alone, who inculcates anew the strict observance in future of some Zoroastrian law long existing. But that after the expression *ton gè mèn Zoroásren* something is omitted, perhaps some such word as *aidoumenos* "fearing, venerating," which has been already suggested by Valesius and Coray (see *Orelli, Supplementa*, note p. 42), whilst Müller expounds: "as to Zoroaster the Persians have . . ." However Welcker is not justified in supporting a contradiction between the *Majiká* and the *Ludiaká*; for nobody ascribes the *Majiká* to Dionysius Scytobrachion.

We are, therefore, confirmed in our opinion that the authentic Xanthus could simply relate in his *Ludiaká* concerning Crœsus nearly what Nicolaus, according to his manner, has embellished, and that, consequently, the mention of the Zoroastrian prohibition against the burning of the dead bodies can be drawn from him. We must not, however, forget that Nicolaus does not explicitly quote from the book of Xanthus, but that it is only most probable[1] that he has drawn from that source.

---

[1] *Vide* Creuzer, "History of Greek Fragments," p. 202. Müller, "Fragments of Greek History," I, p. 40.

Nor do we think it strange that Xanthus should have written the *Magikà*, or at least treated of Zoroaster and his time, after the Cuneiform Inscriptions have informed us that the Auramazdian religion had predominated under the Achæmenidæ, and thus it was perfectly known to the Lydian Xanthus by personal observation.

However, it might be objected, how is it possible that the older Xanthus made mention of Zoroaster and his laws, whilst the later Herodotus, who treats in so detailed and expert a manner of Persian life and Persian religion, entirely keeps silent upon this matter? Here I will lay no stress upon the fact that Herodotus, too, contains some information drawn from Xanthus, as, *e. g.*, the prohibition against burning corpses (Bk. III, 16); the marriage with one's sister (III, 31) which he traces back, it is true, to Cambyses. Rather we must insist upon the fact that all those who either consider Zoroaster to be far older than, or contemporary with the father of Darius, all those who think Xanthus to be either authentic or forged, have to solve the enigma. The Auramazdian religion existed as early as the time of Darius and predominated in the Persian Empire, and yet Herodotus does not mention Zoroaster or Ahura-Mazda. This problem cannot, I believe, be explained by those who make Zoroaster a contemporary of Hystaspes, the father of Darius. For, how could it be possible that Herodotus had not mentioned so powerful a religious crisis happening hardly two generations before his birth?

However, not taking into consideration the Zarathushtrian epoch, how was it possible that Herodotus did not even know the prophet Zoroaster, whilst Plato, who flourished 55 years after Herodotus, was accurately informed about Zarathushtra, and apparently must have drawn from sources which were at least as old as Herodotus? The description given by the latter concerning Persian customs and religion (Bk. I, 131-140) contains, moreover, a series of features truly Zarathushtrian ; as, for instance, the worship of the deities without images or temples ; the offering of sacrifices to Zeus (who is evidently Ahura Mazda), to the Sun, Moon, Earth, Fire, Water, and Winds (*vide* Yasna XVI, 4) ; the worship of Anâhita, whom he calls Mithra ; the description of the sacrifice at which a Magus standing near sings the theogony, which points to sacrificial prayers, such as the Yasna and the Yashts ; the victims which were, according to him, bulls, horses, camels, and asses, whilst the poor offered " small pieces of mutton," just as in the Yashts horses, cattle, and smaller animals are offered (Abân Yasht., § 21), and in Vendidâd, Farg. XXII, § 3, horses, camels, cattle, and smaller animals are vowed.[1] The stress laid on the begetting of children, on veracity and freedom from debts ; the religious observance done to the rivers, and the prohibition against making water in them or in the presence of another person ; the interdict against the burning of corpses (Bk. III, 16) ; the marriage with one's sister (Bk. III, 31)[2]; the necessity of exposing

---

[1] Heraclides Cumanus, a writer of uncertain date (*comp.* Müller, *Fragm. Hist. Graec.* II, p. 95), who has treated of Persian customs, religion, laws and history in a work entitled *Persika*, consisting of at least two books. He says in one of the Fragments in *Athenaeus* IV, p. 145:—"The Persian king offers 1,000 sacrificial animals every day ; among these are horses, camels, oxen, asses, stags, and plenty of sheep ; also many birds are sacrificed." Here the number " one thousand" victims is given as in the *Yashts*.

[2] *Vide* note 1, p. 78. *Eng. Trans.*

the corpses that they may be eaten by dogs or birds before the bones are consigned to the charnel-house; the zeal with which the Magi destroy ants, serpents, and other vermin, whilst they are forbidden to kill dogs and men; all these and other features indisputably prove that Herodotus well knew the Magian belief, as it is expounded in the Avesta texts, although here and there he misunderstood it. That he does not mention the name of Zarathushtra, whose religion he interprets, is, we may hence infer, a mere matter of chance, or he had some special reason unknown to us, perhaps because Xanthus had already treated of it. Or should we conceive that Herodotus became acquainted with the Magian belief merely from oral tradition recounted by men who were not well disposed towards the Magi, and who, therefore, kept secret the name of the founder of their religion? Suffice it to observe that in the silence of Herodotus concerning Zarathushtra we have a remarkable instance of how little value is to be attached to the *argumentum a silentio*, even where, as here, the most direct occasion of mentioning him might be given.

After Xanthus the Lydian had explicitly treated of Zoroaster, after Herodotus had described the religious system founded by him, and after Plato's predecessors in philosophy, Pythagoras and Democritus, had been in intercourse with the Magi, we should not be surprised if we find Zoroaster and the God proclaimed by him in the works of Plato[1] (*vide supra*, p. 82).

---

[1] The story of Er, son of Armenius (so the words, *ton Armenion* "of the Armenian Er," are explained by the Scholiast), of the Pamphylian race, is related by Plato in his book called the *Republik* (X, p. 614. B. *seq.*), that he fell in the battle and revived again on the funeral bed, and proclaimed the mysteries of the other world. This story is as-

The fact indeed need not be ignored that the authencribed by Clemens Alexandrinus (*Stromata* V, p. 711) to Zoroaster, who is directly identified with Er:—"The same Plato, in his tenth book on the *Republik*, mentions *Er*, the Armenian (or son of Armenius), a Pamphylian, that is Zoroaster (in all four passages *Zoroastres*). At any rate Zoroaster himself writes:—' These things have been written by Zoroaster, son of Armenius, a pamphylian, who died in battle, arrived in Hades and was taught there by the gods.' As to this Zoroaster, Plato recounts that he lay on his funeral bed on the twelfth day and revived. He here perhaps metaphorically implies a resurrection, as well as the idea that through the way across the 12 zodiacal signs the soul is taken up, and says that by the same way the souls come down when they come into (material) existence." Whence this mistake arose in Clemens, may be guessed from the words:—"These things have been written by Zoroaster." Probably in one of the Greek Pseudo-Zoroastrian books Zoroaster is represented as relating the story of Her. Or can Her have been reckoned as a Zoroastrian and called himself *Zarathushtrish* (*comp.* Yasna 1, § 23)? From which reasons have the later writers made him Zoroaster himself? The story itself scarcely contain any Zarathushtrian reminiscences. Neither Plutarch, (*Sympos. Probl.* IX, 5, 2):—"That they speak of the intellectual nature of Heaven and the harmonious course of the universe as a winged chariot, and further more they call that messenger from Hades, the Pamphylian, the son of Armenius by the name of *Er*……..", nor Justinus (*Cohort, ed Gent.* 27), nor Origenes (*adversus Cels.* II., 16), nor Augustin (*de Civitate Dei* XXII, 28) who relate the story of *Her*, know anything about his identity with Zoroaster (*Cyrillus, VIII, adv. Julian. Theodoret. Serm.* 11, p. 653). As for the rest Arnobius, too, makes use of this passage (*adv.* G. I, p. 31, ed. Lugdunensis Lyon). Macrobius in *Somn. Scrip.* I, 1:—"This relater of mysteries in Plato is a certain Er, a Pamphylian by birth, and a soldier by profession. He seems to have died of the wounds which he had received in battle. On the 12th day after his death he was to have been honoured with the last rites of the pyre together with others who had fallen victims with him; but suddenly he revived or had perhaps retained his life. He proclaimed to mankind whatever he had seen or done during this time. Cicero, as if he were conscious himself of its truth, regrets the ridicule cast upon this tradition by unlearned people, and while believing it to be true, he prefers the idea of awakening to that of reviving, as if he would avoid the reproof of dulness." To this Mai, p. 311 (Stuttgart edition), adds the following observation :—"As to the name and kindred of Er (by some called Zoroaster), many excellent things have been written by Proclus whose work I shall publish. In this work Proclus mentions his own and Zoroaster's work, and the authors Cronius and Theodorus Asinæus."

ticity of this dialogue is contested by several critics, while it is defended by others (*e.g.*, Hermann, *Geschichte und System der Plat. Philos.*, "The History and System of Platonic Philosophy," I, p. 439). For our purpose it will suffice to assume that Zoroaster was known in Greece in the time of Plato. The assertion of later writers[1] that Plato had travelled to the country inhabited by the Magi and the Persians, is opposed by that of Diogenes of Laërte[2], that Plato had intended going to the Magi; but that he was prevented from doing so by the wars then raging in Asia. However, both these statements presuppose that Persia and its religion had excited a very high interest among inquiring Greeks of that period. For this reason an important contemporary of Plato, Eudoxus of Cnidus, who is said by Apollodorus (*comp.* Diog. Laërt., VIII, 90) to have attained his youth about B. C. 368 (Olympiad, 103), and who was distinguished as lawgiver, physician, and astronomer, treated in his last work: *Gês Periodos* ("The Revolution of the Earth") of the Magi (*comp.* Plutarch, *De Isis et Osiris, ibid*) as is attested by Diogenes of Laërte (Proem. 8). If we might take the words of Diogenes literally, they would imply

---

[1] Lactantius, *Institutiones* IV, 2: "I must wonder at the fact that Pythagoras, and afterwards Plato, who had been stimulated by the love of truth, went to the Egyptians, the Magi, and the Persians, in order to learn their religions and ceremonies (thinking that wisdom was to be found in their religions); but they did not go to the Jews. *Comp.* Plinius, *Hist. Nat.*, XXX, 1. 2.

[2] III., 7:—"Plato resolved to pay a visit to the Magi, too, but he did not fulfil that resolution, fearing the war in Asia."—Apuleius, *de habitud. doctrin. Plat. Phil.*, p, 569, ed. Florid.:—"He would have directed his attention to the Indians and the Magi but for the Asiatic wars."

that Eudoxus' asserts just as Aristotle does some years later, that the Magi were older than the Egyptians. According to the Magi there are two principles, the good and the bad genii, Oromazdes and Areimanios. According to Pliny (XXX, 1, 2), Eudoxus also agreed with Aristotle in placing Zoroaster 6,000 years before Christ. But a distinguished historian of those days, Dino,[1] the father of Clitarchus, the companion of Alexander, has written towards the end of the Persian Empire (yet he mentions an incident relating to Ochus B. C. 350) a work entitled *Persiká* ("Persian Matters"), divided into three *suntáxeis* or volumes; the first part was called *Assuriaká*, the second *Mediká*, and the third *Persiká*. Each volume contained several sections. From this excellent source a great deal is drawn that we read in Cornelius Nepos and Plutarch, and some fragments prove to us that he enlarged also on the religious side of Persian life. I pass over the mere historical statements found in the fragments of Dino's writings, and speak of only those notices which relate to the religion. In the fifth fragment (II, p. 90, I) edited by Müller,[2] Dino says that the Magi did not know the

---

[1] Comp. Müller, *Fragmenta Historia Gr.* II, p. 88 *seq.*

[2] Diogenes Laërtius, *Proem.* I, 8:— "Yet they were not versed in mantology by witchcraft, as stated by Aristotle in his book *Magiká*. Dinon says in the Fifth Book of his *History*, that the word Zoroaster should be translated the 'adorer of stars.' This is also confirmed by Hermodorus." Menage and Bochart would rather spell the name *Astrotheaten* " a beholder of stars," " a star-gazer" (instead of *Astrothuten* "a worshipper of stars"). Toup has *Astrotheten* " a commander of stars"; yet the ordinary reading is determined by the *Scholiast* of Plato, *Alcibiades*, p. 122. I add here the *Scholion* to this passage of *Alcibiades* in the Scholiast (Plato, Tome VI., p. 281, ed. Stam.):—"Zoroaster is said to have been older than Plato by 6,000 years; some say that he was a Greek, or a man of that nation which came from the Continent on the other

mantic magic, which is entirely correct; as the Avesta texts abhor, and are opposed everywhere to the nature of the sorcerer (*yâtu*), and designate it as something diabolical (*comp., e.g.,* Vend., Farg. I, §§ 14-15). The translation of the name *Zarathushtra,* however, reminds us of the explanation which travellers are wont to receive from their guides. Probably the interpreter sought in the first syllable *zor* the Persian word *zôr* = Avesta *zaothra* meaning " offering"; while *astres* was identified unhesitatingly with the Greek *astér* " a star." Besides, this attempt at explanation evinces with what interest the Greeks endeavoured to penetrate into the matter in question.

---

side of the great water. He is said to have learnt universal wisdom from the good spirit, that is, from the excellent understanding. His name translated into Greek means *Astrothutes,* 'a star-worshipper.' He recommended the anchoretic life and moderation in living. He left several books from which it is demonstrated that he professed three kinds of philosophy, *viz.,* physical, economical, and political." And in the preceding passage the author states:—" That Zoroaster kept silence from his seventh year, and that he announced the whole philosophy to the Persian King (Vishtâsp) at 30 years of age, and that the number *seven* was sacred to Mithra, whom the Persians chiefly venerate." The references as to Zoroaster having been older than Plato by 6,000 years, are drawn from Aristotle or Eudoxus, and the notice about the signification of the name of Zoroaster from Dino. That Zoroaster had received his instruction from the Good Spirit, *i.e.,* Ahura Mazda, is as correct as the explanation, " that is, from the excellent understanding," as far as this is meant of *Mainyush-khratush,* " the heavenly understanding." Of the anchoretic life of Zoroaster we shall speak in another place. That Zoroaster kept silence from his seventh year, and announced after thirty years his doctrine to the King, is confirmed by other authorities; also the *Syngrammata.* Quite unique stands the statement :—He was a Greek, or one of those who came forth from the Continent on the other side of the great sea. This last expression is very obscure; it sounds too mysterious to designate the Greeks of Asia Minor. Is it perhaps some reminiscence of the passage of the primitive man to the six *keshvars,* which took place under Tahmurap? Or of the Altantis?

The art of divination by magic was, as Dino affirms, abhorred by the Magi, who, he says, on the contrary predict by means of twigs (*i. e.*, rhabdomancy),[1] which might recall to our mind the *Wünschelruthe*, "the divining rod," of German Mythology. But we must rather allude to the bunch of twigs, which play so important a part in the Persian liturgy under the name of *baresman*. According to Anquetil (*Usages*, Vol. II, p. 532), this *barsam* is made of the wood of the pomegranate tree, of the tamarisk, or of the date tree. But the latter *murikinon xûlon* is the wood of the tamarisk with which the Magi, according to Strabo,[2] chanted hymns, holding a bunch of fine twigs in their hands. Dino[3] further relates that the Persian and the Median Magi offer sacrifice in the open air, and that they regard fire and water as the only likeness of the divinities. This statement is quite well founded if it is correctly understood. Images of gods were unknown to the ancient Persians, and the high veneration shown by them to the sacred fire and water must have evoked

---

[1] *Schol. Nicand. Ther.*, 613:—"The Magi and the Scyths prophesy by means of tamarisk wood; in many places they prophesy also by staves. Dinon says, in the third chapter of the first book, that the Median magicians, too, predict by staves."

[2] XV, p. 733:—"They sing their lays for a long time, holding a bunch of small tamarisk twigs."

[3] Clemens Alexandrinus, *Cohertatio*, ed. *Gent.*, c. 5, p. 56, ed. Potter :—" They (*i.e.*, the Persians, the Medians, and the Magi) sacrifice, says Dinon, in the open air, believing that fire and water are the only images of deities." Clemens adds that "after a long period of years" the image-worship of Anâhita was introduced by Artaxerxes Mnemon. It is clear that this opinion presupposes the idea of a higher antiquity of Zarathushtra than the (short period of) two hundred years which intervened between Hystaspes, the father of Darius, and Artaxerxes Mnemon.

in the observing Greek the opinion that fire and water were considered by the Persians as symbols of the Deity.

Two characteristic facts are preserved by Dino,[1] which prove that he drew his information from authentic sources. He says that amongst the heathens, too, there were heroic bards, and that such bards had predicted the valour of Cyrus and his future wars against Astyages. For, when Cyrus went to Persia and Astyages was sailed with his friends, the most celebrated bard named Angares was called in, and he sang the common lays which he concluded with the words:—"A huge beast will be set free in the swamps more formidable than a wild boar; no sooner shall he have sway over his country than he will easily fight against many." But when Astyages asked: "What animal?" He answered[2]:—"Cyrus the Persian." Astyages having been persuaded that the suspicion was well-founded, sent his messenger to call back Cyrus, but in vain.

---

[1] *Athen.* XIV, p. 633. c., wherein mention is made of the bard Phemius in Homer, who celebrated the heroes:—"This usage has been preserved also by the barbarians, as related by Dino in his *Persiká*. For the bards predicted the valour of Cyrus I. and his war against Astyages. For when, he says, Cyrus entered into Persia, he met at first the mace-bearers and afterwards the life-guards; when Astyages was carousing with his friends and Angares, the most famous of the bards who was called in, was singing the ordinary songs. At the end of the feast, he says, a great beast is sent away into the moor, stronger than a wild boar. As soon as he begins to rule in his neighbourhood, he easily combats with many. But when Astyages questioned: "what animal?" He replied:—"Cyrus, the Persian." Astyages believing that this suspicion was well-founded, sent people to call back Cyrus, but in vain."

[2] ["A mighty beast, more fierce than wildest boar,
　Is to his marshes gone, why should he go?
When master of the country all around,
　To hunters he will prove a deadly foe.—*Tr. n.*"]

It is highly interesting to see Dino mentioning an old lay on this king of the Ophidian dynasty, which is said by Moses of Chorene to have been celebrated *(vide Zor. St.,* p. 138) by the popular songs of the Armenians. The name of the bard Angares reminds us of the Vedic *Angiras;* but the lay contains an idea common in the Avesta texts, personifying victory (*Verethraghna*) in the shape of a formidable boar with sharp claws and tusks (see Windischmann, *Mithra,* p. 41).

Another similar fact from Dino has been preserved by Cicero[1]. Cyrus sees in a dream the sun at his feet, and thrice attempts in vain to take hold of him, until the sun contracts and disappears. The Magi predict to him from this threefold attempt a reign of thirty years. This sun is evidently the *hvarenô ahvaretem* (or *kâvaem,* for both are adequate), the majesty originating in God, the splendour, the fortune of kings, so often spoken of in the Avesta texts, and which is said (in *Zamyâd Yasht,* §§ 56 *seq.*) to have been thrice sought for and seized in vain by Afrâsiâb, and to have been borne away each time to the Lake *Vouru-kasha*. The parallel is too striking to be misunderstood. I do not hence conclude that Dino himself had passages like those of the *Yasht* cited above, lying before him, yet I may infer that his statements were drawn from sources such as those old songs, allegories, and expressions, which

---

[1] *De Divinatione.* I., c. 23 :—" Shall I recount from the *Persiká* of Dino what the Magi have interpreted to the famous King Cyrus? For, when he was sleeping the sun appeared to be at his feet, and he sought three times in vain to touch him with his hand, when the sun rolled back and disappeared then the Magi (*i.e.,* wise and learned men in Persia) predicted to him from this triple attempt on the sun, that Cyrus would reign for 30 years. So it was; for after having begun to reign at 40, he lived to 70 years."

correspond to our Avesta texts; and that Dino consequently bears testimony to the antiquity of the contents of the latter. It is uncertain whether Clitarchus, the son of Dino, has spoken of it in his history of the Magi; for the long fragment cited by Diogenes appears to belong to others, only the words, "the gymnosophists condemned to death," seem to appertain to the physician in ordinary to Alexander the Great. However, the passage is certainly taken from an able author, and will be mentioned below. Though somewhat younger than Dino and Plato, Aristotle devoted his attention so much the more to the Magi, because, as we have seen, Greek philosophers and historians had found an intimate acquaintance, for nearly two centuries, with this feature of Oriental life, and had partly described it. In his "Metaphysics" (X., p. 301, 8th edition by Brand[1]) he once touches slightly upon the doctrine of the first causes. According to Diogenes of Laerte,[2] he has written a special book entitled *Magikós*, which is, however, ascribed by others to Antisthenes or Rhodon,[3] and he has enlarged upon the doctrine of the Magi in a larger work entitled *Peri Philosophias* ("On Philosophy"). Valuable is, indeed, the fragment

---

[1] "Others, too, explain the first causes as cleverly as the Magi."

[2] Proem. 1.:—"There are Magi among the Persians, as Aristotle says in his book *Magiká*." Ibid 8:—"They did not know that prophecy was executed by sorcery, said Aristotle in his book *Magiká*, and Dino, etc." (see above).

[3] Suidas *sub voce Antisthenes*, "the first book on *Magiká*, which treats of the Magian Zoroaster who invented philosophy; but the invention of philosophy is also ascribed by some to Aristotle, by others to Rhodon." *Cfr.* Brandis, "History of Philosophy," II, 2, p. 84. *seq.*

preserved by Diogenes,[1] wherein Aristotle says: "The Magi are older than the Egyptians, and there are two first causes, the good genius and the evil genius." The one is called Zeus and Oromazdes, the other Hades and Areimenios, which is the first mention particularly of the evil genius of the Magi, expressly made by the Greeks. Besides, Pliny[2] traces back to Aristotle the opinion that Zoroaster lived six thousand years before the death of Plato. Indeed we have to regret very much the loss of these books of Aristotle, the master of philosophy, as they contained not only historical and highly trustworthy dates, but also treated of the speculative conception of Magism.

Not the less should we regret the loss of that book which the renowned historian Theopompus, in his great work *Philippiká*, devoted to Zoroaster and the Magi. Born about B. C. 378, he wrote 12 books on *Hellenika* and 58 books on *Philippiká*; of the latter 53 were still existing in the time of Photius (*Cod.* 176, p. 390), and in the eight of these books he enlarged upon Zoroaster and the Magi,[3] bearing testimony not merely to what

---

[1] Proem. 8:—"Aristotle in his first book on Philosophy relates that the Magi are older than the Egyptians, and that they believe in two first causes, a good spirit and an evil spirit. The first, they say, is called Zeus and Oromazdes, the second Hades and Areimanios." The latter form of the name sounds already nearly alike to Neo-Persian Ahriman; and there exist many other symptoms to indicate that the vulgar Irânian idioms had been already formed in that period.

[2] *Hist. Nat.*, XXX, 1, 2:—"Eudoxus who thinks that they are among the most celebrated and useful section of philosophers, narrated that Zoroaster lived 6,000 years before the death of Plato, and so did Aristotle."

[3] The eighth book existed during the life-time of Photius. Perhaps, it might still be found somewhere. Diogenes Laertius, Proem. 8, adds, after *Areimanios*, to the words cited above:—"This is related also by Hermippus in his first book on the Magi, by

has been quoted above from Aristotle regarding Ahura-Mazda and Angrô-Mainyush, but also the Resurrection doctrine of the Magi of which we shall speak further on. From him drew also Plutarch,[1] who quotes him by name. What he has besides preserved in his work, *De Iside et Osir.*, *ch.* 46 and 47, on the doctrine of the Magi, may partly have been borrowed from Dino, Aristotle, Eudoxus, Hermodorus, Hermippus and Sotion; however, we will consider Theopompus as his principal authority. Here I add, therefore, those invaluable fragments of Greek knowledge on Magism, abstaining from any detailed explanation concerning those points which are or will be treated of by me in other places.

" Some believe," so says Plutarch following his authors, " that there are two divine powers working in opposition to each other, the one is the creator of the good, the other is the creator of the bad ; some call the better one God, the other Demon, like Zoroaster the Magus, who is said to have lived 5,000 years before the Trojan war.[2] He called the one Oromazes, the other Areimanios, declaring that the former, more than any other thing perceptible through the senses, resembled light, the other, on the contrary, darkness and ignorance ;[3] but between these two stands Mithra, who is for that

---

Eudoxus in his Travels, and by Theopompus in the eighth chapter of the *Philippika*. Theopompus also says that, according to the Magi, men will revive again and be immortal, and that things and names will keep together."

[1] On *Isis and Osiris*, 47:—In the eighth book of Theopompus is also contained an allusion to Pythagoras (*see Athen.*, V, p. 213 *seq.*)

[2] This is borrowed from Hermodorus.

[3] In other passages, too, these contrasts are mentioned by Plutarch.

reason called by the Persians "Mithra the Mediator." He taught to offer supplications and thanksgiving to the former, but deprecations and gloomy sacrifices to the latter. Pounding a certain herb, called *omomi*, in a mortar,[1] they invoke Hades and Darkness, and then mix it (*i.e.*, the juice of the herb) with the blood of a slain wolf, and take it to a place which is not illumined by the sun, and cast it away. For, some of the plants they regard as pertaining to the good God, while others to the evil Demon; and some of the animals, as *e. g.*, dogs, birds, and hedgehogs, as belonging to the former, but water-mice to the latter; for which reason that person is called happy who kills most of them (*viz.*, the evil creatures)."

"But they (*i. e.*, the Magi), too, relate many wondrous things about the divine existences, as for example the following:—Oromazes emanating from the purest light, and Areimanios from darkness, fight against each other. Oromazes created six *Amesha-Spentas*: the first that of bounty, the second that of truth, the third that of good government; but of the remaining he made one the spirit of wisdom, another that of riches, and the last that of the pleasures of the beautiful creations in Nature. Areimanios made an equal number, as it were, of antagonists. Afterwards Oromazes enlarged himself threefold, and withdrew from the sun as far as the earth is remote from the sun, and decorated the heaven with stars; but one star, namely, Sirius, was placed by him before all as

---

[1] It has long since been observed that this fully agrees with the preparation of the *haoma*-juice, and that these "round stones" are the *hâvanas* of stone and iron, in which the sacred plant is pounded.

guardian and forerunner. And when Oromazes created 24 gods, he placed them in an oval body, but as many evil spirits as were created by Areimanios perforating it entered into it......(a gap), for which reason good is intermixed with evil. There will come a predestined time during which Areimanios, who brings pestilence and hunger, will entirely perish at the hands of the good genii, and will disappear; for when the earth has become even and level, there must appear *one* life and a community of all happy men, who will likewise speak one language. But Theopompus says that, according to the Magi, one of these divine powers will reign by turns for three thousand years when the other will be swayed over; for another 3,000 years they will combat and war against each other, and the one will destroy the creation of the other. But at length Hades will succumb and men shall be happy, neither wanting food nor throwing a shadow. The Supreme Power, who is to effect this, will rest and repose for a time, though long in itself, yet moderate for the God as if He were a sleeping man."

It has already been observed elsewhere (*vide* Windischmann, *Mithra*, p. 56 *seq.*) that whatever is said about the opposition of the two spirits, about their nature as light and darkness, about *Mithra* and the *Andarvâî*, literally harmonizes with the Avesta texts and the Bundahish which is based on them. What is said concerning the *haoma*-offering, ought to be correctly understood. Every Magian offering is in itself partly an appeasing of Ahura Mazda, partly a counteracting of the evil spirits; but, moreover, we find along with the *euktaia* " invocations," and *chariséria* " prayers" unto Ahura and the *yazatas*, also *ápotropia kai skuthropá* " deprecations and execrations" against Angrô-Mainyush and the Demons (*cf. e. g. Vendidâd*, Farg. X, §§ 9,10,13,16 ; XI, § 8, *seq.*) ; it is especially said with regard to the *haoma*-offering that the least squeezing out of the *haoma*-juice, the least eulogy of the *haoma*, the least drinking of the *haoma*, serves for a " thousand killings of the *daevas*" (*Yasna* X, § 6). We must not put stress, therefore, upon the word *thúein* " to offer," as it would not be correct to say that something is offered to Angrô-Mainyush ; on the contrary, rather *thúein* is joined here by a zeugma with the next proposition to which it is not adapted. But the word *anakalountai* " they are called upon aloud," is quite appropriate, referring to the imprecations against the *daevas*, which have been alluded to above. It is also true that the wolf is an Ahrimanic animal ; that among the prayers addressed to *haoma* in the hymn (*Yasna* IX, § 21), there is the entreaty that the wolf may be seen in due time lest he surprise man ; and that wolves are among the evil creatures which are to be fought against (see *Yasht* III, § 8). But it is not affirmed by the Avesta texts. On the contrary, it seems to contradict the religious system. That the *haoma*-juice is mixed with the blood of the wolf was, perhaps, a statement derived from some local usage deviating from the Magian rigour; or it was not the juice, but the remaining fibres which were used in this way.

What follows about the distribution of plants and animals between the two demiurgi, can be completely instanced by the texts, specially the Bundahish. How much dogs were esteemed, is proved by the Fargards treating of them. The *échinos chérsaios*, " the hedgehog living on dry land," is that animal which in Farg. XIII, § 2, is designated as the chief antagonist of the demons :—*Spânem sizdrem urvîsarem yim vanghâparem yim mashyâka, avi duzvachanghô duzakem nâma aojaiti.* The Huzvaresh translation gives the name *zûzak* (comp. Bundahish, Westergaard's edition, p. 30, l. 15 :—" the *zaozag* which is called *khârpûsht*," literary "sting-hide"; and p. 49, 1, 1, where it is said :—" the *zûzak* voids its water into all the holes of the corn-training ants, and kills thousands of them." The word *zûzak* is apparently a variation of *duzaka*.) It is the ant-eater: *tachyglossus aculeatus*[1]; *sizdrem* seems to contain in its first part another form of *tîz* (comp. Sanskrit *sigra*), and to mean " stinged," " prickled," or " pointed."

The Ahrimanian animal is here called in the common text: *thous enhudrous*, " one living in water, *i.e.*, an animal," which in contrast to *chersaious*, " one living on land," and with the supplement *échinos*, " a hedgehog," must denote a kind of water-hedgehog ; (*énhudris*, " the otter," being an animal sacred to the Persians, cannot be meant here). Another passage of the same Plutarch[2] shows that here also *mus* "a mouse" is to be supplied, the mouse being an evil animal (comp. *Sad-dar*, chap. XLVII).

---

[1] [A technical term in Natural History; the expression means " stinged sharp tongue."—*Trans. note.*]

[2] *Quaest conviv.*, IV, 5, 2 :—" The Magi, being followers of Zoroaster, esteem in the highest degree the land-hedgehog, but hate water-mice, and call him, who kills most of them, a friend of the good spirits and a happy man."

That the six gods created by Oromazes are the six *Amesha-Spentas,* has been known long ago.[1] Their names, according to their moral value, as for instance, in the Gâthâs,[2] and exclusive of their physical import, are rendered excellently. *Vohu-manô,* "the good mind," is the *demiourgos Eeunoias,* " the demiurgus of benevolence;" according to the physical meaning he is "the lord of cattle and other animals." *Asha-vahishta* is "the best purity or truth." I have elsewhere shown that he is the *Ománes* of Strabo, and that the name *Ochos* is derived also from it; for both of them morally mean *asha,* the *demiourgós Aletheias,* "the demiurgus of truth," and physically imply "the lord of fire." *Khshathra-vairya,* "the excellent or venerable lord," is at the same time "the lord of metals." *Spentâ-ârmaiti* "the humble pious mind," the *demiourgòs Sophias* "the demiurgus of wisdom," is physically "the genius of the earth." *Haurvatât,* "the preserver and feeder," who gives terrestrial blessings, the *demiourgós Ploútou* "the demiurgus of riches," is physically the lord of water. *Ameretât,* the *Amandatos* of Strabo, physically "the lord of trees," is at the same time morally "the genius of reward in heaven."

Quite appropriate is the Greek expression *antitechnous,* "the opposing or opponent," which has been

---

[1] Burnouf, *Comm., Yasna* I, p. 150 *seq.,* and the passage in Neriosengh, p. 146.

[2] *Vôhu-manô* is translated by Neriosengh, in Yasna XXVIII, § 2, by the words:—*uttamam manas. Ash. vah.* in Ys. XXVIII, §§ 4 and 6, and Ys. XXIX, 2, by *dharma;* yet in verse 11 also by *satyatâ*; *Khshathrem* by *rájyam*; in Ys. XXIX, 11, the names *Ashavah, Vohu-manô* and *Kshathra-vairyô* are explained by *puñyam, uttamammanô,* and *rájyam.* Ys. XXXI. 4: *punya=Ash. vah.* [*Ârmaiti=sumpûrnamânasa* XXVIII, § 8; and XXXIV, 9 *Haurvatât=sarvapravrtti; Ameretât=amrtyupravrtti,* XXX, 6.]

chosen to designate the adverse nature of the Ahrimanian (evil) genii, and to render the Avesta word *paityâra* (comp. Haug, *Gâthâs*, p. 223); for in contrast to these six *Amesha-Spentas* literally stand the evil spirits, *Akôman, Andar, Saurva, Taromat, Tarich* and Zarich in the Pahlavi Bundahish (Westergaard's edition, p. 76, l. 6 compared with p. 5, l. 9), whose statements are based on the original Avesta texts, as for example the *Zamyâd Yasht*, § 96.

The triple enlargement by Oromizes, which reminds us of the triple enlargement of the earth by *Yima*, seems to refer to the three heavens through which, as through stages, it is possible to reach the highest habitation of God; (see *Yasht Fragment* II; and Spiegel, *Parsi Grammatik*, p. 188). The *Yasna* XIX, § 6, also seems to point to this triple growth. The term of distance, "as far as the sun is from the earth," is truly Avestic.

The great eulogy of Sirius, *i. e.*, the Avestic *Tishtrya*, is confirmed by the sacrificial hymn on this *yazata*, and it is very remarkable that in the Bundahish, p. 77, after describing the creation of the stars, *Tishtar* is called the first leader in their rising.

The remaining twenty-four good genii are the *yazatas*, whose number can be variously given. Twenty of them, besides *Ahura Mazda* and the six *Amesha-Spentas*, give their names to the days of the month (comp. *Yasna* XVI, § 3 *seq.*) To these four others might easily be added, as for instance, *Nairyô-sangha, Airyama-ishya, Anâhita* (if this is not already included in water), *Haoma*, etc.

Truly I know no Avestic passage in which the universe is represented as an egg (a conception very common with the Indians); yet the idea of a heaven by which everything is surrounded cannot be explained but by a special shape. However, in the Pahlavi[1] *Mainukhrad*, chap. XLIV, § 8 *seq.*, the world-egg is explicitly mentioned:—

(8) ⸺⸺⸺⸺⸺
⸺⸺⸺⸺ (9) ⸺⸺⸺⸺
⸺⸺⸺⸺ (10) ⸺⸺⸺⸺
⸺⸺⸺⸺⸺

"The sky and earth and water and everything else within them, resemble a fried-egg, for example the egg of a bird. The sky is arranged above the earth, like an egg, by the direct help of the Creator Aûharmazd; and the semblance of the earth, in the midst of the heaven is just like the yolk amid the egg."[2] The perforation and penetration of Ahriman into the terrestrial creation and the intermixture of good and evil resulting from it, is described verbatim in the Bundahish, p. 9, l. 13. The remaining part of this passage will be explained below. Here I have only to remark that Eudemus the Rohdian is also mentioned by Diogenes[3] as an authority on the Magian doctrine

---

[1] (8) *Aigh, âsmân va Zamîk va âv va avârig kôlâ memar, andarûn khâiyaginîh aêdûn hûmânâk chêgûn morûân khâiyak* 1. (9) *Va âsmân azpar zamîk khâiyak hûmânâk pavan yedman-kârîh î Dâtâr Aûharmazd vînârd yeka-vimûnêd;* (10) *va Zamîk bên miyân î âsmân angûshîdak aêdûn hûmânâk chêgûn zardak miyân î khâiyak*. [I have here quoted the original Pahlavi text instead of giving Windischmann's transliteration of the Pazend. *Trans. note.*]

[2] Comp. Dr. West, S. B. E., vol. XXIV.

[3] Proem. 9 :—"This is also related by Eudemus the Rhodian."

of the Resurrection. Eudemus was one of the best disciples of Aristotle (comp. Jons. *Scriptorum Hellenicorum Phil.*, I, 15, 2). He has written a history of astronomy (*Astrologikai Historiai*), where he might very probably have made mention of Zoroaster. A book of Heraclides Ponticus, who was a disciple of Plato and Aristotle, bore, as is alleged by Plutarch (*Adversus Colot.*, p. 1115-A), the name of Zoroaster. Among other books enumerated therein by Plutarch, he mentions also *Herakleidou ton Zoroástren, to peri tôn en Hadou, to peri ton phusikos aporoumenon,* "the Zoroaster of Heraclides upon infernal things or persons, and upon things physically problematical." We might, hence, be tempted to conjecture that, on account of the juxtaposition of the book on Zoroaster and the book on Hades, the story of Er, son of Armenius, had, perhaps, been introduced here and put in the mouth of Zoroaster. This, however, is only a possibility. Clemens of Alexandria also quotes elsewhere a passage from Heraclides. Another disciple of Aristotle, Clearchus of Soli (Jons. I, 18, 1), who flourished under Ptolemæus Soter, asserted in his book *Peri Paideias* ("On Education") that the gymnosophists were the offspring of the Magi (see Diogenes, Proem 9). One of the Platonists, Hermodorus (when he lived is unfortunately unknown to us), has written a book, *Peri Mathematon* ("On Science"), and he is mentioned by Diogenes[1] as bearing testimony to the opinion that Zoroaster had lived 5,000 years before the fall of Troy.

To this Hermodorus I trace back (as has been already said above regarding Xanthus), whatever else

---

[1] Proem. 2.

is found in the passage of Diogenes,[1] *viz* : —" That the Platonist Hermodorus says in his book on the *Mathemata*,—' From the Magi, beginning with Zoroaster the Persian, to the fall of Troy, there are 5,000 years.' That, on the contrary, Xanthus the Lydian says :—' Up to the campaign of Xerxes in Hellas it is 600 years from Zoroaster, and after him there flourished many Magi who succeeded each other, *viz.*, the *Ostanes, Astrampsychs, Gobrys,* and *Pazats,* until the dissolution of the Persian Empire.' "

Nevertheless, we shall soon observe that Zoroaster was placed 5,000 years before the Trojan War by Hermippus too ; and further on we shall comment upon the opinions regarding the age of Xanthus.

A succession of the Magi beginning from Zoroaster, is entirely founded on original indigenous documents,

---

[1] Plutarch, *On Isis and Osiris*, 46 :—" Like Zoroaster the Magian, who is said to have lived 5,000 years before the Trojan War; " probably taken from Hermippus. Proem. 2 :—" From the Magi, whose first teacher was Zoroaster the Persian, to the conquest of Troy, there were 5,000 years as stated by the Platonist Hermodorus in his book *Peri Mathematon* ('About Sciences')." But Xanthus the Lydian says :—" Till the campaign of Xerxes in Greece there was a period of 600 years from Zoroaster, and after him there flourished very many Magi succeeding each other, *viz.*, the *Ostanai*, the *Astrampsychoi, Gobryai,* and *Pazatai* up to the destruction of the Persian Empire by Alexander." This passage lay before the eyes of Suidas, who writes under the word Magi, that they were " the Persian philosophers and theologians, whose teacher was Zoroaster, and after him there succeeded the *Ostanai* and *Astrampsychoi*." Under the word *Ostanes* he remarks :—" They were formerly called Magi by the Persians, afterwards *Ostanai.*" And under the word *Zoroaster,* he calls him " a Perso-Median philosopher, who first introduced among the Persians the name of Magi, and lived 500 years before the Trojan war " (500 instead of 5,000). And Phevarinus says :—" The Ostanes were formerly called Magi by the Persians." The names *Ostanes, Astrampsychos,* and *Zoroastris,* are met with also in *Hippolytus's Philosophy*, p. 130, Oxford edition.

for *Isat-vâstra*, the son of Zarathushtra (comp. *Farvardin Yasht*, § 98), is, according to the Bundahish (p. 79, l. 16), the chief *môbad*, and in line 13 of the same page it is said that all the mobads of Persia are descended from the royal family of Minuchehar.

The name *Ostanai*, which sometimes denotes a species, is given to a Magus who accompanied Xerxes into Greece, and wrote a book on his Magian art (*vide* Plinius, *Historia Naturalis*, "Natural History," XXX, 1, 8)[1], and after him to a Magus in the suite of Alexander. The word seems to be derived from the Avesta *ushta*, expressing a formula of salutation (comp. *Tîr Yasht*, § 29). The second Gâthâ *Ushtavaiti*, too, begins with the word *ushtâ*. That the Magi were named after this formula of benediction, seems to me to be obvious.

The queer expression *Astrampsychoi*, or Astrampsychs, might probably be traced to the purely Avesta name of the third order, *viz.*, the *Vâstryô-fshuyãs* or the farmer. Zarathushtra is explicitly called, in the *Farv. Yt.*, § 89, the chief *Vâstryô-fshuyãs*, and his son *Urvatatnara*, who announced in the *Vara* the holy doctrine, is, according to the Bundahish, the chief of the farmers. Gobryas is known as a proper name of one of the seven connected with Darius, and it is preserved in the *Behistun-Inscription* IV, 84; V, 7, in the form *Gaubruva*.

---

[1] The brother of Artaxerxes is called *Osthanes*. The name of the Magus Ostanes is found also in Tertullian, *De Anima* ("On the Soul"), chap. 57; in Minucius, *Fol.*, chap. 27; in Augustinus, *Contra Donatum*, VI, last chapter; in Eusebius, *Prepar. Evangel.*, IV, p. 119, and Apuleius, *De Magia*, chaps. 27 and 90. In Plinius the manuscripts vary between Osthanes and Ostanes.

A similar name is *Gâurvî* in the *Farv. Yt.*, § 118. The *Pazatai*, or Pazatos, may be allied to the Avesta *paiti zan*, a technical term for the reconciliation of the good spirits. Nay, the brother of the Pseudo-Smerdis is called *Patizeithes*, or *Patizeides*, in Herodotus, Bk. III, 61.

The Alexandrian Sotion had written under Ptolemæus Epiphanes (204-181 B. C.) a huge work entitled : *Peri Diadochon tōn Philosophon* ("On the succession of Philosophers"), from which an abstract was made about Olympiad CL by Heraclides Lembus (*vide* Jonsius II, 10). In the twenty-third book of this work Sotion, as Diogenes[1] says, had praised the very ancient wisdom of the Persian Magi, and referred to marriage between consanguineous relations as a custom of the Magi. If we compare the Proem 1 cited from Sotion, with the Proems 6-8, we are led to assume that the whole passage is taken from Sotion (or Aristotle), and that the quotation from Clitarchus is interpolated only by way of parenthesis. It runs thus :—" Those who assert that philosophy has begun from the heathens (and this is done by Sotion according to his Proem 1), explained also separately the methods of it in the heathen nation. They say that the gymnosophists and druids have philosophized in enigmatical sayings. To venerate the good spirits, to do nothing evil, and to show courage, form the contents of their doctrines. That the gymnosophists condemn also death, is said by Clitarchus in

---

[1] Proem 1 :—"Some say that the work of philosophy began with the heathens. There were the Magi among the Persians, Chaldæans, and Babylonians or Assyrians, the gymnosophists among the Indians, the so-called druids and semnotheists among the Celts and Galatians, according to the testimony of Aristotle in his *Magika*, and of Sotion in the twenty-third book of the *Diadoche*." Comp. *ibid* 7.

his twelfth book. The Chaldæans are occupied also with astronomy and predictions; but the Magi practise the worship of the good spirits, and make offerings and prayers to them, which alone, they asserted, were heard by the deities. They also taught or inquired into the nature and origin of the deities, and considered fire, water, and earth as such. But idols of the gods are contemned by them, particularly by those who fancy the gods to be male and female spirits. They preach also upon justice, and think it illegal to burn dead bodies; nevertheless they permitted consanguineous marriages as Sotion says in the twenty-third book. They practise also mantology and prediction, asserting that the good spirits are seen by them. And the air, according to their opinion, is also full of forms perceptible to the eyes of sharp-sighted persons by means of evaporation. They forbid the wearing of gold and ornaments. Their dress is white; their couch is the soil; their food is vegetables, cheese, and simple bread; their staff a cane with which they pierce the cheese to take it up and eat it. Yet mantical sorcery is quite unknown to them as is stated by Aristotle in the *Magikos*, and by Dino in the fifth book of his History."

We observe here a series of points confirmed, which we have found already in Xanthus, Herodotus, and Dino. We cannot better describe the nature of the Magi than by calling it an occupation *theōn therapeiai, thusiai*, and *euchaī* " with divine service, sacrifice, and prayer." As to the conceptions (see above) of the *yazatas* of fire and water, they resemble that of the earth, the *Armaiti* of the Avesta texts. It is literally incorrect to say that the Magi knew no male and female *yazatas*, if we are permitted to consider as old Magian deities *Mithra* and *Anâhita* for example, who are quite certainly male and female beings. Moreover, it is true that the Magi knew no divine propagations or generations, and genealogies like the Greeks. The appearance of the *yazatas* is sufficiently confirmed by the Avesta texts; but those *eidola* or forms which are visible to sharp-eyed persons, are probably the *Fravashis*; however, they are apparently too materialistic in their conception. The statement as regards the food of the Magi reminds us of what is related about Zoroaster that he had lived for a long time on cheese.[1]

I conclude with Hermippus this remarkable list of the Greek authors who lived before Christ. That an author of this name had written a work on the Magi which contained several books, has been remarked above (p. 279) on the authority of a passage quoted there from Diogenes. Regarding the contents of this work we are indebted to Plinius,[2] whose words will soon occupy our attention. Who this Hermippus was, or when he lived, is nowhere mentioned. Notwithstanding this, *Hermippos Kallimacheios* has been considered nearly unanimously, and not without reason, as the

---

[1] Plinius, *Hist. Nat.*, XI, 42, 97 :—" They relate that Zoroaster lived in the desert for 30 years on cheese, and so temperately as not to feel old age." Compare Porphyrios "On Abstinence," IV, 16, p. 348 *seq.*

[2] *Hist. Nat.*, XXX, 1, 2 :—" Hermippus, who wrote very accurately on this art (of magic), and explained 2,000,000 verses composed by Zoroaster, and who made also an index of the volumes, has related that Agonaces was the teacher by whom he (Zoroaster) was informed, and that he had lived 5,000 years before the war of Troy."

writer of the book on the Magi (see Jonsius, *De Script. Hist. Phil.* II, 9, 3; and Lozynski, *Hermippi Fragmenta*, p. 46). Because it is very probable that a learned man like Hermippus, who had occupied himself so much with the History of Philosophy (I refer only to his work on the "Seven Sages of Greece"), should have also written a work on the Magi after so many excellent preparatory labours. This Hermippus, the disciple of the celebrated Callimachus (who lived when very old under Ptolemæus Energetes, and who died about 240 B. C.), had displayed his great literary activity in the second part of the third century before Christ; and since he mentions the death of Chrysippus (who died in 207 B. C.), his last works must belong to the end of the third century. Probably he is identical with the Peripatetician Hermippus cited by Hieronymus in *De Scriptoribus Ecclesiasticis.*

Müller (*vide* his *Historia Græcorum Fragmentorum,* "History of Greek Fragments," III, p. 36), on the contrary, differs from the common opinion, according to which Hermippus, the disciple of Callimachus, wrote the book *Peri Mágon* ("On the Magi"), and ascribes that work to one *Hermippos o astrologikos,* "Hermippus the Astrologer," who seems to be alluded to in Athenæus[1], and who has also written *Phainómena.*

---

[1] *Hist. Nat.,* p. 478 a :—" Nicomachus says in the first book on the Egyptian festivals :—The drinking cup is Persian (the next two lines are very obscure) from which the wonders and fruitful things on earth come forth." Casaubonus corrects the text [the language being obscure]. Pursan reads it quite otherwise :—"Was like the world of which Hermippus the philosopher says that the wonders of gods, etc." I must acknowledge that I doubt very much whether the name of Hermippus is here in its right place. I believe that we have here

Yet Müller avers that this astrologer Hermippus must have been contemporary with the Callimachian, and that both might also be identical; so the question, whether the two Hermippi are one and the same person or not, is without any importance as to the age of the book in question.

If the statement of Hermippus concerning Persian matters is obscure and uncertain in Athenæus, another quotation from the former in Arnobius[1] is no less so.

---

the name of some astrological vessel (or instrument) . . . "it was an astrological tripod like the world." The word *kondu* is used (in Genesis, xliv, 2, 4, 12, in the *Septuagint*) of the drinking cup of Joseph. Or we must read it thus :—" In the beginning was, as says Hermippus, an astrological world." Certainly it appears to me very doubtful whether the predicate 'astrological' refers to Hermippus. According to Anquetil, *Usages*, T. II, p. 533, the water vessel used in the liturgy is called in Guzarati *kouri* [rather "*kundi*"], Sanskrit *kandu*, "an iron pan."

[1] *Adversus Gentes* ("Against the Heathens") I, chap. 52, p. 31, ed. Lugd. :—" There may now come (here there are great variations in the manuscripts) on the fiery way from the interior path the Magian Zoroaster, the Bactrianus, as the author Hermippus calls him; may he come to the meeting, whose deeds are recounted by Ctesias in the first book of his *History*; Armenius, the nephew of Zostrianus, and Pamphilus, the friend of Cyrus; Apollonius, Damigero and Dardanus, Velus Julianus and Bæbulus, and any other person who is said to have excelled in these things." Instead of *Zostrianus*, which occurs in the MSS., some editors read the word *Ostanis*. They are followed by Lozynski and Müller too. They (as well as Oehler and Orelli) have a punctuation after *auctori*, and connect the word *Bactrianus* with the following *Bactrianus et ille*. Desid. Heraldus in his *Animadv. ad Arnobius* p. 52, would read thus :—" There may now come some Magian Azonaces from the interior orbit; so that we assent to the author Hermippus, that the Bactrian also may come." This Bactrian is, in his opinion, Zoroaster, whose name, he imagines, was first written on the margin and thus found its way into the first sentence.—The words : *Armenius Zostriani nepos et familiaris Pamphilus Cyri*, ("Armenius, the nephew of Zostrianus, and Pamphilus, the friend of Cyrus") are, I think, corrupt. They refer to the Her mentioned above. Perhaps we should read : *Armenii filiis Zoroastris nepos et familia Pamphylus Herus* ("a nephew of Armenius, the son of Zoroaster,

Whether the statement expressed by the words: *quis super igneam zonam magus interiore ab orbe Zoroastres*, " which Magus over a fiery zone from the inner orbit was Zoroaster "—the meaning of which I cannot understand[1]—is testified to by Hermippus, or (if *Bactrianus*

and Her, a Pomphylian by birth"). I see that a similar conjecture has already been made by Cotelier in *Recogn. Clement.*, IV, 27 (*Patres Apostolici*, I, p. 542), who reads: *Armenius Zostriani nepos et familiaris Pamphylus Her*, " Armenius, the nephew of Zostrianus and the Pamphilian Her, his friend." Zostrianus is mentioned by Porphyrius in his Life of Plato.—The Bactrian Zoroaster is mentioned by Arnobius in another passage too (chap. 1. p. 5) :—" Is it also to be laid to our charge that one day under Ninus and Zoroaster as their chiefs the Assyrians and Bactrians fought against each other not only with swords and forces, but also with the magical and mysterious art of the Chaldæans ? " Evidently Oxyartes is here meant, the king of Bactria, who is mentioned in Diodorus Siculus II, 6, as succumbing to Ninus after a valorous resistance.—Eusebius, *Chron.* II, p. 35, ed. Auch. (concerning the seventh year of Abraham) says:—" There is some Zoroaster, the Magian, who is reckoned a famous king of Bactria, against whom Ninus fought."—Eusebius, *Prep. Evangel.*, X, 9 : " According to whom Zoroaster the Magian reigned over the Bactrians."

We find the same Magian and King of the Bactrians in Moses of Chorene. Theo Progymnast in the book on " Comparisons," says:— "For, if Tomyris is stronger than Cyrus, or Semiramis stronger than the Bactrian Zoroaster, we must not, therefore, conclude that a female is stronger than a male." *Justinus*, *Hist.*, I. 1.

[1] Arnobius, *Adv. Gent.*, I, 52:—The codex has, according to Oehler, the words *quae super* "which above "; *quis super* "who above", in Orelli, Lozynski, and Müller; *quaeso per* "I pray through" is a conjecture of Salmasius, adopted by Oehler. The words: *super igneam zonam magus interiore ab orbe Zoroastres*, "above the fiery zone from the interior circle the Magus Zoroaster," are very obscure. *Ignea zona*, " the fiery zone," has been considered by Salmasius as the Libyan (or African) glowing zone, which is impossible. *Interiore ab orbe*, " from the inner orbit," might perhaps mean " from the central orbit," in opposition to Bactrianus; but it might also denote the inner magical circle out of which Zoroaster comes from the burning mountain through fire, or above the fire-circle. Then we have to compare the passage in Dio Chrysostom in his " Borysthenian Oration" (see below), and in this case we should have Hermippus bearing testimony to this fiery apparition. Or *interiore ab orbe* might perhaps refer to the opinion which represents Zoroaster as an offspring of the Greeks (see *supra* the *Scholiast* of

belongs to the first part of the sentence) whether the origin of Zoroaster was from Bactria, is doubtful; the former, however, is more probable. It perhaps alludes to what the later Greek fabulists narrate concerning the death of Zoroaster by lightning and the preservation of the fire glowing in ashes, as a symbol of dominion.

We will, however, go back to the passage of Plinius, in order to learn more certain data about the work of Hermippus. Herein three things are related of Hermippus: — (1) that he placed Zoroaster three thousand years before the Trojan war, wherein he agrees more or less with other Greek authors; (2) that he called Agonaces (an obscure name) the teacher of Zoroaster; and (3) that the manuscripts of Plinius have the variants: *Agonaccen, Agoneten, Aganacen, Abonacem, Agonsiscen*, which sufficiently prove that the passage in question is corrupted. Since the Avesta texts and tradition know no other teacher of Zoroaster than Ahura-Mazda Himself, I assume that Hermippus rendered the name *Oromazes* or *Cromasdes* in some form corresponding to the Avesta, perhaps *Agoramazdes*, giving the Avesta *h* by the Greek *g*, or perhaps only *Agomazes*. If this hypothesis is correct, it proves the independent investigation of Hermippus and his knowledge of the (Avesta)

Plato), or *ignea zona* is perhaps a translation of *Atropatene*, or *Aderbiján, Atropatene* originally signifying the fire-land. Strabo, XI, p. 523, derives the name of this province, which he calls *Atropatene* or *Atropatia*, from *Atropates* who had preserved this province from the Macedonian dominion. *Athró-paiti* means in Avesta "the master of the fire," or *áthró-páta* "the protector of the fire," or "he who is protected by fire," or as in the *Farv. Yt.*, § 102, one of the sons of Vishtáspa so called. In the Bundahish the country is called *Atró (Atún)-pátkán*. The birth of Zarathushtra is said to have taken place at Urmi in Atropátene.

language. The Greeks knew right well that Ahura-Mazda Himself was the teacher of Zoroaster ; for in no other way must the Platonian words *Zoroastres o tou Oromázes,* "Zoroaster the Disciple of Oromâzes," be understood, as the explanation of the scholiasts correctly indicates ; and, moreover, we have the explicit assertion of Plutarch[1] who derived from the best sources whatever he said as to the Magi, for he says in his Life of Numa that the Deity had intercourse with Zoroaster.

The third thing asserted by Hermippus, according to Plinius, is regarding the existence and number of Zoroastrian writings, which were known to Hermippus, and illustrated by him with a synopsis of the contents of the several books. It is evident that the word *explanavit* ("he has explained") must not be urged, or taken to mean "translated." This expression is rather used to elucidate what is obscure and uncertain. Most probably Hermippus became acquainted with a synopsis of the contents of the twenty-one Nasks of the Avesta. The contents of one of these nasks are still surviving, and Lassen[2] has excellently indicated a parallel between the expression "the twenty-fold composition or interpretation of 100,000 verses" and these Nasks, which correspond to the twenty-one words of the prayer : *Yathâ ahû vairyô.* Only a small remnant of

---

[1] Num. c. 4 :—"While agreeing in this, is it worth while not to believe that the Deity conversed with Zaleucus and Minos and Zoroaster and Numa and Lycurgus, who had governed empires and established kingdoms ? Or is it probable that the gods have earnest intercourse with these men to instruct and admonish them in what is best, but that with poets and lyric warblers such dealings as they have are only in sport ? "

[2] *Indische Altertumskunde* " Indian Antiquities," III, p. 440 note-

these Nasks has been preserved. The whole mass must have been very numerous. In the register given by Anquetil and Vullers (" Fragments of the Religion of Zoroaster," p. 15) 825 chapters on the whole are indicated of the 21 Nasks ; the smallest having 17, the largest 65 chapters. For the Vendidâd 22 chapters are correctly stated, and we have no reason to doubt of the accuracy of the other numbers.

In the edition of Spiegel these 22 chapters of the Vendidâd have about 4,485 lines, each chapter, therefore, having about 205. In the lithographed codex of the *Vendidâd Sâ le* there are 560 pages, of which a little more than the half, *i.e.*, 292 pages belong to the Vendidâd. Each page in it has 19 lines, and the whole book amounts to 5,548 lines, consequently each chapter has on average 252 lines. If the volumes described by Hermippus were perhaps in form and handwriting of the same extent as that codex (we may believe that in an older time they were still larger, grander, and more extensive) ; and if we assume that the same average is applicable for all the 825 chapters of the Nasks, the whole sum of the *stichoi* or lines of the Nasks amounts to 207,900 ; or, if some chapters were shorter, to about 200,000 verses : *vicies dena milia versuum* (Gr. *eikosákis murioi stichoi*), "two hundred thousand verses." Should we read in Plinius, wherein possible mistakes as to numbers are so obvious, just the same (*vicies dena milia versuum*) instead of *vicies centum milia versuum*, "20 times 100,000 verses," we should see a striking harmony between the statement of Hermippus and the register of the Nasks and of the manuscript of the Vendidâd. But if Plinius has actually written on the authority of Hermippus, *vicies centum milia versuum;* "twenty times 100,000 verses," either the other Nasks must have had much longer chapters, or the oldest manuscripts must have been written in a way much more extended, or there lies at the bottom an Oriental exaggeration.

That the division into Nasks is no invention of later writers, is proved by the well-known Avesta passage, *Yasna* IX, § 22 W. ꜟꜟꜟꜟꜟ

"Haoma grants more sanctity and greatness to those who have long sat reading the *Nasks*."[1]

Consequently, the statement of Hermippus is as unobjectionable as important. *In the third century before Christ the Greeks had access to original Zoroastrian Texts of such a quality and extent as we should expect them to be from the still existing Avesta books, wherein is clearly comprehended almost everything that we see hitherto handed down to us by the ancients as Magian doctrine.*[2]

Such is the result of the informations of antiquity, which date back a long time before the Christian era, and consequently before the time when there was an intermixture of religions in the Roman Empire, when the fantastical mysteries of the later Magi and fictitious

---

[1] Burnouf, *Etudes*, p. 289, *seq.*, compares Av. *frasaōnghô* with Sanskrit *prasâshah* from *sâsh* "to speak." Neriosengh renders it by *adhyayanam kartum*.

[2] Besides this Plinius asserts that the Magian *Ostanes* wrote books in the time of Xerxes.

books on Zoroastrian subjects[1] written in Greek, were in vogue—circumstances which must render us very cautious with respect to the informations of later authors, when their statements do not expressly refer to those older documents, or at least cannot be traced to them with some probability.

---

[1] Suidas *sub-voce Zoroastres*. There existed a Greek book under the name of Hystaspes (at the end of the second century). Clemens Alexandrinus (*Stromata* VI, p. 761, ed. Potter), says that the heathens have also had their prophets, and alludes to a word of the Apostle Paul borrowed either from tradition or some Paulinian apocryphal book. "Besides the word of Peter, the Apostle Paul also proclaims saying: 'Take the Greek books; study Sibylla, which declares the oneness of God and future things; take Hystaspes, too, and read it, and you will find that the son of God has been written of very farseeingly and clearly, and that many kings will make opposition to Christ, hating him and his followers.'"

Lact. Inst., VII, 16 :—"Hystaspes, too, a king of the Medians in the earliest time, from whom a river has derived its name of Hystaspes, has handed down to posterity a wonderful dream with the interpretation of a boy gifted with prophecy; that the Roman name and Empire would be taken away from the earth, was predicted by him a long time before the Trojan people existed." Hence it follows that Lactantius placed this Hystaspes a long time before the foundation of Rome, and consequently before Darius Hystaspes. Justinus, *Apol.*, I, 20, says:—"Sibylla, as well as Hystaspes, said that the perishable things will be destroyed by fire." *Ibid*, c. 44 : "By the energy of the evil gods death was constituted, as is stated by those who read the books of Hystaspes and Sibylla and the Prophets, that through fear they might turn aside men who were attaining to a knowledge of the good, and keep them in bondage to themselves, which thing at the end they were made to effect." Justinus wrote this apology about 151 years before Christ.

The contents of the work were, as it seems, to the following effect:— Hystaspes had a dream about things to come, which was interpreted to him by a prophetic boy. In this was a description of the son of God, and how the kings of this earth persecuted him; besides the decay of the Roman Empire and the destruction of the world in fire. According to the context of *Apology*, I, 44, the book must also have treated of the fate of man after death.—The book must have been known at any rate in the first century before Christ.

Among the authors of the period of the Roman Empire, the first place is taken up by Strabo. He draws a parallel[1] between the Magi and the Indian philosophers, saying that the former gave instruction like the latter in divine things. In another passage he describes them as a tribe of the Persian people, and calls them zealous students of a holy life. That the Magi were of *one* tribe, although not of the Persian, is stated in the Bundahish, p. 79, l. 12, where it is said that Maidhyômâh, the cousin of Zarathushtra, had first adopted the holy doctrine, and that all Mobads of Persia are to be traced back to the family of Manushchithra (Minúchehr).

The detailed description of the Persian customs and religion, given by Strabo[2] in the same book, is partly based on autopsy, and partly on the testimony of other historians. We must consider the whole passage which runs as follows[3]:—

"The Persians do not erect any statues or altars. They offer sacrifices on an elevated place, thinking the heaven to be Zeus. They venerate also the Sun (whom they call Mithra), the Moon, the Aphrodite, fire, earth, winds and water. They offer sacrifices also in a pure place with prayers, standing near the garlanded animal which is to be immolated" (or "standing garlanded near the victim," if we read with Herodotus *estemmenoi* "garlanded"), and when the Magus who

---

[1] XV, p. 717:—"They are informed about divine things (by the philosophers of India) as the Persians by the Magi." *Ibid*, p. 727:—" In that country there live tribes called *Patischoreis*, and *Achaimenidai* and the *Magoi*; these latter are devoted to a pious life."

[2] XV, p. 733:—"The former we have seen ourselves, the latter you can read in histories."

[3] XV, p. 732.

performs the holy act has cut the flesh into pieces, they distribute and give it away without offering any portion of it to God, for God wishes for the soul of the animal sacrificed, and nothing else. Nevertheless, they lay, as some say, a small portion of the intestines (or fat) on the fire."

Hitherto we have an abridged extract from Herodotus, which I think wants correction here and there (Herodotus I, 131-133). The words "whom they call Mithra," are an incorrect addition made by Strabo who, following the opinions of his time, confounded Mithra with the Sun. He is right, however, in dropping the words of Herodotus: *oute pur ánakaiousi* "neither do they illumine fire." The concluding portion beginning from the words "for the soul," is a singular and quite certainly an authentic insertion taken from another source.

"In a different manner," continues Strabo, "they sacrifice to fire and water; certainly to the fire by depositing dry wood without the bark, and laying some fat upon this wood. Then they kindle it and add fuel to it not blowing but fanning it. They kill those who blow out the fire, or lay a corpse, or anything dead or filthy, on the fire. They sacrifice to the water by going up to a lake, river or fountain, where they form a ditch, into which they kill the animal, taking care that nothing of the neighbouring water gets bloody, and causes thereby any contamination. Afterwards they dismember the flesh and place it on myrtle or laurel, and the Magi touch it with fine staves, singing, pouring out oil mixed with milk and honey, not into the fire nor into the water, but on the soil, and while they are singing they hold for a long time a bunch of fine tamarisk-twigs." We observe that here, too, Strabo follows Herodotus. Whilst he abridged his statement before, he now enlarges, as I believe he does, upon what he has seen himself or borrowed from first rate sources. The laying on of dry wood to venerate the fire (*Vend.*, Farg. XIV, 2-3; XVIII, 19), the strict prohibition against putting dead or impure objects on fire, or of mixing it with water, the classical description of the *baresma* (vide *supra* the passage of Dino), and the long hymns connected with its gathering—all these things are completely confirmed by the Avesta texts. The oil here spoken of may doubtless be identified with the *haoma* juice, which was mixed with milk. Honey, too, is mentioned in the Avesta, if according to my supposition in the discourse on "Mithra," p. 72, the *madhu* employed in offerings does not mean "wine," but "honey."

What now follows especially refers to Cappadocian Magism, and we are fully entitled to consider it as an account of what the Cappadocian Strabo had seen with his own eyes.

" But in Cappadocia where there is a large number of Magi who are called fire-burners or fire-priests, and where there are many sacred places of Persian deities, they do not sacrifice with the sword, but they strike with a log of wood as with a club. There are also fire-burning places, certain remarkable inclosures, in the midst of which stands an altar full of ashes, on which the Magi preserve inextinguishable fire ; daily they enter it, and sing for nearly an hour, holding a bundle of *baresma* before the fire, their heads covered with cocked tiaras, which go down on both sides so far as to touch the lips. The same thing is customary in the temples of Anais and Omanus. They, also, have enclosures, and the picture of Omanus is borne in a procession. These things we have now seen, but those previously mentioned are related in historical books just like the following."

"The Persians do not make water in a river, nor do they wash or bathe in it, nor cast into it dead bodies or whatever produces contamination. They always first adore the Fire before making an offering to any other deity."

After mentioning several features of private life, which are partly related by Herodotus, too, Strabo continues :—"They inter corpses surrounded with wax; but the Magi are not interred. The latter are suffered to be devoured by birds (from Herodotus) ; . . ."

Strabo gives us here a most accurate description of the Magian fire-hearths and the divine service connected with them, such as is described in the original texts. He translates the Avesta word *âthrava*[1] very accurately with the Gr. *puraithos* "fire-hearth," and the Pers. *âtashgâhs* with the Gr. *puraitheia* "fire-temples."[2] To the description of the *barsam* he adds here that of the *paitidâna* (*Vend.*, Farg. XIV, § 8 ; *Abân Yt.*, § 123) or *penom*. Of Anâhita and Omanus I have treated in another discourse, and I can, therefore, pass over the Strabonian passages concerning them, and also those about Mithra.

---

[1] Gen. *athaurunô*; dat. *athaurunê*; acc. *âthravanem*.

[2] In the Bundahish (p. 40, l. 20) *Atûn (âtrô) gâs* "the fire place." The *âdityô gâtush* of the fire is found in the eighth Fargard of the Vendidâd.

So we have a testimony as to the whole offering service of the Magi, and the prayers and songs used in it, which confirms the holy texts no less than it is confirmed by these texts to the minutest point.

Still another feature has been preserved by the geographer Strabo[1] in describing the Bactrians:— "Their customs have been somewhat milder than those of the Sogdians; but of them also many evil things are recounted by Onesicritus and his followers, as for example, those who are debilitated by old age or sickness are thrown by them (i. e. the Bactrians) before living dogs which are fed expressly for this purpose, and which are called in their languages 'buriers in solitude' (Gr. *entaphaiastas*). The place outside the wall of the capital of the Bactrians appears clean; but inside every place is filled with human bones."—Strabo mentions as his authority Onesicritus of Assypelæna, a writer of the time of Alexander, who is certainly not regarded as a great authority. Nevertheless, what he states here is true in itself, though painted in too striking colours. Porphyrius also[2] mentions the facts, and the later Agathias[3] enlarges upon this subject describing how the ceremony was performed by the Magi in his time:—"If people of lower rank in the army fall victims to any bad disease," says he, "they are brought away from the city while living and conscious; and when a soldier is exposed in this way, a piece of bread, water, and a stick are placed by him.

---

[1] XI, p. 517.

[2] "On Abstinence," IV, 21:—"The Hyrcanians cast living persons before devouring birds and dogs, the Caspians dead persons. The Bactrians cast old men living before dogs."

[3] II. 23, p. 114, ed. Bonn.

"As long as he is able to eat of the bread, and has strength enough, he drives away with the stick the approaching animals, and repels the hungry guests. If his life is not yet fully extinct, but he has grown so invalid as to be unable to move his hands, the beasts devour the unhappy man who is half famished and already rattling in his throat, and deprive him of the hope at any rate of escaping from his illness. For many have already recovered and come back to their homes as one in a theatre or a tragedy arrives from the gates of darkness, emaccerated and meagre enough to terrify persons meeting them. If some one returns home, all turn aside from him, and run away from him as though he were contaminated in the highest degree, and as though they were still with the infectious dead. He is not allowed to partake of the ordinary manner of living before he is purified by the Magi from the contamination of the expected death, and before he has as it were regained fresh life."

According to Agathias, people of the lower ranks were treated in this way, who in the army contracted evil maladies. According to Onesicritus, sick and old people in general were so treated. The Avesta texts, however, confine this treatment to those who bear corpses (singly), and contaminate themselves by doing so. The *Vendidâd*, Farg. III, § 15, says:—" What shall be the place of the man who bears corpses [alone]?"—" Thereupon Ahura Mazda answered:—' Wherever the earth is most waterless, treeless, cleanest, driest, and the least passed through by cattle and team, and by the fire of Ahura Mazda, and by the *baresma* spread in purity, and by the faithful man.'"—(16) " How far from the fire? How far from the pure or clean water? How far from the spread *baresma*? How far from the faithful men?" (17) "Thereupon Ahura Mazda answered:— 'Thirty steps from the fire, thirty steps from the water, thirty steps from the spread *baresma*, thirty steps from the faithful man.' (18-19) 'Thus the Mazdayasnians shall there erect an enclosure, and therein shall these Mazdayasnians bring the coarsest food, therein shall these Mazdayasnians bring the most worn clothes; such food he shall eat, such clothes he shall put on; so long as he grows old and sick, and quite invalid.' (20) 'But when he has grown old or sick, and quite invalid, the strongest, swiftest, and most skilful Mazdayasnians are to lead him on a mountain, and to cut his head off from the breadth of his back, and deliver his corpse to the hungry and corpse-devouring creatures of the Holy Genius, *i.e.*, to the birds *kahrkâsa*, saying: This man here repents of all evil thoughts, words and deeds, and if he has done other vicious deeds, he is pardoned (by his repentance); but if he has done no other vicious deeds, this man is absolved by his repentance for ever and ever.'"

Hence we observe that the *Greeks did not fully understand the Persian practice*, or exaggerated this kind of interpretation; unless the practice had been more cruel than the law. It is important for us to know that from the time of Alexander to the sixth century after Christ this strange custom of the Magi, as contained in the original texts, had been fully verified.

Plinius (living 23-79 years after Christ) had, in his great work on "Natural History," frequent opportunities of speaking upon magic, the Magi, and Zoroaster. In his first book, in which he enumerates the sources and contents of all books (*Tome* 1, p. 87 ed. Sill), he cites Eudoxus, Aristotle, and Hermippus among the extraneous authorities for his thirtieth book, wherein the well-known passage about the Magi is found. And in this thirtieth book itself (1, 2) he again refers to these authorities, particularly Hermippus. So we are fully justified in ascribing to Hermippus those notes on the Magi and Zoroaster, which are given by Plinius without specially mentioning his authority.

Besides those passages in Plinius, which have just been mentioned in Eudoxus, Aristotle, and Hermippus, we have here to dilate upon that passage[1] wherein he calls Osthanes, the companion of Xerxes in Greece, the first writer on magic, who had sown the seeds of this marvellous art wherever he went. But further on he states that a short time before this Osthanes another Zoroaster of Proconnesus had lived as some trustworthy writers have related. Osthanes had awakened an ardent desire for learning this wisdom among the Greeks. There were also a tribe of the Magi who were descend-

---

[1] *Hist. Nat.*, XXX, 1, 2 :—"As far as I can find, one Osthanes, who accompanied Xerxes on his campaign in Greece, first wrote about it (*viz.*, witchcraft). He sowed the seeds of this miraculous art wherever he went, and the world was infected wherever they reached; but some very accurate authors state that Zoroaster, another Proconnesian, lived a short time before him. It is certain that this Osthanes chiefly excited the Greek nation to that pitch (not of eagerness but of frenzy) for this art, although I see that in the earliest time, and nearly always, the greatest literary glory and excellence was sought in this art.—There is also another magical sect depending on the Jews : Moses, Jannes and Lotapea ; but it was many thousand years after Zoroaster; still younger is the Cyprian (art). In the period of Alexander the Great, great importance was given to this art by a second Osthanes who had the honour of accompanying him (Alexander), and of peregrinating with him in the whole world."

ed from the Jews, *viz.*, Moses, Jannes, and Lotapea (*Ilitopata*) who lived many thousand years after Zoroaster. What is called the Cyprian magical art flourished still later. In the time of Alexander, too, a second Osthanes, as pre-eminent as his companion, had given no small importance to this art. I have treated of this Osthanes in another discourse. According to Plinius, there can be no doubt as to the reality of his person and books. We wish that Plinius had more enlarged on the Proconnesian Zoroaster, and on those *diligentiores* "more zealous persons," who had adhered to him.

The Miletian colony on the island of Proconnesus in the Propontis, may be traced back to very high antiquity; for Herodotus (*vide* Bk. IV, 15) places Aristeas of Proconnesus 340 years before his time, that is, in the beginning of the eighth century before Christ, or, if the reading *diekosioisi* is correct, in the beginning of the seventh century. The miraculous story of Aristeas is related by Herodotus: he died at a tanner's house, who had shut him up in his shop, and announced his death to his relations; that he had been seen by some one while on his route to Cyzicus, and had not been found either living or dead on opening the workshop; that he had reappeared seven years afterwards in Proconnesus, had composed some poem entitled *Arimaspi*, and disappeared a second time. Three hundred and forty years after this second disappearance he appeared again in Metapontus and ordered an altar to be built to Apollo, and a statue to be erected on the side of it bearing the name *Proconnesius Aristeas*, for Apollo had come to them alone in Italy, and he now being

Aristeas, had then followed that god in the shape of a raven[1]—and after that he had disappeared. Strabo also mentions him (XXII, p. 589), speaking of Proconnesus:—"Here," he says, "was born Aristeas, the author of the *Arimaspian Epos* (*cfr.* I., p. 21 ; Plinius VII, 2, 2), a magician (*anèr goes*) if there was any magician in the world." In the XIV p. 639, he mentions the opinion of some writers, that Aristeas the Proconnesian had been the teacher of Homer. Origenes in his work *Adversus Celsum*, III, 26 *seq*, relates the whole story of Aristeas from Herodotus. He adds the name Pindar, too, as one of his authorities.

We gather from this narrative that Proconnesus was a seat of mystical things, and it is possible that just as Er, son of Armenius, who revived on the funeral pile, happened to be transformed into Zoroaster, so the reviving Aristeas gave origin to the story of the Proconnesian Zoroaster. What is said by Plinius about the two Osthanes, may well be connected with the "succession of the Magi," which has been treated of above. There can be no doubt that his determination of the chronology by placing Moses and the Egyptian magicians (of the Christian Bible, *cfr.* II, Timotheus 3, 8) many thousand years after Zoroaster, is an exaggeration, even if we suppose that Zoroaster lived 5,000 years before the Trojan War.

Plinius[2] commemorates two remarkable features of the life of Zoroaster, one of which he refers to his birth,

---

[1] Plinius VII, 52, 53 :—"Also (the soul) of Aristeas had been seen flying out of his mouth in the image of a raven."

[2] *Hist. Nat.*, VII, 16, 15 :—"We have heard that Zoroaster was the only man *who laughed on the same day on which he was born* ; his cerebellum is said to have palpitated so much as to push back the hand laid on it—a proof of his future knowledge."

viz., he laughed on the day he was born, and his cerebellum palpitated so as to push back the hand laid upon it, a presage of future knowledge. The next feature is the life of Zoroaster in the desert.[1] He had lived there for thirty years on cheese prepared in a way that his old age could not be marked. The first feature is also found in the *Zartusht Nâmah*, chapter VI; the second is likewise confirmed by the original texts on the life of Zoroaster in the desert already spoken of elsewhere, as well as by the passages of Eubulus in Porphyrius, which refer to it, and of Dio Chrysostom. Plutarch,[2] too, mentions that Zoroaster lived on food made of milk.

In the thirty-seventh book of Plinius there is a series of quotations from the book of Zoroaster: *Peri Lithon*, mentioned by Suidas. In the eighteenth book, § § 24, 56, there is a statement of Zoroaster about sowing, and in the twenty-eighth, 6, 19, some dogma about the *gomez* ("the consecrated cow's urine").

As far as we can rely upon the extracts made by Eusebius[3] from Alexander Polyhistor, and by the latter from Berosus, the contemporary of Alexander, this Chaldæan writer has placed after the deluge a set of eighty-six kings in Babylon, the two first of whom were Euechius and Chomasbelus (to the former he gives four *neri*, to the latter four *neri* and five *sossi*), and who are said to have reigned 33,091 years. After this the

---

[1] *Hist. Nat.*, XI, 42, 97 :—"They recount that Zoroaster lived for 30 years on cheese so moderately as not to feel old age."
[2] *Quæst. Sympos.*, IV, 1, p. 660 :—"I do not remember, said Philo, that Philinus adduces to us Sosaster, who is said to have used no other beverage or food, but to have lived on milk during all his life."
[3] *Chron.* I., p. 40 *seq.*

Medians (it is related) had taken Babylon, and then eight Median tyrants had reigned 224 years, whose names have been preserved by Berosus; afterwards eleven kings ("48 years" stands on the margin of the manuscript; Gutschmidt supposes 248); then forty-nine Chaldæan kings for 458 years; then nine Arab kings for 245 years. Then he has related the story of Semiramis who had reigned over the Assyrians, and then explicitly again the names of 45 kings who had reigned for a period of 526 years. Afterwards Phul had been the king of the Chaldæans. Whereas the kings who reigned in succession immediately after the deluge, prove by the reckoning by *sari, neri,* and *sossi,* and by the immense number of years, to be a mythical supplement of a period of 36,000 years. The Median rulers over Babylon and the kings who followed them down to Phul, seem to be historical facts; and learned men of modern times place the commencement of the Median dynasty 2,458 or 2,447 years before Christ. As the first of these eight Median kings mentioned by Berosus, Syncellus[1] (who lived about 800 years after Christ) names a Zoroaster. In this statement he follows, as he

---

[1] *Chronograph.* T. I, p. 147. ed. Bonn :—" From this time " (the year of the world 2405) " the same Polyhistor introduces eighty-six Chaldæan kings (the two first of them Euechius and Chomasbelus), and eighty-four Median kings; but Zoroaster and the seven Chaldæan kings after him are said to have reigned during 107 solar years, not during *sari* and *neri* and *sossi* and other nonsensical mythical terms, but for solar years. For mythologists thinking earlier kings to be gods or demi-gods, and leading their successors into error, make them to have reigned during an infinite time, believing that the world existed from eternity, in contrast with the Holy Scripture. The later kings, on the contrary, who are known to everybody, being mortals were represented as reigning during solar years, and not, as it seems to Panodorus and some others, because the years of the kings were at last measured by solar years, since the solar years were calculated by Zoroaster from the years of Enoch."

says, the opinion of Alexander Polyhistor. From the words of Syncellus it likewise follows that Panodorus, too, calls Zoroaster the first king, and ascribes to him astronomical calculations. If we consider only the contradiction between the Polyhistor of Eusebius, who evidently distinguishes the eighty-six kings from the Medians, and the Polyhistor of Syncellus who enumerates those eighty-six kings among the Median rulers, but afterwards designates Zoroaster and the seven kings after him as Chaldæans, and gives them 190 solar years, whilst the Polyhistor of Eusebius reckons 224 (or 234) years, we must aver that either the text of Syncellus is corrupt, or that he has himself made arbitrary alterations. It is, therefore, also problematical whether Alexander Polyhistor and his authority Berosus had actually called the first of the Median tyrants Zoroaster, or whether it is an interpolation of the later writers. It is not at all certain that this Median Zoroaster, who reigned over Babylon, was the celebrated prophet of this name, and if we admit the correctness of the statement of Syncellus, it is not improbable that several persons have had the name of Zarathushtra. We have a proof of this in the statements of the Chroniclers as to one Zoroaster having been king of the Bactrians and reputed as a contemporary of Ninus and Semiramis. According to the Armenian translation of the *Chronicle* of Eusebius,[1]

---

[1] I. p. 43., ed. Auch :—"'I begin to relate what others also have recounted, principally the story of Hellanicus the Lesbian, and Ctesias the Cnidian, then Herodotus the Halicarnassian. At first there reigned in Asia the Assyrians, of whom the first was Ninus, the son of Belus, during whose time very many and very splendid achievements had been performed.' Further on he adds the birth of Semiramis and a narrative of the combat and defeat of the Magus Zoroaster, King of Bactria, by Semiramis ; and that Ninus had reigned for 52 years and

Cephalion has related that the Assyrians first ruled over Asia. He has also treated of Ninus and his achievements, of the birth of Semiramis, of the Magus Zaravesht, King of Bactria, of his war against and defeat by Semiramis. Ninus, Cephalion says, reigned 52 years, after him Semiramis 42 years. The latter surrounded Babylon by a wall, and then undertook the unlucky war against India. Syncellus[1] (I, p. 315) abbreviates and, as it seems, disfigures this passage, provided his text is not corrupted. For whilst Eusebius makes Cephalion state the age of Ninus to be 52 years, Syncellus places the birth of Semiramis and Zoroaster in the fifty-second year of Ninus, which is evidently absurd. Moreover, *etei* "in the year" is an emendation of Scaliger; the manuscripts having *ete te* "years and." Somewhat differing information concerning the Magus Zoroaster, the contemporary of Semiramis, is given by Moses of Chorene (I, p. 87, Venice edition). Semiramis, he says, as she spent the summer in Armenia, made the Magus and Median ruler Zradasht governor of Assyria and Niniveh, consequently she became his enemy and attacked him; but she fled before him into Armenia, and afterwards Ninyas killed her and took possession of her empire. Moses of

---

then died. After Ninus reigned Semiramis, and fortified Babylon in the form which has been described by many authors, *viz.*, Ctesias and Zeno and Herodotus and some writers after them. Then he relates that Semiramis waged a war against the Indians, but was defeated and put to flight, *etc.*"

[1] "I begin to relate . . . . . (just as before) . . . . . 52 years. (The manuscripts have *Zoroastrobatu* 'instead of Zoroaster.' *Zoroastru magu* 'of the Magus Zoroaster' has been conjectured by Scaliger; perhaps we should read instead *Bactrianu*). After him, he says, Semiramis fortified Babylon in the form related by many, *viz*, by Ctesias, Zeno (Müller reads *Dino*), Herodotus and the writers after them; and her campaign in India and her defeat," *etc.*

Chorene is here expressly attacking the addition of Cephalion. The latter relates, as many others, first the birth of Semiramis, then her war against Zoroaster in which Semiramis was conqueror, and, lastly, the Indian campaign. Maribas of Catina, he says, has drawn the facts from Chaldæan sources, which are confirmed by the Armenian tradition. Next he continues (I, p. 39) :—"A certain Zradasht, a Magian and King of Bactria, that is Media, says, that *Zervan* was the beginning and father of the deities ; and many other things he has fabled about him which cannot be repeated here."

Let us go back to Cephalion, whose age we regret cannot be determined (Müller, *Fragm. Hist, Gr.,* III, p. 68 and p. 625). He expressly names Ctesias among his authorities. We must, therefore, trace back to Ctesias the whole story of the war of Semiramis against Zoroaster so much the more, since it is also found in Diodorus, though under another name. The latter relates the conquests of Ninus (Bk. II, 2 *seq.*,) wherein he expressly cites Ctesias, and says that Bactria alone resisted him. Further, that he then delayed the war against Bactria and founded Niniveh in the meanwhile. After that by way of episode (in chapters IV and V) the birth of Semiramis is asserted, as Diodorus states in harmony with Cephalion (in chapter V :—" But what tradition says about the birth of Semiramis is this.") Then follow the preparations for war made by Ninus, his invasion of Bactria, the stratagem of Semiramis by which the town was taken, the marriage of Semiramis and Ninus, the birth of Ninyas, and the death of the founder of Niniveh; then the foundation of Babylon by Semiramis, her expedition into India, and her death. We clearly observe that whatever is quoted from Cephalion, is only a dry and much shortened synopsis of the contents of what is related more diffusely from Ctesias by Diodorus. Yet Diodorus, in following Ctesias, calls the King of Bactria *Oxyartes*, without hinting anyhow at his identity with the Magian Zoroaster, whilst Cephalion, according to the authority of Eusebius, Moses of Chorene, and Syncellus taken from the *same* Ctesias, designates the Magian Zoroaster as the Bactrian King in question. Considering that Cephalion is little trustworthy, we might be led to conjecture that he had, on his own account, altered the *Oxyartes* of Ctesias into *Zoroaster*. But many reasons controvert this hypothesis:—Firstly, that Maribas, the authority of Moses, has also related of the Magian *Zradosht* and his combat with Semiramis. Secondly, the passages in Justin, Arnobius,[1] and Theo already mentioned above, cannot one and all be traced back to the single authority of Cephalion. Consequently, we must either think that the name is spelt incorrectly in Diodorus, and *Zoroasteres* must have been substituted for *Oxyartes*; or that Ctesias has really named Oxyartes, the King of Bactria, who was, according to him, a contemporary of Ninus and Semiramis, whilst the other sources from which Cephalion and others drew their informations called him Zoroaster. So the later authorities at least, if not Ctesias himself, placed the Magian Zoroaster in the age of

---

[1] He expressly introduces Ctesias as his authority for the Bactrian Zoroaster, quotes the book in which the passage was found, and speaks of the magical means wherewith the Assyrians and Bactrians had fought, which he could neither have drawn from Diodorus nor from Cephalion, just as he has stated to us.

Ninus and Semiramis. If the latter lived about 1273 B.C., as is now believed (see Gutschmid, p. 100; Brandis, "On the Historical Gain from the Decipherment of the Assyrian Inscriptions," p. 15), *we have as the period of Zoroaster the middle of the thirteenth century before Christ*, whereas those chroniclers who co-ordinate Ninus and Abraham mention Zoroaster in the seventh year of Abraham; (compare Eusebius, *Chron.* II, p. 35 ed. Auch; *Praep. Evang.* X, 9—a difference of 700 to 800 years).

A circumstance which might in particular render doubtful the account of the Greeks, which makes the Magian Zoroaster a contemporary of Semiramis, is the position of a *Bactrian King* which is attributed to him; for nowhere in the original texts Zarathushtra has royal dignity (or kingship), though he is said to be the lord of all ranks and orders. On the contrary, *Vishtâspa* is expressly mentioned as the king in whose reign Zoroaster flourished, and who spread the holy Doctrine. This difficulty could only be solved by calling *Vishtâspa* a follower of the Prophet Zarathushtra, and by taking the former for the latter, so that we must regard Zoroaster-Vîshtâspa himself as the Bactrian king abovenamed.

If the statement of Syncellus be true, we should have a Median Zoroaster, King of Babylonia, who is placed about 2,458 B.C., and a Bactrian King Zoroaster, who is placed about 3,000 B.C., or in 1,273 according to the era of Ninus. But therewith all the difficulties do not come to an end. The authors of the "Pseudo-Clementinian Recognitions"—the Latin Translation of which is still preserved—and of the false "Clementinian Homilies" (which are, likewise, now extant in Greek, and which were written at least in the second century after Christ), who have, it is true, many intrinsic similarities, but who, too, differ from one another in manifold ways, as is proved by the passages cited below,[1] identify Zoroaster with *Mesraim*, son of *Cham* (*vide* "Recognitions"), or with Nimrod (*vide* "Homilies of Clemens"). Later eccle-

---

[1] *Recogn. Clement.* IV, 27: "One of these (the sons of Noë) named Cham, delivered to one of his sons called Misraim "Egypt," from whom the Egyptian, Babylonian and Persian people took their origin, the ill-acquired art of magic. He was called Zoroaster by the heathens of those times, and admired as the first master of the magical art, under whose name exist very many books upon this art. A very great observer of the stars, he wished to be regarded as a divine being and began to elicit sparks from the stars and to show them to the people (comp. *Anonymus ror Malalas*, p. 17, ed. Bonn), wherewith dull and stupid people were amazed as with a wonder. Wishing to enhance his reputation he repeated this practice very often until he was burned by God himself whom he troubled too much." 28 "But the stupid men instead of rejecting as they ought to have done this belief about Zoroaster, extolled him so much the more, notwithstanding they saw that he had been punished by death. For they built in his honour a monument and ventured to adore him as if he were a friend of God, and had been raised up to heaven in a chariot of lightning. They also venerated him as a living star. Hence he was called after his decease Zoroaster, *i.e.*, "the living star," by those who had learned the Greek tongue after one generation (*i. e.*, 30 years). For this reason many of those who are killed by lightning, are honoured with a monument, as if they were friends of God. After he had begun in the 14th generation, he died in the 15th, in which the (Babylonian) Tower was erected and the languages of men were divided (into many varieties)." (Here follows the passage about Nimrod). 29 "And he was burned by the wrath of the God to whom he had been too troublesome as is said above; yet his ashes were collected, as if they were the remnants of the lightning, by those who were first deceived and brought to the Persians, to be preserved by them in constant watches, as godlike fire fallen from heaven, and to be adored as a heavenly God."

Clem. Homil., IX., 3:—"One of these was Cham called Mizraim, from whom the Egyptian and Babylonian and Persian peoples take their origin." (4) "From this family came forth one who had inherited the magical art in succession. He was called Nebrod (Nimrod?), and being a giant he chose to be an antagonist to God. Him the

siastical writers are still more at variance in this question, calling now *Cham* (*Historia Scholastica* in Genesim, 39), now *Chus* (*Gregorius Turonius Historia*, I, 5), now *Assur* (Epiphanius, *Panar.*, p. 7 ; Procopius, *Gaz. in Gen.*, XI.) by the name of Zoroaster. The " Recognitions " say :—" This Zoroaster began his life in the fourteenth generation, and died in the fifteenth, at the time when the Tower (of Babel) was built, and there was a confusion of languages." But these fourteen generations are the ten from Adam to Noah inclusive, then Cham, Chus and Nimrod ; but which generation is further added, is not clear. All these identifications of Zoroaster are connected with Genesis X, 6, and tend to the belief that every magical art was the original property of the family of Cham. As Zoroaster was regarded as the representative of Magism, he was consequently

---

Greeks call Zoroaster. After the great Deluge he longed for empire, and being a great *Magus* (here "sorcerer") he forced by magical arts the horoscopic star (here the readings vary much) . . . . to give him empire. But when he was as it were ruling, and had authority from the star which he had forced, he poured out the fire of the empire in pride, that he might act according to his oath and revenge himself upon him who had first compelled him." (5) " By this lightning which had fallen from heaven on the earth Nimrod was destroyed, and from this accident he was surnamed *Zoroaster* on account of the living stream of the star. Yet the ignorant people of those times, thinking that his soul was taken up by the thunderstroke owing to his love of God, interred the remains of the body, but honoured the tomb by a temple built in Persia where the bringing down of fire had taken place. He was honoured like a god, and after this example others, too, who died there by the thunderstroke, were interred like the friends of God and honoured with temples, and statues were erected in the individual forms of the dead persons . . . . ." (6) " The Persians first took coals from the thunderbolt which had fallen from heaven, watched and nourished them at home and venerated the fire like a god, being the first to adore it ; and by means of this fire they first had the honour of domination. After them the Babylonians stole coals of this fire, and preserved them in their houses and adored it, and they got the empire subsequently."

set back, without hesitation, into this primeval time of Cham, although it was well-known, as is proved by the passages cited, that Zoroaster was of the Medo-Persian tribe. The origin of the Medians from Japheth, which is attested by the very passage in Genesis X, 2, is here overlooked. In order to maintain their hypothesis, these authors of the "Recognitions" traced the Persians back to Cham and Mezraim, whereby they forgot at the same time that the Chamitical Magism, which consisted of astrology and sorcery, very widely differed from the Zoroastrian Magism. It is possible that the reminiscences of a Median king Zoroaster in Babylon, or of the relations in which Ninus, who was thought identical with Nimrod, stood to Zoroaster, King of Bactria, had floated before the minds of these authors. It is certain that no historical trace could be found in all these combinations; but they are only useful in showing the extent to which the conviction prevailed in antiquity that Zoroaster lived in far older times than the reigning family of the Achæmenidæ.

There is a remarkable difference between the statements of the "Recognitions" and those of the "Clementinian Homilies" as regards Zoroaster. The former represent him as drawing rays of light (or flash of lightning) from the stars,[1] and state that in consequence of his repeating this act too frequently, as he was urged to do so by the *daēva* by whose strength he performed it, he was killed through fire (*i. e.*, lightning). The "Clementinian Homilies," on the contrary, represent him as requesting the gift of domination from the star of that *daēva* who rules over this world with

---

[1] This reminds us of the *pairikas*, which, according to the *Tir. Yt.* § 8, fall down as shooting stars between heaven and earth.

magical arts, after which the *daeva* pours down the fire of dominion by which he (*viz.*, Nimrod-Zoroaster) is immediately devoured. This death by lightning has led to the apotheosis or glorification of Zoroaster, over whose body a temple (?) was erected in Persia. The Persians, it is said, had nourished the cinders of this lightning, and adored the fire as a deity. By this means they first obtained domination,[1] and after them the Babylonians who had also stolen cinders of fire and then become rulers. The latter circumstance is somewhat shortened by the "Recognitions." But both documents have essentially in common a whimsical explanation of the name Zoroaster, though there is here also some small deviation. The "Recognitions" render Zoroaster by the Lat. *vivum sidus* (Gr. *Zoronastron*) "living star." The "Clementinian Homilies" explain it by *zosa roë tou asteros* "a living stream of the star." I need not remark how very absurd these derivations are. But the fire, and indeed the fire coming from Heaven, is a symbol of dominion, which is a genuine feature of the statement. For the *hvarena* of kings is a brilliancy of light which originates from God *Ahura*.

Dio Chrysostom of Prusa in Bithynia, a friend of Plutarch, who was exiled under the Emperor Domitian,

---

[1] The later fabulists describe the death of Zoroaster in a similar manner. So *Cronicon Pasch.*, Vol. I, p. 67, ed. Bonn :—" From his family (of Ninus) issued the very illustrious (Chaldæan) Zoroaster who on the point of death requested to be devoured by heavenly fire, saying to the Persians : 'if the fire destroys me, take up and preserve some burning bones, and the domination shall not disappear from your country as long as you keep my bones.' And he prayed to Orion, and he was destroyed by heavenly fire. And the Persians did as he had bidden them, and they still keep the ashes of him which remain until our days." Comp. *Cedrenus*, v. I, p. 29, ed. Bonn ; *Anonymus vor Maluhas* (I, p. 18, ed. Bonn) and Suidas, *s. v. Zoroastres*.

but had great authority in Rome under Nerva and Trajan, has preserved in his "Borysthenian Oration" (Tome II, p. 60 *seq.*, edition of Dindorf) an alleged myth of the Magi, which is worthy of closer investigation. I quote here this passage dropping what is not essential, or what is purely rhetorical ornamentation. After speaking of the Divine Empire over the Universe, Dio Chrysostom goes on to state :—"Another marvellous myth is sung in the mysterious consecrations of the Magi who praise this God as the first and perfect Conductor of the most perfect Wagon. For the car of Helios," he says, " is younger than this and visible to the whole world, its course being apparent. The strong and perfect team of Zeus has never been praised so worthily by the Greeks, neither by Homer nor by Hesiod ; but Zoroaster and the sons of the Magi that were his disciples, celebrated it (worthily). Zoroaster is said by the Persians to have left society owing to his love of justice and wisdom, and to have lived a solitary life on a mountain. Then this mountain had begun to burn on account of the huge quantity of fire falling from Heaven, and had continued so to burn ; wherefore the King with the chiefs of the Persians had approached thither, intending to adore the Deity. Then it was that Zoroaster had come forth unhurt from the fire and approached them gracefully, bidding them not to be afraid (of the awful prospect) ; but to offer some offerings unto God, since He had visited their territory. Then Zoroaster had intercourse not with all of them, but with those only who were most qualified for truth and most apt for an intercourse with God, and whom the Persians called Magi, *i. e.*, such as understood how to serve the Divine Being,[1] but not sorcerers, as the Greeks called them from their ignorance of the name. Beside other functions fixed by the holy ordinances, the Magi are to nourish for Zeus a team of Nisæian horses (these are the finest and largest in Asia), and for Helios only one horse. But they developed the myth with great boldness saying:—"It is only a conducting and car-driving of the Universe, which is executed with the greatest expertness and strength, always and unceasingly in the unceasing period of time. The courses of the Sun and Moon are only partial movements, and so more apparent, whilst the motion of the Universe is unknown to the common people." Dio hesitatingly dares to sing the pagan song of the horses of this team along with the pleasant Hellenic songs. It appears to him so extravagant. The first horse is of extraordinary beauty, greatness and swiftness, winged and sacred to Zeus. He has the colour of purest light, Sun and Moon are his marks, the other stars including. The second horse, who is next to him and yoked with him, is called after *Here*. He is tame and soft and much inferior in strength and swiftness to the first, black by nature, only that part is shining which is illumined by *Helios*. The third is sacred to *Poseidon*, and slower than the second. Poets call him *Pegasus*. But the fourth and most improbable of all is stiff and immoveable, unwinged and belonging to *Hestia*. Nevertheless, they (the Magi) do not dismiss the image, but they say that this horse, too, is yoked to the wain. He remains in his place champing a bit of diamond. He clings to his place with all his parts, and the two others near him bow towards him;

---

[1] The same definition is given by Dio elsewhere.

whilst the first and most distant horse always moves round the remaining as round the goal of an arena. Commonly they are peaceable; but now and then a strong pull of the first causes a conflagration of the world, like that of the Hellenic *Phaethon*, or some vast sweat of the third causes a flood like that of *Deucalion*. All this, however, is no fortuitous accident, as people fancy, but it is executed after the design of the Wise Driver of the Wagon. Beside this movement of the Universe there is also a movement and transformation of these four that changed their form, until they all adopted one nature, vanquished by the stronger. This motion also is compared by them in a still bolder image with wagon-driving, as if a wonder-working man forms horses of wax, taking away and turning off from each one and adding to the other, until he combines all four into one, and works up one form of the whole mass. But it is not as though the demiurgi were working from outside on lifeless images, and changing the materials; but they, as it were, themselves endured the same as in a struggle for victory in a great and true combat. This victory is naturally gained by the first, strongest, and swiftest horse which was at the beginning designated as the chosen one of Zeus. For this horse being the strongest of all, and naturally all fiery, devours the others in a very short time, as if they were indeed made of wax; but they seem infinite according to our calculation. The first horse takes into himself the whole essence of others. He appears much larger and brighter than before, having turned out the vanquisher in the greatest combat, not through any one of mortals or immortals, but through himself. Again he stands proud and haughty, glad at his victory and needing larger space on account of his strength and valour. Having arrived at this point of the narration the author is afraid of naming the real nature of the animal, which is simply the spirit of the Wain-driver and Lord, or rather His understanding and guiding essence."

So far, it seems, runs the description of the Magi in Dio Chrysostom. It is difficult to decide how much of this mythical discourse is drawn from a true Magian document, and how much has been added by the Greek panegyrist, as such additions are to be presumed on account of the occurence of the names of Zeus, Here, Poseidon, Hestia and Pegasus, and from the references to Phaethon and Deucalion. Or it may be that the whole matter has been invented by Dio, and ascribed to the Magi. The latter, however, does not seem probable. On the contrary, it is possible that Dio, who speaks of the mysterious initiations of the Magi, has drawn this matter from the " Mithraic mysteries " which prevailed at Rome in those times. The idea of a wagon with four horses being driven by God is not opposed to the Magian mode of belief. We find in the original Avesta texts that *Anâhita* drives in a chariot with four white horses (*Abân Yt.*, §§ 11, 13), which are afterwards designated as Wind, Rain, Cloud, and Lightning (*ibid* § 120). *Mithra*, too, has a team of four white horses, whose fore-hoofs are shod with gold, the hinder ones with silver. (*Mihr Yt.*, § 125). The same thing is mentioned of *Sraosha* (*Yasna* LVII, § 27), though he is drawn by falcons of all surpassing swiftness. It is not, therefore, impossible that such a team of four horses was ascribed to Ahura Mazda, too, in some Avesta text which is now lost.

The horses of the team are easily to be interpreted as light, air, water, and earth. The combination of light and air reminds us of the combination (so frequently found in the Avesta texts) of *Mithra*, the representative of light, and *Râma Qâstra* (*vayush uparo kairyô*), the genius of air, who likewise appears personified in the *Râm Yt.*, § 54, *seq.* As they were so well represented under the image of mighty warriors, they might as well also be represented under the image of horses; for we see *Tishtrya* and *Verethraghna* take the shape of horses in the *Yashts* dedicated to them (*Tir Yt.*, § 18; *Bahrâm Yt.*, § 9).

Moreover, we have the description of the wain of Zeus, who is evidently identical with Ahura Mazda, in Xenophon's *Cyropædia*, VIII, 3, 12, where a white wagon—the colour refers to the horses of the wagon—with golden yoke and sacred to Zeus, is conducted in a procession.

What is said by Dio Chrysostom of the bright horse reputed to be the soul of the chariot-driving God, this, too, is Magian in my opinion. It is the *Fravashi* of Ahura Mazda, that is spoken of in the *Fravardin Yt.*, §§ 80, 81, as we have seen above.

Most important is what Dio says about Zarathushtra. He had lived from love of justice and wisdom in solitude on a mountain burning with fire which fell from Heaven. Out of this burning mountain the prophet had made his appearance to the King[1] and commenced his Revelations. Whence has Dio drawn this? The

---

[1] By the bye, I remark that Dio, or his authority, does not mean to identify this king with the father of Darius.

life of Zoroaster in the solitude and on a mountain is I think, founded, as has been already presumed by me in my discourse on *Mithra*, p. 63, on a statement of *Vend. Farg.* XIX, 4, compared with the Bundahish, p. 53, l. 5, p. 58, l. 5, and p. 79, l. 10. Porphyrius in *De antro nymph*, c. 6., describes after Eubulus the Mithraic cavern which Zoroaster had consecrated on the mountain in the neighbourhood of Persia.

The burning mountain from which Zoroaster came forth, reminds us of the burning *thorn-bush* of Moses; I cannot recall any similar thing in the Avesta texts, though a passage in the Bundahish might be pointed at with regard to this allusion.

THE ALLEGED PAHLAVI LETTER OF TANSAR TO THE KING OF TABARISTÂN.[1]

In his disquisition upon a Pahlavi letter of Tansar said to have been addressed by him to the king of Tabaristan during the reign of Artakhshatar-i-Pâpakân, M. Darmesteter gives very great prominence to a supposed Persian rendering of that Pahlavi letter, and attempts to point out from certain incongruous statements which are made in it, and interpreted by him according to his preconceived opinion, that the antiquity of the extant Avesta literature is not as remote as is established by most of his contemporaries in science, *viz.*, Geiger, Geldner, Mills, etc. Darmesteter's observations on the Persian of the alleged letter of Tansar, run briefly as follows :—

ᛞᛟᛋᚨᚱ Tansar or Tôsar, the *Aîrpatân Aîrpat*, *i.e.*, the head of the priests, has taken a very important part in the religious renaissance which characterized the epoch of *Artakhshatar* or Artakhshîr, the founder of the Sâsânian Empire. It is stated in the Dinkard, that this Tansar was not only authorized "to collect the sacred texts upon which Zoroastrism is based," but also *de restituer l'Avesta perdu ou mutilé* "to restore the lost or mutilated Avesta." This Tansar receives in the Dinkard the epithet of a *pôryôtkêsha*. The statement of the Dinkard that Tansar was "also ordered to restore the lost or mutilated Avesta"[2] is not an isolated one,

---

[1] *Vide* Journal Asiatique, Neuvième Série, Tome III, *Lettre de Tansar au Roi de Tabaristân*, par M. J. Darmesteter, pp. 185-250, 502-555, Paris, 1894. Here I have rendered to a certain extent Darmesteter's own views upon the authenticity of the Pahlavi letter.

[2] The rendering seems to be inaccurate.

but it is confirmed and made clear by an independent Arabic authority. In his "*Prairies d'or*," Masoudi alludes to the report that Ardashîr was assisted at the commencement of his reign by a pious personage of royal blood, named *Bîshar* بشر, who belonged to the Platonic sect. In the *Kitâb et-tanbih*, Masoudi refers again to this Bîshar as the mobed or apostle of Ardashir. According to the Arab writer, Bishar or Tansar was one of the *Mulûk ut-tavâif*, and reigned in the province of Persis or Fars. When he became an adherent of Platonism, he abdicated the princedom of Pârs, and embraced a religious life. Afterwards he preached upon the advent of Ardashîr, sent missionaries to do the same in different provinces, and facilitated thus the triumph of the prince over the *Mulûk ut-tavâif*. Masoudi adds that Tansar composed fine treatises on the administration and religion of the Sâsânian kingdom, wherein the latter justified the political and religous innovations which Ardashir had introduced, and which the preceding monarchs had not been able to undertake. In support of this assertion the two letters of Tansar, one addressed to the king of Tabaristan and another to the king of India, are chiefly cited by Masoudi who has preserved a fragment of Tansar's letter to the king of Tabaristan.

The (alleged) letter is not preserved in its primitive form, which was the Pahlavi; only the Persian translation is surviving, which is not made from the original Pahlavi text, but from an Arabic version which is now lost, and to which the quotations from Masoudi refer. This Arabic translation is supposed to be the work of Ibn al-Moqaffa, a Zoroastrian convert to Mohammedanism, under the first Abbassides. He died about the year 760 A. D. Ibn al-Moqaffa was entrusted with the task of rendering into Arabic, the language of the Mohammedan conquerors, the principal national works of Sâsânian Persia. The Persian translation, which was produced five centuries later, is the work of Mohammed bin ul-Hassan bin Asfandyâr, who wrote about A.D. 1210.

This Mohammed bin ul-Hasan was a native of Tabaristan, who has written a history of his native country. One day having been at Khvârizam, then the grand centre of erudition and literature, he discovered on the shelf of a library a letter translated by Ibn al-Moqaffa from Pahlavi into Arabic, and originally written by Tansar, "the Persian sage and high priest of Ardashîr Bâbagân," in response to a letter from Jasnasf Shâh, the then ruler of Tabaristân. Finding it full of edifying thoughts, he translated the Arabic letter into Persian, and inserted it in the introduction to his history of Tabaristân.

If this letter is authentic, that is to say, if it really represents, throughout both the Arabic and Persian translations, a text which emanated from the chaplain of Ardashir, it constitutes (says Darmesteter) the most ancient monument of Persia after the inscriptions of Darius and the Avesta. It can be even more ancient than the Avesta in its last and complete form, if we admit that a part of the Avesta was written out under the first successors of Ardashir. The principal question is: *Is it authentic?*

(To this question the French savant's reply is): *It is not so in its present form, not only as to the language, but also as to the main points of thought.*[1] It

---

[1] See p. 189 : Elle ne l'est pas dans sa forme présente, non point seulement quant à la langue, ce qui va de soi, mais aussi quant au fond.

does not appear that the Persian translator has added anything of his own to the principal facts that he found in his Arabic original, save perhaps the anecdote on the fatalist king Jihang, which is cited by him at the end of his translation for the purpose of throwing some light upon the relations between free will and destiny. It is, however, clear that the Arabic translator has inserted a number of new things in the original now lost, whatever the materials were which he had before him. *Ibn al-Moqaffa had* with the object, no doubt, of rendering the old Zoroastrian text more appreciable to his Musulman readers, *interpolated in the letter some quotations from the Koran and some from the Bible, which stand out from the context, and which were besides, not meant to form part of the Pahlavi original.*[1] It is also to be remembered that Ibn al-Moqaffa's mind was also occupied with the translation of the Pahlavi book entitled "*Kalila* and *Dimna*," and he has thereto added, in order to please its reader, a long fable which is found in the *Panchatantra*, and which undoubtedly appertained to his Pahlavi translation of the *Kalila*. Let us add to this list of interpolations the description of the anarchy, the history of the generation in the small chest, the explicative commentary of the judicial term *abdâl*, the history of the fatalist king Jihang, and the Arabic quotations reproduced and translated by Mohammed bin ul-Hasan.

These interpolations having been deducted, there remains (according to Darmesteter) a text which, in reference to its fundamental ideas, is anterior to Ibn-

---

[1] Ibn al-Moqaffa, sans doute pour rendre le vieux texte guèbre plus respectable à ses lecteurs musulmans, y a glissé des citations du Coran et de la Bible qui se detachent d'ellesmêmes du contexte et qui, d'ailleurs, n'ont jamais eu la prétention d'appartenir à l'original.

al-Moqaffa, and cannot be his original work. Its gene
ral authenticity is as clear as daylight, because it i
teeming with details of which the authenticity i
guaranteed to us on the one hand by their conformit
with what we know directly by means of the extan
Pahlavi texts, and on the other hand by the new thing
which instruct and throw their light on the obscuritie
of those very Pahlavi texts.

We do not see why Ibn al-Moqaffa, while writin
for the Musulmans, should have forged such a text a
had only a historical and archæological interest. Ib
al-Moqaffa is before all an antiquarian, who wishes t
know what he can of the past and to familiarize th
Musulmans with that past, in order to make his writing
interesting to them if possible. Here he continues o
what he has done in his translation of the *Khudâi-nâma,*
the *Kalila* and *Dimna,* and other national old works o
the anti-Islamic period.

Besides, *we cannot ascertain that he had before h:
eyes the Pahlavi original of Tansar himself.*[1] He give
himself a statement of his authority in a line o
which the sense is unfortunately somewhat ambiguou
According to Masoudi, the kolophon states

از بهرام بن خورزاد و او از پدر خویش منوچهر موبد خراسان
علماء پارس

That is to say: "According to Bahrâm, son o
Khûrzâd, and the latter according to his father Manu
chihar, Mobed of Khorâsân, and according to th
sages of Persia." In this indication of the source on
thing only is absolutely clear, *viz.*, that the Ara
translator has worked upon a text which he discove

---

[1] Mais on ne peut assurer pourtant en toute certitude qu'il e
sous les yeux l'original pehlvi de Tausar même.

ed in a book belonging to a Zoroastrian named Bahrâm, son of Khûrzâd Now the question arises: Whence Bahrâm himself got this text? According to the analogy of the kolophons which are found in same old Pahlavi MSS., and which give the genealogy of the copies, it seems probable that Ibn al-Moqaffa gives us here the kolophon abridged from the text of Bahrâm, that is to say, from the successive copies of the text. In other words Bahrâm copies a MS. emanating from his father Khûrzâd, and transcribed from a MS. written by Khûrzâd's father Manûchihr, a Mobed of Khorâsân; the last copy having been derived from a MS. emanating from the copyists of Fârsistân. If this interpretation is the right one, the Arabic version of Ibn al-Moqaffa goes back to a Pahlavi MS. of the letter of Tansar.

But the short Arabic kolophon, which is translated into Persian as above, is susceptible of another meaning. It can denote not only the successive originals of an anterior text, which from copy to copy came into the hands of Bahrâm and of Ibn al-Moqaffa; but an *ensemble* of the sources on the basis of which Bahrâm *composed the Pahlavi that is rendered into Arabic by* Ibn al-Moqaffa. In this case (as Darmesteter avers) *our text is not the work of Tansar, but the work of Bahrâm, son of Khûrzâd.*[1] But even then (says he) the letter of Tansar is not less authentic although in a different sense; because the details, which it contains, bear so far the stamp of truth that it must be inferred that Bahrâm worked on some excellent historical sources.

The epoch of Bahrâm is not known to us; but, according to Darmesteter, that matter is of relatively secondary importance for the question of the authenticity of the text.

---

[1] Dans ce cas, notre texte n'est plus l'œuvre de Tansar, mais l'œuvre de Bahrâm, fils de Khûrzâd.

In fact, Ibn al-Moqaffa died at the commencement of the second century of the Hegir era, scarcely a century after the close of the national dynasty. Now, two centuries later, in the epoch of Masoudi, Pahlavi was flourishing as a written language, and whether Bahrâm belonged to the Sâsânian period or to the Arab period, he at least lived in a period when the old Pahlavi literature was yet intact.

We now come to the analysis of the alleged Persian version of Tansar's letter (which is given by Darmesteter as follows) :—

After a historic preamble on the history of the conquest of Alexander, which describes the traditional legend about the origin of the provincial princes (*Mulûk ut-tavâif*), Ibn al-Moqaffa relates that at the time when Ardashîr overpowered Ardavân and re-established the unity of the Irânian Empire, Tabaristan was ruled by a prince, whose name was Jasnasf-Shâh, whom Ardashîr did not like to reduce by violence, bearing in mind that the ancestors of Jasnasf-Shâh had conquered their province of Tabaristân under the lieutenants of Alexander, and remained faithful to the dynasty of Persia. However, Jasnasf-Shâh seeing his independence afterwards menaced, wrote to Tansar, the high-priest of Ardashîr—who had formerly served as an intimate adviser to his father—a letter containing a " veritable act of accusation against Ardashîr, against his cruelty, his practice of inquisition and espionage, his tyrannical laws, and his religious innovations." The Persian text of the letter is the reply of Tansar, which was judged to be decisive, for Jasnasf-Shâh sent in his submission, and thereby retained his province under the suzerainty of the Sâsânidæ.

(Darmesteter divides the Persian letter into the following fourteen sections :—)

I. Tansar commences his letter by explaining why he quitted the world, and embraced an ascetic life. It was to induce the kings and nations of his time, who seeing him detached from selfish interests might believe in his advice. He renounced everything in order to have greater authority for the purpose of reforming the world according to the true religion.

II. The duty of Jasnasf-Shâh is to surrender himself without any delay to the court of Ardashîr, and to lay his crown at his feet. Thus only lately the king of Kirmân and Qabûs has done, who in return of his obeissance, has kept his royal title. The King of Kings allows the title and right of kingship to all those of the provincial kings who would recognize him as their head.

III. Jasnasf-Shâh remonstrates with Ardashîr for wrongly representing himself as the restorer of the ancient law. Indeed, the sacred texts have been destroyed by Alexander, and there only remain of them a few traditions and legends, which are so much corrupted by the vice of men, by the taste of novelties and unauthenticated stories, that there survives nothing authentic in them. In order to revive religion, therefore, an upright and honest man was required. Is there a man who is so capable for the purpose as the *Shahân-Shâh?*

IV. Jasnasf-Shâh reproaches Ardashîr with the rigid division of men into four classes, and the laws regarding handicrafts. Tansar enlarges upon the necessity of a hierarchy of classes and upon the evils arising from mixing up the ranks of society. The king besides authorizes promotion in rank from an inferior class to a superior class, but that is done after the examination and guarantee of individual merit.

V. Jasnasf-Shâh accuses Ardashir of cruelty. Upon which Tansar remarks: a king may be cruel although he executes only a few persons, and he may not be cruel even if he spilled floods of blood. The number of executions only proves the public corruption and the extent of evil to be suppressed. Ardashîr, on the contrary, is more merciful than the ancient kings in cases of crimes against God, against the king, or against particular individuals. Formerly immediate death was the punishment inflicted for crimes against religion ; but since Ardashir's time the heretics are imprisoned for one year, during which time some of the scholars daily preach to them and catechize them. It is only in those cases where they remain obstinately blind that capital punishment is inflicted upon them. Before Ardashir's reign, the rebels or fugitives were never treated with forbearance. At present the king is satisfied with decimating them in order to hold others in suspense between terror and hope. In ancient times the delinquency against individuals was punished with mutilations which diminished public strength, without bringing any advantage to the individual accuser, to the people who wished to be compensated for it. In Ardashir's time punishment or fine takes the place of mutilation.

VI. A justification of the sumptuary laws as distinguished from the classes.

VII. A justification of the laws of inheritance established by the king.

VIII. Ardashir is accused of sacrilege for having extinguished the sacred fires of the *Malúk ût-tavâif*. Not he but the fires were sacrilegious.

IX. Ardashir is found fault with for the practice of espionage. But it is necessary that the king should know all about the conduct of his subjects, for which he ought only to choose honest informants. The honest people have simply to congratulate themselves upon this practice of espionage, which will cause their merit to be made known to the king, and render him favourable to them.

X. Why has the king not appointed his heir? In reply to which Tansar states the laws concerning the election of the king and the rules of sacerdotal consultation in the matter.

XI. Virtue and grandeur of ancient Persia. The history of the fall of the dynasty. The legend of Dârâ and Rastîn (related by the king of monkeys).

XII. The place of Persia in the world. The superiority of the Persian race which united the merits of all other races.

XIII. The preparations made by Ardashir against the Romans, the successors of Alexander, whom he attacked in order to conquer the provinces which the latter had formerly taken from his ancestors.

XIV. The relationship of Jasnasf-Shâh to Ardashir does not make him his equal.

XV. The genius of Ardashir, the prodigious grandeur of his work, would last for ever. Do we not know from religious sources that the abandonment of his laws one day will cause universal ruin?

OBSERVATIONS.

The discovery of a Persian version of the so-called Pahlavi letter of Tansar, addressed to Jasnasf-Shah, by the late M. Darmesteter, is a subject of high interest to the student of Irânian antiquities. However, the light that has been thrown upon the question of its authenticity as well as the non-existence of the Pahlavi original, does not persuade us to regard the surviving Persian text of the letter as an indigenous authority for fixing the date of the Avesta. Darmesteter's arguments, which are mostly derived from the extant Persian letter, may be summarized and replied to as follows :—

1. Tansar, the writer of the alleged Pahlavi letter, had taken a very important part in the Sâsânian renaissance of the Zoroastrian religion, and he had been authorized not only "to collect the sacred texts," but "to restore the lost or mutilated Avesta," as is evidenced by the Pahlavi Dînkard and Masoudi. [According to the passage of the Dînkard referred to by Darmesteter, and quoted and translated below, it cannot be proved that the high-priest was ordered "to restore the lost Avesta." No Pahlavi expression in the text points to such an idea or import. The original Pahlavi only indicates that he was entrusted with the task of collecting all the scattered fragments of the copy (*ham nipîk min pargandagîh ôl aêvak jîvâk ydityûnt*) which had fallen into the hands of the Greeks, and to compile (*bûndakînîdan*) the whole of the sacred work with the help of the Pahlavi version or tradition preserved by the people. At the same time, we cannot infer from the statement of Masoudi that Tansar, having belonged to the Platonic sect, must have introduced Platonic ideas into the Avesta. Do we not learn as to Greek philosophy that much of it was suggested by ideas borrowed from the East? Plato is said to have been born B. C. 429 at Athens and to have travelled for twelve years to Cyrene, Egypt, Sicily, and

Italy. He died in B. C. 347. So in Egypt he had good opportunity for learning much about Egyptian and Eastern philosophy; and we know from historical testimony that the chief advances in Greek philosophy took place after the Greeks came in contact with Eastern nations, including the ancient Persians. Socrates lived in B. C. 468-399. Hence, undoubtedly, the resemblances in the Avestic and the Greek philosophy were to some extent the outcome of the close study of the ancient Irânian literature by the Greeks. The Ameshaspend-doctrine is certainly old and purely Zoroastrian, and not influenced by Philo the Jew.* Strabo may be quoted to show that the glorification of the Ameshaspends must have been recognized long before the beginning of the Christian era. The divinities whose elaborate worship is described by Plutarch, can be none other than *Vohumanô* and *Ameretât*, since the elaborate ceremony of their worship in Cappadocia does not imply a historical development of any considerable time.]

2. Neither the Pahlavi original text of Tansar's letter nor its direct Arabic translation is surviving; but only the Persian version of the Arabic of Ibn al-Moqaffa. Besides this, the Persian rendering is not authentic in its present form, not only in respect of the language, but also of the main points of thought; and

---

*Comp. Max Müller, "The Contemporary Review," Vol. LXIV, p. 870 *seq*:—" We are told that Tansar was a Platonist, and it is in order to account for the Neo-Platonist ideas which M. Darmesteter discovers in the Gâthâs that he places the Gâthâs in the first century of our era, about the time of Philo Judæus. If so, why not place them in the third century or in the time of Clement of Alexandria and Origen? Could Parsi priests in the first century have composed in the ancient metre of the Gâthâs which existed nowhere but in the Gâthâs? . . . If the ancient monotheistic religion had become dualistic as early as Aristotle, who knew the names of *Oromasdes* and *Areimanios*, what could have led Tansar to re-introduce Ahura-Mazda as the name of the one supreme deity? How could he have discovered the very name of Ahura-Mazda, in two words, which even in the inscriptions of Darius, had dwindled down to one word, *viz.*, Auramazda?"

it contains many interpolations. However, after deducting these interpolations, there remains, according to Darmesteter, a text which is teeming with details of which the authenticity is guaranteed to us. [The latter statement is a mere sweeping assertion, made without proving by quotations and references, that there are some new things in Tansar's letter which throw light on certain obscure passages of the extant Pahlavi literature. In the absence of the Pahlavi original it is, of course, very difficult to distinguish Tansar's text from the later additions and interpolations. We do not, consequently, understand where to draw the line or what the extent is to which the letter is forged or true. Again, Ibn al-Moqaffa finds, as he alleges, the Pahlavi letter in some book or MS. belonging to a Zoroastrian, named Bahrâm, son of Khûrzâd. In that case, as Darmesteter himself avers, the text in Bahrâm's MS. may not be the work of Tansar, but perhaps of Bahrâm himself. There are, therefore, no authentic grounds to indicate that the Pahlavi letter which is attributed to Tansar in Bahrâm's book, is genealogically descended from the original in Tansar's own hand-writing. In short, the Persian letter put forth in the name of Tansar by the French savant, seems to be entirely unauthentic. If we were to believe Ibn al-Moqaffa, and to grant that a Pahlavi letter had been discovered by him in the MS. belonging to Bahrâm, son of Khûrzâd, which Ibn al-Moqaffa translated into Arabic, still there exist no historical data for calling the alleged letter the genuine work of Tansar, the high-priest of the Sâsânian monarch Artakhshatar.]

[To this I may be allowed to add that "the age of Gâthic composition had so long passed away in the time of the earliest Sâsânian monarchs, that the sages whom they appointed to collect and rearrange the sacred literature, were unable to fully understand many of the stanzas they had to translate into

Pahlavi, much less could they have added to their number." (*Vide* S. B. E., Vol. XXXVII, int., p., 42).]

3. There is one important point which draws our attention. It is Darmesteter's argument that as "*Haoma* overthrew the usurping *Keresâni* who arose, longing for sovereignty, and said : 'Henceforth no priest will go at his wish through the country to teach the law,' and as the epithet *Keresâni* is transcribed in Pahlavi *Kilisyâk*, the Keresâni usurper was neither a *dêv* nor a Turânian, he was a Greek, he could be no other than Alexander." [The name *Keresâni* occurs only once in the Avesta, *Yasna* IX., 24, where it is represented that the usurper was dethroned by Haoma. Now there is nothing in the history of Alexander to prove that the latter had ever been dethroned by an Irânian prophet or monarch. It is true that owing to the scantiness of the Pahlavi alphabet the transcription of the proper name *Keresâni* quite resembles the spelling of the Pahlavi word *kilisyâk*, but hence it does not follow that the signification of the *kilisyâk* commonly used in Pahlavi literature ought to be attached to the Avesta proper name. The mythical idea connected with the Vedic *Krishânu*, archer and demi-god who guarded the heavenly Soma (Av. *Haoma;* Mills, p. 237), suggests to us some old Arian origin of this picture of *Keresâni* in the Avesta and the Vedas. Compare the Rigveda, Hymn CLV., § 2 :—

> "Your *Soma*-drinker keeps afar your furious rush, Indra and Vishnu, when ye come with all your might.
>
> That which hath been directed well at mortal man, bow-armed *Krishânu's* arrow, ye turn far aside."]

The Pahlavi statement regarding the state of the Avesta literature in the time of *Artakhshatar î Pâpakân*, which is contained in the last chapter of the third book of the *Dînkard*, runs as follows :—

[*Vide* chapter 420, page 450 of Dastur Peshotanji's forthcoming Edition of the Dînkard, Vol. IX.]

[Transliteration] *Va bên vazand î min mar î dûsh-gad man Aleksandar ôl Aîrân shatrô dîn khûdâêîh mat; va zak î ôl Dêz î Nipisht ôl sûzishnô, va zak î pavan Ganj î Shapigân ôl yedman î Arûmâkân mat; avash ôlich Yûdandîk hûzvân vidhârd pavan âkâsîh î min pishînik gûftô dîd. Ôlmanî î Artakhshatar î malkâân malkâ î Pâpakân mat ôl lakhvâr ârâstârîh î Aîrân khûdâêîh, ham nipîk min pargandagîh ôl aêvak jîvâk yâîtyûnt; va pôryôtkêsh aharôb Tôsar î aîrpatân aîrpat yehevûnt madam mat, va levatman paêtâkîh min Avistâk lakh- vâr andâkhtan va min zak paêtâkîh bûndakînîdan fra-*

mûd, va hamgûnak kard[1], *angûshîdak min brâh min bûn rôshan, pavan Ganj î Shapîgân dâshtan, va pachîn pasîjagîhâ frâkhnînîdan framûd âkâsîh.*

[Translation] " And in the subversion which happened to the religious sovereignty of the country of Irân (Pahl. *Aîrân*) that (literature) which was (deposited) in the *Dîz î Nipisht* 'Fortress of Documents or Manuscripts,' came to be burnt, and that which was in the 'Treasury of Shapîgân' fell into the hands of the *Arumâns* or Greeks, and it was rendered in the Greek language, too, as the knowledge that was derived from the tradition and observation of the ancients; and (thereafter) when he who was Artakshatar, King of Kings, son of Pâpak, came for the restoration of the (religious) monarchy of Irân, the same copy (which had fallen into the hands of the Greeks) was brought into one place from the different places where it (*viz.*, the copy) was thrown loosely about; and there happened to be (in his time) a *pôryôtkêsh*, the pious Tôsar, the high-priest, who was ordered (by Artakhshatar) to rearrange it (*viz.*, the copy) together with the (Pahlavi) exposition or interpretation of the Avesta, and to compile it (*viz.*,the sacred work) with the help of that exposition. This was accordingly done. And like unto the brilliance or flame of the Original Light the sacred intelligence was ordered (by the king) to be preserved in the 'Treasury of Shapîgân,' and to be propagated by means of true[2] copies of it."[3]

---

[1] In the MSS. ⟨Pahl.⟩ *va zimânak kard* "and a certain time was appointed (for the task)." This expression occurs in the *Bundahish*, chap. I.—[2] ⟨Pahl.⟩ *pasijagîhâ*, *lit.* "in a pure manner." ⟨Pahl.⟩ may mean *lit.* " to be developed," " to be extended."—[3]Cfr. Dastur Dr. Peshotanji's Pahlavi Grammar, Introduction, p. 7 (Bombay Edition, 1871.)

Jede Religion, wo und wann sie auch entstanden sein mag, hat ihre Geschichte und ihre Entwickelung. Keine Religion tritt plötzlich als etwas vollkommen Neues und Unerwartetes in die Erscheinung. Das Auge des Forschers, welcher jedes Ereignis in der Geschichte der Menschheit nach Ursachen und Wirkungen zu prüfen und zu verstehen sucht, wird erkennen, dass jeder neu gestifteten Religionsform eine Zeitperiode vorher geht, welche wir als die Zeit der Vorbereitung bezeichnen können. Es zeigen sich in dieser Zeitperiode gewisse Erscheinungen auf dem Gebiete des geistigen, sittlichen und wirtschaftlichen Lebens des Volkes, welche auf eine bevorstehende Umwälzung der Anschauungen hindeuten. Diese Erscheinungen häufen sich und verstärken sich, das Bedürfnis nach einer Reformation des gesamten Lebens wird immer stärker und mächtiger, bis, man möchte sagen: mit einer gewissen Naturnotwendigkeit, die Persönlichkeit hervortritt, welche dem Verlangen und Hoffen des gesamten Volkes Ausdruck zu verleihen vermag und so zum Stifter einer neuen Lehre wird. Dem Zeitgenossen freilich mag diese Lehre als etwas ganz Unerwartetes, Unerhörtes erscheinen, da er eben die Ereignisse, die er selber miterlebt, noch nicht nach Ursache und Wirkung erfassen kann; der Geschichtsforscher aber, der dies vermag, wird den Erscheinungen nachspüren, welche ein solch bedeutsames Ereignis vorbereiten, und er wird sie überall und immer auffinden, mag er seine Aufmerksamkeit der Geschichte des Christentumes oder des Islam, des Buddhismus oder des Zoroastrianismus zu wenden.

Wie aber jede Religion ihre Vorgeschichte hat, so sie auch ihre Entwickelung. Nicht nur die Naturreligionen der Wilden Afrikas, Amerikas und Australiens sind in einer beständigen Umgestaltung und Veränderung begriffen, es ist dies auch, wenngleich in geringerem Masse, bei den sogenannten Buchreligionen der Fall, d. h. bei den Religionen, welche auf heiligen Urkunden als Kompendium ihrer Lehren, als Norm und Richtschnur für das Leben ihrer Bekenner

---

* A Discourse written by Dr. Wilhelm Geiger, of the University of Erlangen.

beruhen. Selbst in der jüdischen Religion,[1] so wie wir sie aus dem alten Testamente kennen, finden sich Spuren von Wachstum und Verfall. Auch sie ist nicht von Anfang an als etwas Fertiges und Vollendetes ins Leben getreten, sondern ist der Verderbnis ebensowohl wie auch der Entwickelung und Vervollkommnung zugänglich gewesen.

Der Forscher nun, welcher den Inhalt und die Geschichte einer der Religionsformen zum Gegenstand seiner Darstellung gemacht hat, wird die Aufgabe haben, die Idee der Entwickelung nie aus dem Auge zu verlieren und dem Gange dieser Entwickelung nachzuspüren. Er wird sich die Mühe geben müssen, wenn möglich die ursprüngliche Form der Religion festzustellen und das Älteste zu scheiden von dem, was im Verlaufe der Zeit hinzugekommen ist, was notwendig hinzukommen musste. Ich sage notwendig; denn da die Religion eines Volkes zu dessen wichtigsten Kulturgütern gerechnet werden, muss so wird sie im Verlauf der Jahrhunderte gleich allen anderen Kulturgütern gewisse Veränderungen erfahren. Die allgemeinen Lebensverhältnisse des Volkes werden umgestaltet, die wirtschaftlichen Zustände verändern sich, selbst die Wohnsitze können gewechselt werden; damit erfahren aber auch Ideen und Anschauungen, Denken und Wissen ihre Umwandelungen, und das, was der Mensch als das höchste und heiligste Gut bewahrt, seine Religion wird diesen Umwandelungen sich anpassen. Der Inhalt, das Wesen und der Kern der Sache, bleibt der gleiche, woferne nicht ein Volk überhaupt mit Herkommen und Tradition bricht und vollständig neue Wege aufzusuchen sich bemüht; aber der alte Inhalt wird in neue Formen eingefügt, und es muss dies geschehen, wenn die Religion nicht ihre Bedeutung als treibende und immer wieder Geister und Herzen belebende Kraft im Kulturleben des Volkes verlieren soll.

Selbstverständlich ist es nur dann möglich, den ursprünglichen Inhalt irgend einer Religionslehre aufzufinden und festzustellen, wenn litterarische Quellen vorhanden sind, welche entweder von dem Begründer der Lehre selbst herrühren, oder doch wenigstens in dessen Zeit zurückreichen und dabei den Stempel der Wahrhaftigkeit und Zuverlässigkeit tragen.

Wenn wir nun auf den folgenden Seiten den Versuch machen wollen, die zoroastrische Lehre, welche nach einem Bestande von sicherlich 2½ Jahrtausenden und nach einer reichen Geschichte von

---

[1] Max Müller, Vorlesungen über Ursprung und Entwickelung der Religion, S. 149, 150.

Kämpfen und Siegen, Verfolgungen und Erfolgen noch heutzutage von rund 100000 Personen bekannt wird,[1] auf ihre älteste und ursprünglichste Gestalt zurückzuführen, so entsteht vor allem die Frage, ob dies überhaupt noch möglich ist. Besitzen wir Dokumente, deren Verfassung ihrem Stifter zugeschrieben werden darf, oder welche doch wenigstens seinem Zeitalter und etwa dem Kreise seiner ersten Anhänger und Freunde entstammen? Wir können diese Frage mit Ja beantworten; denn wir sind in der That noch im Besitze einer solchen Urkunde, und *diese Urkunde sind die Gâthâs, d. h. die heiligen Hymnen, welche den ältesten Teil des Awestâ, des Religionsbuches der Zoroastrier ausmachen.*

Es ist hier wohl überflüssig, Form und Inhalt der Gâthâ's eingehender zu charakterisieren. Sie bilden, wie bekannt, einen Teil des Yasna, des zur Rezitation bei der Opferhandlung bestimmten Handbuches. Sie stehen aber mit demselben in keinem inneren Zusammenhange, sondern sind ganz lose und ohne Verbindung mit dem übrigen Texte an der Stelle in den Yasna eingefügt, wo ihr Vortrag während des Gottesdienstes dem Ritual entsprechend stattzufinden hat. Somit bilden die Gâthâs ein selbständiges Ganzes für sich, wie auch das sakrale Gesetzbuch, der Vendidâd, dessen Abschnitte in durchaus analoger Weise in den Handschriften des sog. Vendidâd-sâde zwischen die einzelnen Stücke des Yasna eingeschoben werden. Vom ganzen übrigen Awestâ aber, dem Yasna sowohl wie dem Visperad, Vendidâd und den Yashts, unterscheiden sich die Gâthâs schon äusserlich durch die metrische Form, in welcher sie verfasst sind, und welche vielfach an die Metrik der Hymnen des Rigveda uns erinnert, sowie durch ihre Sprache, die von dem gewöhnlichen Awestâ-Dialekte nicht unerheblich abweicht.

Der Umfang der Gâthâ's ist leider nur ein geringer. Aus meinen Berechnungen ergeben sich folgende Zahlen, deren Mitteilung nicht ohne Interesse sein dürfte:

1. Gâthâ Ahunavaiti   300 Zeilen, rund 2100 Worte (Ys. 28-34)
2. Gâthâ Ushtavaiti   330   ,,   ,,   1850 ,,   (43-46)
3. Gâthâ Spentâ-mainyû 164   ,,   ,,   900 ,,   (47-50)
4. Gâthâ Vohû-khshathrâ 66   ,,   ,,   450 ,,   (51)
5. Gâthâ Vahishtô-ishtish 36 ,,   ,,   260 ,,   (53)
Sämtliche Gâthâs 896 Zeilen, rund 5660 Worte.

---
[1] *Dosabhai Framji*, History of the Parsis, Vol. I., S. 91, 92.

Dies ist an sich nun schon wenig genug. Die Sache gestaltet sich aber noch ungünstiger durch die erheblichen Schwierigkeiten, welche die Interpretation der Gāthā's an vielen Stellen bietet. Manche Verszeilen, manche Strophen sind so dunkel, dass es schwer ist eine definitive Übersetzung aufzustellen, oft genug wird man zugeben müssen, dass sowohl die eine als die andere Übersetzung möglich ist, keine als unbedingt richtig, keine als unbedingt falsch gelten kann. Solche Strophen und Zeilen dürfen aber nicht oder doch nur mit grösstem Vorbehalt als Beweise für irgend eine sachliche Auseinandersetzung beigezogen werden. Oft genug wird auch ein Übersetzer etwas für sicher und zweifellos ansehen, was andere bestreiten. Unter allen Umständen ist äusserste Vorsicht in der sachlichen Verwertung der Gāthās dringend geboten.

Aller dieser Schwierigkeiten sind wir uns wohl bewusst gewesen. Nichts desto weniger kann man behaupten, dass auf grund der Gāthā-Texte die ursprüngliche Form des Zoroastrianismus, die philosophische und religiöse Anschauungsweise seines Begründers und seiner ersten Bekenner wenigstens in den allgemeinen Grundzügen dargestellt werden kann, und dass ein solcher Blick in die frühesten Zeiten einer der reinsten und erhabensten Religionen, die es je gegeben, als überaus lehrreich bezeichnet werden muss.

Wir begegnen hier aber gleich im Beginne unserer Untersuchung einem Einwande, welcher entkräftet sein muss, ehe wir auf die Sache selbst eingehen können. Es handelt sich um nichts Geringeres als um die Frage, ob denn die Gāthās von Zarathushtra oder seinen ersten Jüngern und Schülern herrühren, ob sie wirklich in die Urzeit des Zoroastrianismus zurückreichen, ja ob sie überhaupt älter sind als das übrige Awestā. Es gibt unter den Awestā-Forschern in Europa manche, welche das bestreiten, welche Zarathushtra zu einer "mythischen" Persönlichkeit machen möchten, welche die Verschiedenheiten zwischen den Gāthās und dem übrigen Awestā nicht als solche des Zeit sondern vielmehr des Ortes auffassen. Sie nehmen also an, das die Gāthās in einem anderen Teile von Irān verfasst seien als etwa Yashts und Vendidād und dass sich namentlich der Unterschied der Dialekte aus diesem Umstand zur Genüge erkläre. Es scheint übrigens doch, als ob in neuerer Zeit diese Anschauung mehr und mehr an Boden verliere, und gerade der letzte Übersetzer der Gāthā's, Mills, vertritt deren Altertümlichkeit mit grosser Entschiedenheit.

Die metrische Form der Gāthā's darf man allerdings kaum als Beweis für deren höheres Alter beibringen. Denn auch im übrigen Awestā finden sich zahlreiche Stücke, welche ursprünglich metrisch verfasst wären; vielfach ist das Metrum auch noch ungestört erhalten; an anderen Stellen freilich muss der Text erst von den bei der schliesslichen Redaktion des Awestā gemachten Zusätzen und Einschiebungen gereinigt werden. Von grösserem Gewichte wäre schon der Umstand, dass das Versmass in den Gāthās so gut erhalten ist, unvergleichlich besser als in den metrischen Stücken des übrigen Awestā. Dies beweist sicherlich, dass man bei der eben erwähnten Redaktion die Gāthā's für etwas Heiligeres und Unantastbareres ansah als die sonst überlieferten Texte.

Auch der abweichende Dialekt der Gāthā's beweist uns nicht, dass sie älter sind, als das übrige Awestā. Jener Dialekt zeigt allerdings manche altertümlicheren Formen, daneben aber auch solche, die mehr abgeschliffen und verändert zu sein scheinen. Alles dies erklärt sich weit besser durch einen örtlichen als durch einen zeitlichen Unterschied beider Dialekte.

Das was die Gāthās aber unzweifelhaft vom ganzen übrigen Awestā scheidet und sie als weit älter kennzeichnet, ist ihr Inhalt—ihr Inhalt, der uns deutlich hineinführt in die Zeit der Gründung der neuen Lehre, in die Zeit, wo Zarathushtra und seine ersten Anhänger noch lebten und wirkten, während sie für das jüngere Awestā ohne Zweifel Persönlichkeiten einer fernen Vergangenheit sind.

Dies wurde früher schon aufs entschiedenste hervorgehoben[1] und unseres Wissens noch auf keine Weise widerlegt. Neuerdings spricht Mills[2] den nämlichen Gedanken aus : "In the Gāthās all is sober and real. The Kine's soul is indeed poetically described as wailing aloud, and the Deity with His Immortals is reported as speaking, hearing, and seeing, but, with these rhetorical exceptions, everything which occupies the attention is practical in extreme. Grehma and Bendva, the Karpans, the Kavis, and the Usij's are no mythical monsters. No dragon threatens the settlements, and no fabulous beings defend them. Zarathushtra, Jāmāspa, Frashaoshtra, and Maidhyō-māh, the Spitāmas,

---

[1] Civilization of the Eastern Irānians in Ancient Times, by Darab Dastur Peshotan Sanjana, B. A., Vol. II., p. 116 ff.
[2] The Zend-Avesta, Part III. : The Yasna, etc., translated by L. H. Mills (Sacred Books of the East, Vol. XXXI.), p. xxvi.

Hvōgvas, the Haēcat-aspas, are as real, and are alluded to with a simplicity as unconscious, as any characters in history. Except inspiration, there are also no miracles."

Wir werden noch oft genug Gelegenheit haben, auf diesen, ich möchte sagen, aktuellen Charakter der Gāthā's hinzuweisen, und die Richtigkeit der von uns oben aufgestellte These, dass die Gāthās in die Gründungsperiode des Zoroastrianismus gehören, wird dann wohl jedem Leser sich von selbst ergeben. Sie ergibt sich namentlich dann, wenn wir die Rolle ins Auge fassen, welche Zarathushtra und die Persönlichkeiten in den Gāthās spielen, die in der Tradition der Parsen als dessen Zeitgenossen gelten.

Die spätere Legende von Zarathushtra, seinem Leben und seinen Wirken hat ungefähr folgenden Inhalt, wobei ich von allen Ausschmückungen absehe, die sich als solche sofort erkennen lassen.[1] Zarathushtra stammt aus königlichem Geschlechte; sein Stammbaum führt auf Minucheher zurück; zu seinen Ahnen gehören Spitama und Haēcat-aspa, Pourushaspa ist sein Vater. Von Ahura Mazda wird ihm die heilige Religion geoffenbart, zu welcher als der erste von allen Maidhyô-māh, der Sohn von Zarathushtra's Oheim Ārāsti. Auf Gottes Befehl begibt sich Zarathushtra an den Hof des Königs Gushtâsp von Baktrien, um hier seine Lehre zu verkündigen. Minister des Königs ist der weise Jāmāspa. Es gelingt dem Propheten, diesen sowie dessen Bruder Frashaoshtra, dann auch den König selbst und dessen Gemahlin für sich zu gewinnen, und damit fasst der neue Glaube festen Boden. Zarathushtra vermählt sich mit einer Tochter des Jāmāspa, Hvōvi. Hochbetagt stirbt er, nachdem es ihm beschieden war, die ersten Erfolge seiner Verkündigung zu erleben.

I.
DIE AUTORSCHAFT DER GÂTHÂS.

Werfen wir nun einen Blick auf die in den Gāthās vorkommenden Personennamen, so ist es an sich schon bemerkenswert, dass sie alle der Zarathushtralegende, wie wir sie kurz zusammengefasst haben, angehören. Es finden sich genannt: Zarathushtra, Vīshtāspa, Jāmāspa, Pourushaspa, ausserdem Maidhyō-maōgh, von familiennamen Hvōgva, Spitama und Haēcat-aspa, die Geschlechter des Jāmāspa und des Zarathushtra selber. Erwähnt wird endlich die Tochter des Propheten. Dagegen findet sich mit einer einzigen

---
[1] F. von Spiegel, Eranische Altertumskunde, T. I. S. 681 ff.

Ausnahme keiner der in der iränischen Heldensage wohl bekannten und auch im übrigen Awestā oft genug vorkommenden Namen, weder Thraetaona noch Keresāspa, weder Haoshyagha noch Kavi Husrava noch Arjat-aspa. Nur Yima wird an einer einzigen Stelle genannt.

Ist das ein blosser Zufall? Oder ist nicht doch die Annahme wahrscheinlicher, dass die Gāthā's eben von Zarathushtra selbst und seiner Umgebung herstammen und die Erlebnisse, Hoffnungen, Wünsche und Befürchtungen des engen Kreises schildern, aus welchem sie hervorgegangen sind? Diese Annahme wird aber wohl dem Unbefangenen zur Gewissheit, wenn man die Stellen, wo jene Namen vorkommen, eingehender prüft.

Zarathushtra wird, meines Wissens im ganzen sechzehnmal genannt und zwar in sämtlichen Gāthās, in der Gāthā Ahunavaiti dreimal, in der G. Ushtavaiti fünfmal, in der G. Spentā-mainyū zweimal, ebenso oft in der G. Vohū-khshathrā und endlich verhältnismässig am öftesten, nämlich viermal, in der G. Vahishtô-ishti. Gerade diese letzte Gāthā jedoch scheint mir die jüngste zu sein. Die einleitenden Strophen in welchen Zarathushtra, Kavi Vīshtāspa, des Zarathushtra Tochter Pouru-cista, und Frashaoshtra erwähnt werden, scheinen mir einen Rückblick auf die zoroastrische Epoche zu enthalten; dass sie unmittelbar aus der selben stammen, glaube ich nicht.

Von grosser Wichtigkeit sind nun die Stellen, wo Zarathushtra von sich selbst in der ersten Person spricht. *Wer mir in Frommigkeit Gutes zu erweisen sucht*, heisst es z. B. Ys. 46, 19, *mir, dem Zarathushtra, dem werden die himmlischen Geister das als Lohn gewähren, was das Erstrebenswerteste ist, nämlich die ewige Seligkeit.* Ich meine, es liegt am Tage, dass wir hier Worte des Zarathushtra selber vor uns haben. Eine solche Stelle unterscheidet sich vollkommen von Stellen des jüngeren Awestā, wo nicht der Prophet selber spricht, sondern der Verfasser ihn sprechen lässt. Man vergegenwärtige sich nur unter anderem etwa den Anfang von Ys. 9, der ohne Zweifel auch ein altes Lied enthält, sich aber auf den ersten Blick als lange nach Zarathushtra entstanden ergibt, wenn es heisst: Um die Morgenzeit kam Haoma zu Zarathushtra, da dieser das Feuer weihte und die Gāthās rezitierte. *Und es fragte ihn dieser: Wer bist du denn?* u. s. w.

Wir sind gewiss berechtigt, aus der ganz verschiedenen Art, weil Zarathushtra in dieser und in jener Stelle erwähnt wird einen

Schluss auf ihr relatives Alter zu ziehen. In analoger Weise unterscheidet Oldenberg neuerdings zwischen älteren und jüngeren Hymnen im Rigveda, je nach dem die Ausdrucksweise der Dichter eine solche ist, die ihn gleichzeitig zu gewissen geschichtlichen Ereignissen erscheinen lässt oder nicht. So hebt sich Rv. VII. 18 aus den übrigen Hymnen des nämlichen Buches als weit älter heraus, weil sein Verfasser von der grossen Schlacht, die König Sudās schlug, als von etwas eben erst geschehenen spricht, während in anderen Liedern von der nämlichen Schlacht als einem Ereignisse der vergangenen Zeiten die Rede ist.

Gilt aber die Strophe Ys. 46, 19 für zarathushtrisch, so können wir das ohne Zweifel von dem ganzen Liede behaupten. Dasselbe ist aber ungemein reich an persönlichen Anspielungen. In der 14 Strophe wird Zarathushtra angeredet mit den Worten: O Zarathushtra, wer ist dein Freund? Dies steht jedoch unserer Annahme dass der Hymnus von ihm selber herrührt, keineswegs im Wege. Der Dichter lässt eben in echt dichterischer Lebhaftigkeit diese Frage aufgeworfen werden, auf die er selbst dann die Antwort gibt: Er selber ist es, Kavi Vīshtāspa. Mit anderen Worten ausgedrückt bedeutet die Stelle also eben nur: Ich habe keinen besseren Freund und Anhänger gefunden, als den Vīshtāspa.

Im weiteren Verlaufe wendet sich dann der Dichter, d. h. Zarathushtra, an seine eigene Familie, die Spitamiden, er erwähnt den Frashaoshtra und den Dē Jāmāspa, um eben zum Schluss in den oben angeführten Worten von sich selbst in der ersten Person zu reden und allen denen, die ihm sich anschliessen, das Paradies als Lohn ihrer Treue zu verheissen.

Bleiben wir zunächst bei der Gāthā Ushtavaiti, so begegnet uns in derselben noch ein anderer Hymnus, der uns lebhaft an den eben besprochenen erinnert, nämlich Ys. 43. Auch hier lässt der Dichter an sich selbst die Frage gerichtet werden: Wer bist du denn und wessen Sohn? Und er gibt wieder selbst die antwort: "Zarathushtra bin ich, ein offener Feind aller Bösen; aber den Frommen will ich ein kräftiger Beistand sein, so lange ich es vermag." Und der Dichter schliesst diesmal, indem er von sich in der dritten Person sagt: "Jetzt entscheidet sich für die Welt des Geistes Zarathushtra und (mit ihm entscheiden sich dafür) alle die, welche dem Ahura Mazda anhängen" (Str. 16).

Diese anwendung der dritten Person, wenn der Dichter von sich selbst spricht, darf uns nicht befremden. Sie findet sich gerade so im Rigveda. Hier heisst es: "So hat der Vasishtha, d. h. ich der Sänger aus dem Geschlechte der Vasishtha, den gewaltigen Agni gepriesen" (VII. 42, 6) und dann wieder: "Wir, die Vasishtha's wollen deine Verehrer sein" (VII. 37. 4) und so oft genug, bald in der einen, bald in der anderen Ausdrucksweise. Offenbar war es also in der alten Hymnendichtung durchaus gebräuchlich, dass der Verfasser sich selbst in der dritten Person nannte, und dieser Gebrauch ist auch in unserer modernen Poesie durchaus nicht unbekannt.

Von der Gāthā Ushtavaiti gehen wir über zur Gāthā Ahunavaiti. Hier begegnet uns nun eine auffallende Erscheinung. Der Dichter spricht Ys. 28, 7-9, von sich selbst in der ersten Person, es unterliegt auch keinem Zweifel, dass er zur Zeit der Stiftung der neuen Lehre lebte; allein ich möchte annehmen, dass nicht Zarathushtra der Verfasser ist, sondern einer von seinen Freunden und Zeitgenossen. In den drei erwähnten Strophen betet nämlich der Sänger so der Reihe nach zu Gott: "Gib du *dem Zarathushtra* kraftvolle Hilfe *und uns allen!*" dann: "Gewähre du *dem Vishtāspa* Kraft *und mir;*" und endlich, "Um das beste Gut flehe ich dich an *für den Helden Frashaoshtra und für mich.*" Der Parallelismus in diesen drei Stellen ist so deutlich, dass wir nur annehmen können, der Dichter stellt sich hier neben Zarathushtra, neben Vishtāspa, und neben Frashaoshtra. *Er war also nicht Zarathushtra selbst.*

Wie das Lied Ys. 28, so stammt nach meiner Meinung auch Ys. 29 nicht von Zarathushtra selbst, sondern von einem seiner Anhänger. In diesem Hymnus lässt der Verfasser Geush-urvan, die "Seele des Rindes," zu den himmlischen Geistern um Beistand flehen und um Errettung aus der Not und Bedrängnis, welche ihr durch böse Menschen zu teil wird, die Himmlischen aber stellen ihr die Sendung des Propheten Zarathushtra in Aussicht durch dessen Lehre jenen Übelständen Abhilfe geschafft werden solle. Allein Geush-urvan ist mit dieser Verheissung nicht zufrieden; denn nicht einen ohnmächtigen Menschen hat er sich als Helfer und Retter gewünscht. Meiner Ansicht nach ist nun am Schluss des Liedes eine Strophe abgefallen, in welcher Ahura Mazda verspricht, er wolle in dem Schwachen mächtig sein und den Zarathushtra mit seiner Gnade und Kraft erfüllen, damit er seine schwierige Aufgabe doch auszuführen vermöge. Wie dem aber auch sei, ob das

Lied in der etwas unbefriedigenden Weise abschliesst, wie dies in seiner jetzt vorliegenden Gestalt der Fall ist, oder ob eine Schlussstrophe verloren gegangen: jedenfalls erscheint es viel passender, nicht den Zarathushtra als Verfasser zu denken, sondern einen seiner Freunde, welcher auf den Propheten hinweist als auf den Mann, welcher von Gott auserwählt und in die Welt geschickt ist, um die Werke der Bösen zu vernichten.

Die übrigen Lieder der Gāthā Ahunavaiti geben keine festen Anhaltspunkte für die Autorschaft. Einmal (Ys. 33, 14) wird Zarathushtra in der dritten Person genannt; doch ohne dass sich etwas Bestimmtes daraus folgern liesse. Gewiss ist, dass alle diese Lieder der Zeit Zarathushtra's angehören. Sie setzen alle die Lebensverhältnisse und Zustände voraus, welche, wie wer später sehen werden, für jene Zeit bezeichnend sind. Ob aber der Prophet selbst ihr Verfasser ist, erscheint ungewiss. Mehrfach ist ihr Ton und Charakter ein lehrhafter, die Dogmen der zoroastrischen Religion werden ausführlich dargelegt. Das scheint mehr für die Annahme zu sprechen, dass ein Schüler des Propheten sie verfasste, welcher das, was er unmittelbar aus Zarathushtra's Mund gehört hat, nun in eine feste und bestimmte Form kleidet und dem gesamten Volke überliefert.

Ys. 49·8 in der Gāthā Spentā mainyū nennt sich der Dichter zusammen mit Frashaoshtra, ohne jedoch seinen eigenen Namen anzugeben. Im folgenden wird dann Jāmāspa genannt, und zwar in Verbindung mit einem anderen Anhänger der neuen Lehre, unter dem vielleicht Vishtāspa verstanden werden darf.[1] Es stünde nichts im Wege, Zarathushtra für den Sprechenden zu halten, gewiss ist jedenfalls, dass der Dichter im zarathushtrischen Zeitalter lebte. Das Lied schliesst dann ab mit den Worten: "Was für eine Hilfe hast du für Zarathushtra, der dich anruft?" Was durchaus nicht gegen die Autorschaft des Propheten selber spräche.

Von grosser Wichtigkeit ist nun aber der folgende Hymnus Ys. 50, 5 6; eine Stelle, auf deren Bedeutung Mills[2] zuerst hingewiesen hat. Hier wird von Zarathushtra in der dritten Person gesprochen als von dem, welcher die Lieder und Sprüche, die māthra, an Ahura Mazda und die Himmlischen vorträgt, und bittet dann: "in guter Gesinnung möge er *meine* Verordnungen (regulations) verkündigen." Deutlich steht hier der Verfasser neben Zarathushtra, ganz so,

---

[1] So nach *Mills*, Yasna, S. 166.
[2] Yasna translated, S. 167 ff.

wie wir Ys. 28, dies schon gesehen haben. Vielleicht ist es Vishtâspa der hier spricht, vielleicht Jâmâspa; jedenfalls scheint es weniger ein Priester zu sein, als vielmehr ein Fürst oder Grosser im Lande, der sich des gewichtigen Ansehens Zarathushtras bedient, um im Bunde mit ihm in der politischen und sozialen Ordnung der Dinge irgend welche Neuerungen einzuführen. Wir werden sehen, dass Zarathushtra in der That ein ebenso grosser Reformator auf sozialem wie auf religiösem Gebiete ist, so dass ein solcher Gedanke durchaus nicht ferne läge.

Dass die Gâthâ Vahishtō-ishti nach meiner Meinung einer späteren, vielleicht sogar nachzarathushtrischen Zeit angehört, habe ich schon, kurz angedenkt, den noch übrig bleibenden Hymnus Ys. 51, die Gâthâ Vohū-khshatkrem wäre ich wieder geneigt, dem Zarathushtra selbst zuzuschreiben. Für diese Annahme spricht schon der Umstand, dass dieses Lied unverkennbare Ähnlichkeiten mit dem Hymnus Ys. 46 besitzt, den wir gleichfalls als zarathushtrisch annahmen. Hierauf hat Mills (S. 182) hingewiesen.

Ganz wie Ys. 46, 14 lässt auch Ys. 51, 12 der Dichter die Frage gestellt werden: " Welcher Mann ist des Spitamiden Zarathushtra Freund?" Er antwortet dann zuerst negativ: " Nicht die lasterhaften Irrlehrer und falschen Priester haben je des Zarathushtra Beifall gewonnen " (Str. 12). Diese werden vielmehr dem Verderben preisgegeben, während Zarathushtra den Seinigen als Lohn das Paradies in Aussicht stellt (13-15). Und nun zählt er seine Freunde alle auf: an erster Stelle nennt er Kavi Vishtâspa, dann die Hvôgviden Frashaoshtra und Jâmâspa und endlich den Spitamiden maidhyō-mâogh. Bezeichnend sind dabei die Worte am Schluss von Str. 18, die doch nur in Zarathushtra's Mund passend zu sein scheinen. "Verleihe *mir*, o Mazda, dass *sie* d. h. Vishtâspa und Frashaoshtra und Jâmâspa *an dir* festhalten." Gott wird also gebeten, den Glauben der ersten Anhänger zu stärken und zu befestigen, dass sie treu festhalten an der Lehre Zarathushtra's, die sie einmal als wahr und richtig erkannt haben.

Die Resultate unserer Untersuchung über die in den Gâthâs vorkommenden Personennamen und insbesondere über die Erwähnung des Zarathushtra in denselben sind folgende:—

(1) Die Gâthâs stammen, vielleicht mit einziger Ausnahme von Ys. 52, sämtlich aus der Zeit des Zarathushtra, und unterscheiden sich dadurch wesentlich vom übrigen Awestâ, welchem Zarathushtra eine Persönlichkeit der Vergangenheit ist.

(2) Einige Stücke aus den Gāthā's—besonders wahrscheinlich ist dies von Ys. 46, 49, 51—haben vermutlich den Zarathushtra selbst zum Verfasser.

(3) Andere Lieder rühren nicht von Zarathushtra selber her, sondern von einem seiner Freunde und Anhänger; dies lässt sich mit einiger Sicherheit erweisen bei Ys. 28, 29 und 50.

(4) Unter allen Umständen aber haben wir es mit einer Sammlung von Hymnen zu thun, in denen allen der gleiche Geist weht, die alle der gleichen Zeitperiode angehören, die alle den nämlichen Wünschen und Hoffnungen, Sorgen und Befürchtungen, der nämlichen Glaubensfreudigkeit und dem nämlichen Gottvertrauen Ausdruck geben. Unser Thema "Zarathushtra in den Gāthās" wird nun genauer so gefasst werden müssen: *Die Reform Zarathushtra's nach den gleichzeitigen Schilderungen der Gāthā's.*

II.

DIE RELIGIÖSE UND SOZIALE REFORM ZARATHUSHTRA'S.

Zarathushtra ist, so satzen wir, ebenso sehr ein Reformator auf sozialem wie auf religiösem Gebiet gewesen. Ein Blick auf den Inhalt der Gāthās belehrt uns darüber zur Genüge. Keine Reform vollzieht sich ohne Kämpfe, und eine Zeit erbitterter Kämpfe ist es in der That, was vor unserem Auge sich entrollt, wenn wir die in den Gāthās geschilderten Zustände betrachten.

Wir können uns die Sache ungefähr folgendermassen vorstellen. Das Volk der Arier, d. h. die noch vereinigten Indo-Iränier, waren vom Oxus herkommend nach Süden gewandert und hatten die Flussthäler nördlich und südlich des Hindukusch in Besitz genommen. Allein hier war nicht genug Boden vorhanden für eine so grosse Menge von Stämmen und Geschlechtern. Neue Massen drängten vom Norden nach und so geschah es dass die am weitesten nach Süden vorgerückten Stämme ostwärts weiterzogen und in die Ebenen am Indus einrückten. Damit vollzog sich eine bedeutsame Scheidung. Aus dem Teile des Volkes, welcher in den früheren Wohnsitzen am Hindukusch zurückblieb, gingen die nachmaligen Iränier hervor, aus dem, welcher nach Osten gewandert war, die nachmaligen Inder. Letztere durchlebten, während sie im Kampfe mit Dāsa und Dasyu das heutige Pendschab eroberten, die Kulturepoche des Rigveda. Aber auch für die Iränier brach nun eine wichtige Periode ihrer Geschichte an. Noch immer erwies sich das Land, das sie im Besitze hatten, nicht als ausreichend, um eine grössere Anzahl von Nomadenstämmen

—denn das waren die Iränier der damaligen Zeit—mit ihren Herden zu ernähren. Auch war das Land wohl in manchen Teilen, wo die Gebirge gegen die Steppen hin auslaufen und allmählich in niedrigere und breitere Höhenrücken übergehen, einem nomadischen Leben günstig; in anderen Teilen aber, wo das Terrain rauher, zerrissener, gebirgiger ist, hinderte es die freien ungebundenen Wanderungen. So musste naturgemäss ein Teil des iränischen Volkes sehr bald zu sesshaftem Leben und Ackerbau übergehen. In Nomaden und Ackerbauern zerfällt nun auch wirklich das Volk der Gāthā's, und in dem scharfen Gegensatze, welcher zwischen beiden besteht, spielt Zarathushtra eine hervorragende Rolle. Wir sehen in zahlreichen Stellen, wie er in den Gāthās sich auf die Seite der sesshaften Bevölkerung stellt. Er ermahnt sie, in ihrer Arbeit nicht zu ermüden, fleissig den Acker zu bebauen und dem " Rinde " die Pflege zu teil werden zu lassen, welche es verdient. Und weiter und weiter breitet das Gebiet der Ackerbauern sich aus und " mehren sich die Siedlungen der Frommen," trotz aller Anfechtungen, aller Verfolgungen und Gewaltthaten, welche sie von Seite der Nomaden zu erdulden haben, die ihre Niederlassungen überfallen, ihre Saatfelder verheeren, ihre Herden ihnen rauben.

Es mag genügen, dies hier mit wenigen Worten anzudeuten, da diese soziale Umwälzung, welche das Awestā-Volk in der Gāthā-Epoche durchlebte, schon an anderer Stelle ausführlich geschildert wurde[1] und wir Wiederholungen vermeiden möchten. Was uns hier im besonderen von Interesse ist, das ist *der Geist und die Gesinnung Zarathushtra's* und seiner Freunde und ersten Anhänger, wie sie dieselbe in jenem grossen Kampfe, soweit sich aus den Gāthā's entnehmen lässt, bethätigen.

Der Kampf zwischen den Nomaden und den Ackerbauern, zwischen den Anhängern des Propheten und seinen Feinden war ein erbitterter und ein wechselnder. Es kamen Zeiten der Mutlosigkeit und der äussersten Bedrängnis, so dass der Prophet in die Worte ausbricht: " In welches Land sol ich mich wenden, wohin soll ich gehen ? " Und er beklagt sich, dass selbst Freunde und Verwandte ihn im Stiche lassen und die Beherrscher des Landes ihm ihren Schutz und ihre Unterstützung versagen (Ys. 46, 1). Allein solche Stimmungen

---

[1] *Darab Dastur Peshotan Sanjana*, B. A., Civilization of the Eastern Iränians in Ancient Times, T. II, S. 119 ff.

sind doch verhältnismässig selten in den Gāthās. Zarathushtra und seine Freunde kennen ja einen Helfer aus aller Not, das ist Ahura Mazda, der sie gesandt hat und der sie auf allen Wegen leitet. An ihn wenden sie sich in Zeiten der Bedrängnis und auf ihn blicken sie *mit festem Gottvertrauen.*

Darum fährt der Dichter nach den eben angeführten Eingangsworten seines Hymnus fort: "Ich weiss ja, dass ich arm bin, dass ich wenig Herden und wenig Gesinde besitze; dir klage ich das, sieh auf mich, o Ahura, und schenke mir Hilfe, wie der Freund dem Freunde sie bringt." (Ys. 46, 2.)

Das Bewusstsein, der Ahura Mazda selbst den Zarathushtra gesendet hat, um der Menschheit die neue Lehre zu verkündigen, und ihm als Berater allezeit zur Seite steht, tritt überall in den Gāthās hervor. Der Prophet spricht es (Ys. 45, 5) geradezu aus, dass Gott ihm das Wort mitgeteilt habe, welches das beste ist für die Menschen. Von Anfang an ist er zu dessen Verkündigung auserlesen (Ys. 44, 11). Er erklärt sich bereit das Amt eines Propheten zu übernehmen: Als euren Verehrer will ich mich bekennen und will es auch bleiben, so lange ich es vermag durch den Beistand des Ascha; und er bittet nur, dass Ahura seinem Werke auch das Gelingen schenken möge (Ys. 50, 1). Mit Stolz nennt er sich den "Freund" des Ahura (Ys. 44, 1),[1] der treu an ihm festhält, aber auch seinerseits auf seine Hilfe bauen kann. An andrer Stelle (Ys. 32, 1) wieder bezeichnen sich Zarathushtra und seine Anhänger als die "Boten" des Ahura Mazda, durch deren Mund dieser seine "Geheimnisse," d. h. seine bis dahin unbekannten und ungehörten Lehren, der Welt verkündigt. Wir werden dabei lebhaft erinnert an den gleichen Ausdruck (*malāk*) im alten Testamente, womit in erster Linie die Engel gemeint sind als die "Boten Gottes," die den Verkehr zwischen Jehovah und den Menschen vermitteln, dann auch die Propheten und Priester, die Jehovah's Stellvertreter auf Erden sind und seinen Willen ausüben, endlich aber sogar das ganze Volk Israel, welches von Gott unter die Heiden gesandt ist, sie zu bekehren. Hier wie dort, bei Israeliten wie bei Iräniern, zeigt sich deutlich das Bewusstsein, dass die neue Lehre nicht das Werk von Menschen ist, sondern dass Gott selbst durch seine Propheten redet, dass sie von ihm ausgehen, dass sie seine Diener, seine Herolde, seine Gesandten sind.

---

[1] Vgl. ähnliches im Rigveda 2, 38, 10; 5, 85, 8; 7, 19, 8; u. a. m.

Dieses Gottvertrauen hat seinen letzten und sichersten Rückhalt in der Überzeugung, dass früher oder später jedem Menschen durch die göttliche Gerechtigkeit doch das Loos zu teil wird, das er vermöge seiner Handlungen verdient. Wenn auch im diesseitigen Leben oft genug der Böse eines unverdienten Glückes sich zu erfreuen scheint, so wird ihm doch die Strafe, die ihm gebührt, im Jenseits ereilen. Ein Leben in Finsternis, Qual und Seelenpein wartet ihrer dort. Andrerseits aber kann der Prophet seine getreuen Anhänger in all ihrer Not, in Kämpfen und Verfolgungen trösten und stärken durch den Hinweis auf die Freuden des Paradieses, die ihnen Gott im anderen Leben bereiten wird (Ys. 30, 4 ; 31, 20 ; 32, 15 ; 45, 7 ; 46, 11 ; 49, 11).

In der That war ein solches festes Vertrauen auf die göttliche Gerechtigkeit und auf einen Ausgleich zwischen Verdienst und Schicksal im Jenseits notwendig zu jener Zeit, wo es allerdings der Feinde genug gab und wo oft genug die gute Sache in höchster Gefahr sich befand und nur wenige Anhänger zählt, die treu zu ihr hielten.

Die Feinde des neuen Glaubens, in erster Linie die Nomadenstämme, welche sesshaftes Leben, Bestellung des Ackers und sorgsame Pflege des Rindviehs verschmähen, beten noch zu den alten Naturgöttern, den *daēva*, den *dēva*'s der indischen Stämme. In den Augen der Anhänger Zarathushtra's werden diese *daēva* selbstverständlich zu bösen Wesen, zu Lügengötzen, zu Dämonen. Die Menschen nun, welche diesen Dämonen anhängen und ihnen Opfer und Verehrung darbringen, werden als "Freunde" der *daeva* bezeichnet (*daevā-zushtā*, Ys. 32, 4, von den *daēva* geliebt), wie andrerseits Zarathushtra und die Seinigen sich Ahura's Freunde nennen. Und noch einen Schritt weiter gehen die Verfasser der Gāthā's: sie sehen in den Ungläubigen die Dämonen selbst verkörpert und legen auch den Menschen den Namen *daēva* bei (Ys. 32, 5, und so oft).

Eine andere Bezeichnung für die ungläubigen Feinde ist das Wort *khrafstra* (Ys. 34, 9) ; dasselbe mag etwa "Schlangenbrut, Otterngezücht" bedeuten. An anderer Stelle heissen sie die "schlangenzüngigen" (*khrafstrā-hizvā* Ys. 28, 6) und in einer dritten Strophe (Ys. 34, 5) werden die *khrafstra*-Menschen unmittelbar und gleichbedeutend neben den Daeva selber genannt. Die Ungläubigen haben auch ihre Priester: die *Usij*, die *Kavi's*, und die *Karapan's*.[1] Sie sind natürlich die erbittertsten Gegner der neuen Lehre, durch welche ihre Götter

---

[1] Vgl. Ys. 44, 20. Die Ungläubigen werden im allgemeinen als die, *dregvantō* bezeichnet, die Frommen dagegen an Stellen wie Ys. 34, 13 ; 48, 9 ; und namentlich, Ys. 48, 12, als *snoshyantō*.

entthront werden und sie selbst allen Einfluss auf das Volk verlieren müssen. Oft gelingt es diesen Lügenpriestern, die Fürsten auf ihre Seite zu bringen. Mit den Fürsten haben sich verbündet die Kavi's und die Karapan's, so klagt daher Ys. 46, 11, der fromme Sänger, um durch Übelthaten die Menschen zu verderben. Selbstverständlich war es von der höchsten Wichtigkeit, für welche Sache die Fürsten sich entschieden; denn wo der Fürst zu der neuen Lehre sich bekannte oder derselben feindlich gegenüber trat, da mag wohl das Volk in der Regel ihm gefolgt sein. Daher preist Zarathushtra die Glaubenstreue des Vīshtāspa immer wieder, daher betet der Dichter zu Gott: "Gute Fürsten mögen über uns herrschen, aber keine bösen Fürsten!"

Zu den Fürsten, welche Zarathushtra feindlich gegenüber traten, dürfte der mächtige *Bendra* gehört haben, welchen Ys. 49,1-2, erwähnt wird. Jedenfalls ergibt sich aus dem Zusammenhange der Stelle, dass er auf der Seite der Ungläubigen stand. Eine Familie oder ein Stamm endlich von fürstlichem Geblüte waren vermutlich die *Grēhma* (Ys. 32, 12-14). Von ihnen heisst es, dass sie im Bunde mit Kavi's und Karapan's ihre Macht einsetzen, um den Propheten und seine Anhänger zu überwältigen; aber höhnend wird ihnen entgegen gerufen, dass sie die Herrschaft, nach welcher sie streben, erst in der Hölle erlangen werden. Mit allen ihren Anhängern den Götzendienern und Afterpriestern, werden sie dem ewigen Verderben verfallen; der Prophet aber, der hier so viel geschmäht wird, wird dereinst mit den Seinigen in die Freuden des Paradieses eingehen.

Es ist nun von Interesse, wie die Verfasser der Gāthā's diesen ihren Feinden sich gegenüber stellen, welche Gesinnungen sie ihnen gegenüber an den Tag legen. Zunächst wird es als heilige Pflicht angesehen, durch Wort und Lehre die Ungläubigen zu bekehren (Ys. 28, 5). Die Religion Zarathushtra's ist eine Religion der Kultur, des geistigen und sittlichen Fortschritts. Sie durchdringt alle Lebensverhältnisse, indem sie jede Thätigkeit, so z. B. die Urbarmachung des Bodens, die sorgsame Pflege der Herden, die Bestellung des Ackers, unter den Gesichtspunkt der religiösen Pflicht bringt. Eine solche Religion oder eine solche Philosophie kann sich nicht auf einen engen Kreis beschränken; die Ausbreitung derselben, die Bekehrung aller Menschen zu ihr liegt in ihrem Wesen selber begründet. Wir finden daher auch ganze Lieder, wie Ys. 30 und 45, die offenbar bestimmt waren, vor einer grösseren Versammlung vorgetragen zu werden, und in welcher Zarathushtra oder einer seiner Freunde die wesentlichen Punkte der neuen Lehre den Zuhörern darlegt. Diese Situation ergibt sich deutlich aus der Eingangsstrophe des letztgenannten Hymnus:

> Verkündigen will ich's; nun hört und vernehmet,
> Die ihr von nahe und von ferne herbeigeeilt seid!
> Jetzt hast du alles offenbar gemacht, o Mazda!
> Damit nicht abermals ein Irrlehrer das Leben ertöse
> Durch falschen Glauben, ein Böser, der Schlimmes redet.

Offenbar hat Vishtāspa oder sonst einer der Gaufürsten sein Volk zu einer grossen Versammlung geladen. In dieser Versammlung mögen die Kavi's und Karapan's ihre Gesänge vorgetragen haben, in welchen sie die *daeva*, die Götter des Sturmes und Gewitters, der Sonne und der Gestirne verehrten. Sie brachten wohl auch Opfer dar, ihren Beistand zu gewinnen für irgend eine Unternehmung oder ihren Zorn zu versöhnen. Nun aber tritt Zarathushtra auf. Seiner siegreichen Beredsamkeit müssen die alten Priester der Naturreligion weichen, und dem lauschenden Volke rings umher seine bis dahin "ungehörte" Lehre von Ahura Mazda als dem erhabenen Schöpfer der Welt und von der finsteren Macht des Bösen, dessen stete Bekämpfung Pflicht aller Menschen ist. Nicht in blutigen Opfern oder sinnlosen Bräuchen besteht der wahre Gottesdienst, sondern in der sittlichen Reinheit der Gesinnung, in eifriger Erfüllung der menschlichen Berufspflichten in Frömmigkeit und Arbeitsamkeit.

Wo nun aber der Prophet auf offenen Widerstand stösst, wo alle Reden alle Vorstellungen fruchtlos geblieben, da tritt er nun auf mit der vollen Wucht eines heiligen Zornes. Der Gute *hasst* das Böse; da gibt es keine Versöhnung, keine Duldung, keine Nachsicht. Jede Duldsamkeit wäre eine Sünde, weil sie dem Bösen Raum schafft, statt es zu vernichten.

In den Gāthā's tritt uns derselbe Geist energischen Hasses gegen das Böse entgegen, wie etwa im alten Testament. Auch hier fordert Moses die Leviten auf, zum Schwerte zu greifen und die Abtrünnigen zu töten, die statt am Dienste Jehovah's festzuhalten, sich ein goldenes Bildnis machten und es anbeteten (2 Mos. 32, 25ff.). Jehovah ist ein "eifervoller" Gott, ein zürnender Gott, der die Götzenbilder der Heiden zu zertrümmern und ihre Altäre umzustürzen gebietet. "Gott der Rache, Jehovah, Gott der Rache, erscheine," so ruft der Psalmensänger (Ps. 94); "erhebe dich, du Richter der Erde, zahle Vergeltung den Stolzen! Wie lange sollen die Frevler frohlocken, Jehovah? .... Sie versammeln sich, zu bedrohen das Leben des

Gerechten und verurteilen unschuldiges Blut. Doch Jehovah ist meine Burg, und mein Gott der Felsen, wo ich Zuflucht finde. Er wird ihnen ihr Unrecht heimzahlen und um ihrer Bosheit willen sie vertilgen. Vertilgen wird sie Jehovah, unser Gott! Jehovah rettet alle, die ihn lieben, die Frevler aber vernichtet er" (Ps. 145, 20). Durch Widerspenstigkeit wird Jehovah's Zorn gereizt; nun erzürnt er sich und gibt dem Schwerte preis die, welche von ihm abfallen (Ps. 78, 56 ff.). Wie die Söhne Korah's gegen Moses sich empören, da spaltet Jehovah die Erde und Korah mit allen den Seinigen samt Häusern und Habe werden von ihr verschlungen (4 Mos. 16, 1 ff.).

Diese Stellen aus dem alten Testamente sind ohne Wahl herausgegriffen. Es wäre ein leichtes, sie um das zehnfache zu vermehren. Der Hass, der den Sünder nicht nachsichtig duldet sondern seine sofortige Bestrafung ja sogar seine gänzliche Vernichtung von der göttlichen Gerechtigkeit fordert und erwartet, ist eben ein Grundzug des altisraelitischen Geistes. Wir können ihm unsere Bewunderung nicht versagen: das ist Kraft und Energie, frei von aller schwächlichen Nachsicht, sich steigernd bis zu Gewaltthätigkeit und Fanatismus. Und wenn nun Zarathushtra ausruft: "Ein Peiniger will ich sein für die Bösen, ein Freund aber und ein Helfer für die Frommen" (Ys. 43, 8) — oder wenn er das Volk auffordert: Keiner soll auf des Frevlers Lehren und Gebote achten; denn dadurch bringt er Leiden und Tod in sein Haus und Dorf, in sein Land und Volk! Nein, greift zum Schwert und schlagt sie nieder!" (Ys. 31,18) — oder wenn er denen, die sich ihm nicht anschliessen, Tod und Verderben ankündigt (Ys. 45, 3): so erinnert uns das lebhaft an den Geist des alten Testamentes.

In der That scheint der Gegensatz zwischen Frommen und Unfrommen, Gläubigen und Ungläubigen oft genug zu offenem Kampfe geführt zu haben. Der Prophet bittet zu Ahura, er möge den Seinigen, "wenn die beiden Heere zusammenstossen" den Sieg verleihen, damit sie eine Niederlage anrichten können unter den Bösen und Leid und Not ihnen bereiten (Ys. 44, 14-15). Wer den Lügner, den Irrlehrer, seiner Macht oder seines Lebens beraubt, der darf auf Ahura's Gnade rechnen (Ys. 46, 4). Jedenfalls aber werden die Frevler dem ewigen Gericht nicht entgehen, und wenn nicht schon im Diesseits, so wird doch im Jenseits Ahura sie strafen und sie in die Qualen der Hölle und der Verdammnis stossen (Ys. 31, 20; 45, 7; 46, 6 und 11; 49, 11).

III.
ZARATHUSHTRA'S MONOTHEISMUS.

Wenn die Reform Zarathushtra's eine lebhafte Bewegung der Geister hervorrief, wenn sie selbst zu blutigen Kämpfen und Kriegen Veranlassung gab, so begreift sich das sehr wohl durch ihren Inhalt. Sie bricht nahezu vollständig mit allen vorhandenen Anschauungen und bietet in der That etwas vollkommen Neues. Sie stellt sich in bewussten Gegensatz zu der aus arischer Vorzeit überlieferten und noch vom Volke gepflegten Naturreligion, und was sie etwa von derselben herübernimmt und beibehält, das erhebt sie in eine weit höhere sittliche Sphäre, durchdringt es mit ihrem Geiste und verleiht so der Form einen neuen Inhalt.

Wir sprechen hier von den Gāthā's und deren Inhalt, nicht vom ganzen Awestā; denn mir scheint und die späteren Ausführungen werden dafür Beweise erbringen, dass gerade die Gāthās den Zoroastrianismus in seiner reinsten und ursprünglichsten Gestalt enthalten, so wie der Stifter dieser erhabenen Lehre sie selber erdacht und mitgeteilt hat. Wollen die jetzigen Bekenner des zoroastrischen Glaubens dessen Inhalt und Tendenz kennen lernen, so wie er von ihrem Propheten selber herstammt, so werden sie immer wieder zu den Gāthā's greifen und in deren freilich oft dunklen und schwierigen Sinn einzudringen versuchen müssen. Ich glaube, dass dies auch praktisch von Bedeutung sein wird, um diesen Glauben als ein seltenes Gut wertzuschätzen und rein zu erhalten.

Der Prophet selbst bezeichnet seine Lehre als "ungehörte Worte" (Ys. 31, 1), oder als ein "Geheimnis" (Ys. 48, 3), weil er selber empfindet, wie sehr sich dieselbe von dem bisherigen Glauben des Volkes unterscheidet. Die Religion, die er verkündigt, ist ihm nicht mehr bloss Sache des Gefühles, nicht mehr bloss ein unbestimmtes Ahnen und Empfinden der Gottheit, sondern *Sache des Verstandes, des geistigen Erfassens und Erkennens*. Dies ist von Bedeutung; denn es gibt wohl nicht viele Religionen von so hohem Alter, in denen dieser Grundsatz, dass der Glaube ein Wissen, eine Erkenntnis des Wahren sei, mit solcher Bestimmtheit ausgesprochen wird, wie in der Lehre der Gāthā's. Die Ungläubigen, das sind die Unweisen, die Gläubigen dagegen die Wissenden (Ys. 30, 3), eben weil sie zu jener Erkenntnis durchgedrungen sind. Jeder der eben geistig zu unterscheiden vermag zwischen dem was wahr und dem was unwahr ist, wird sich auf die Seite des Propheten stellen (Ys. 46, 15). Die Nichtlügenden (*adrujyantô*) und die Lügner: das ist genau der gleiche Gegensatz wie zwischen Gläubigen und Ungläubigen, Anhängern und Gegnern des neuen Glaubens (Ys. 31, 15 und öfters). Es wird dabei aber jedem einzelnen zugemutet, dass er Stellung nehme in der grossen Frage und sich entscheide für die eine oder die andere Partei. "Mann für Mann" soll das Volk prüfen, was der Prophet ihm verkündet (Ys. 30. 2), und dessen Wahrheit erkennen. Dies ist deutlich genug ein offe Bruch mit der Volksreligion. Dem Anhänger des Zarathushtra ist die Religion nicht mehr eine "Abhängigkeit" von unbekannten und mehr oder weniger unverstandenen höheren Mächten; sie ist ihm vielmehr eine "Freiheit" des Geistes, eine Befreiung von allem Aberglauben und Irrwahn, ein selbständiges Durchdringen zu der Erkenntnis der göttlichen Wahrheit, die ihm zuvor ein Geheimnis war. Damit aber dass die Religion aus einem Gefühl der Abhängigkeit ein solches der Freiheit wird, ist der bedeutendste Schritt gethan, der auf dem Gebiete religiösen Lebens überhaupt gethan werden kann.

Wir werden wieder an das alte Testament erinnert, wo ebenfalls Glaube und Erkenntnis, Unglaube und Thorheit als identische Begriffe gelten. Ich brauche nur auf die berühmte Stelle Ps. 14, 1, hinzuweisen: "Der *Thor* spricht in seinem Herzen: es ist kein Gott. Verderbt, abscheulich ist ihre Handlung; keiner ist da, der Gutes thut. Jehovah aber blickt vom Himmel herab auf die Menschenkinder, um zu sehen, ob ein *Kluger* da ist, der Gott sucht; aber alle sind abgefallen, alle verdorben; keiner ist da, der Gutes thut, auch nicht einer." (Vgl. Ps. 53, 2.)

Worin aber besteht nun das Neue, das bis dahin Unbekannte der zoroastrischen Lehre, wie sie aus den Gāthā's uns entgegen tritt? Es besteht in dem *vorherrschend monotheistischen Charakter dieser Religion*. Ihr Stifter hat sich losgemacht von der Vielheit, in welche die Gottheit durch den Volks-und Naturglauben zerspalten hat, und sich erhoben zu der Erkenntnis der göttlichen Einheit, welche in der Natur in vielgestaltiger Weise waltet.

Es ist bekannt genug, dass im zoroastrischen Religionssystem *Ahura Mazda* als der Herrscher und Gebieter im Himmel und auf Erden, als der höchste und erste der Genien gilt. Dieser Doppelname, und zwar in der gegebenen Aufeinanderfolge, kommt im späteren Awestā als die ständige feste Bezeichnung vor; Ausnahmen von diesem Gebrauche finden sich nicht, oder sicherlich nur sehr selten. In den Gāthā's liegt die Sache ganz anders, und ich komme damit auf einen höchst bedeutsamen Unterschied zwischen den alten Hymnen und den jüngeren Stücken der zoroastrischen Urkunden. Ein solcher stereotyp gewordener Name für die Gottheit existiert dort noch nicht. Wir finden bald Ahura, bald Mazda, bald Ahura Mazda, bald Mazda Ahura verwendet. Gott kann ebenso wohl als " Herr " (*Ahura*) schlechthin wie als " Allweisheit " (dies bedeutet vermutlich *Mazdāo*) bezeichnet werden. Es scheint eben, dass in den Gāthā's die appellativische Bedeutung beider Namen noch mehr gefühlt wurde, als in späteren Schriften.[1] Bedenken wir nun noch, dass in den altpersischen Keilinschriften der Achämenidendynastie der Gottesname Auramazdā als ein *einziges* Wort, das nur am Ende flektiert wird, vorkommt, so ergibt sich gewiss, dass wir es hier mit den Ergebnissen verschiedener Zeitepochen zu thun haben.[2] Ursprünglich erfand Zarathushtra überhaupt keinen eigentlichen Eigennamen für die Gottheit; er bezeichnet diese bald mit diesem, bald mit jenem Worte, und wir können die verschiedenen Bezeichnungen, die in den Gāthā's gebraucht werden, zumeist einfach mit " Gott " übersetzen. Später wurde dann die Benennung Ahura Mazda, in dieser Verbindung gerade und in dieser Reihenfolge der beiden Wörter, festgehalten, und damit war nun erst ein wirklicher Gottesname geschaffen, dessen Gebrauch etwa dem des alttestamentlichen Jehovah entspricht.

In noch jüngerer Zeit verschmolzen dann die beiden Namen zu einem Ganzen, eben weil sie stets in der nämlichen Reihenfolge gebraucht wurden. Immerhin fühlte man aus dem Namen Auramazdā noch beide Bestandteile heraus, weil sie in einer einzigen Stelle einer Inschrift des Xerxes beide dekliniert erscheinen. Die letzte Entwickelungsphase repraesentieren dann die Formen des Namens in den mittel- und neuiranischen Dialekten: Pahlavi *Auharmazd* und Np. *Ormazd*. Die Verschmelzung beider Wörter ist hier endgiltig vollzogen derart, dass keines mehr eine selbständige Bedeutung besitzt.

Das Wesen des Polytheismus besteht nun darin, dass der Mensch die verschiedenen Kräfte der Natur einzeln zu Gottheiten erhebt und die Wirkungskreise dieser Gottheiten gegen einander abgrenzt. Wir können also die Religion des Rigveda im allgemeinen eine polytheistische nennen. Indra ist der Gott des Gewitters, Agni herrscht über das Feuer, die Maruts sind die Genien des Sturmes. Es finden sich

---

[1] Dies beweisen u. a. auch die Stellen wo *Ahura Mazda* (Ys. 30,9; 31,4) oder *mazda* allein (Ys. 33, 11; 45, 1) im Plural gebraucht wird. Die *mazdāonjhō* sind dann offenbar die Gesamtheit der himmlischen Geister.

[2] Vgl. *Haug* and *West*: Essays on the Parsis, sec. ed., pp. 301-302.

aber auch in den vedischen Hymnen schon Vorstellungen, welche allmählich vom Polytheismus zum Monotheismus hinüber leiten. Wir können beobachten, wie da und dort auf einen Gott die Wirksamkeit eines anderen oder der anderen übertragen wird. Dies ist namentlich bei manchen von den Varuna-Hymnen der Fall. Varuna gilt in ihnen als Schöpfer des Alls, als Geber alles Guten, als der Hüter der Wahrheit und Rächer der Sünde (Rv. I, 25, 20; II., 27, 10; VII., 86, 1 ff.) In anderen Liedern werden die nämlichen Eigenschaften und Kräfte anderen Göttern übertragen: auch Indra, Soma, Agni können gelegentlich für die höchsten Gottheiten gelten. Von dem letzt genannten heisst es Rv. 3 geradezu, er sei der nämliche wie Indra, Vishṇu, Savitri, Pūshan, Rudra und Aditi; er wird also mit der Gesamtheit der Götter identifiziert.

Wir können so auch im Rigveda beobachten, wie die Sänger und Priester nach dem Erfassen der göttlichen Einheit suchen und nur eben dadurch davon abgehalten werden, dass sie nicht den Mut haben, mit den seit alters überlieferten Vorstellungen, Begriffen und Namen zu brechen. In den Gâthâ's liegt die Sache anders. Der bedeutsame Schritt, den die vedischen Sänger zu thun zauderten ist da gethan: die Vielheit der Naturgottheiten ist beseitigt, an ihre Stelle ist *ein* Gott gesetzt, ebenso alles umfassend, ebenso gross und gewaltig, wie der Jehovah des alten Testamentes, und jedenfalls nicht mehr als dieser anthropomorphisiert.

Im 104 Psalm wird Jehovah als der Schöpfer und Regent der Welt gepriesen: "Licht ist sein Kleid, das er trägt, er spannt den Himmel aus wie ein Zelt; er wölbt mit Wasser sein Gemach, die Wolken macht er zu seinem Wagen und fährt auf den Flügeln des Windes. Die Winde macht er zu seinen Boten und zu seinen Dienern die Feuerflammen. Er stützte die Erde auf ihre Fundamente, dass sie nicht wankt immer und ewig .... Den Mond erschuf er, die Zeiten zu ordnen, die Sonne kennt die Stätte ihres Unterganges. Du machtest die Finsternis, dass es Nacht wird: in ihr regen sich die Tiere des Waldes. Die jungen Löwen brüllen nach Raub und verlangen von Gott ihre Speise. Die Sonne geht auf; da entfliehen sie und lagern sich in ihren Höhlen. Es gehet der Mensch an seine Arbeit und an sein Tagewerk bis an den Abend."

Ich will neben diesen Psalm einige Strophen aus der Gâthâ Ys. 44 stellen, wo Ahura Mazda erscheint als der allmächtige Gott, der das All erschuf und es erhält und regiert. Die Aehnlichkeiten der beiden Stellen springen sofort ins Auge, und man wird ohne Zögern zugeben, dass der Verfasser der Gāthā nicht weniger gut Erkentnis des göttlichen Weltschöpfers durchgedrungen ist, wie der Dichter des Psalmes. In Ys. 44, 3-5, und 7 heisst es :—

Darnach frage ich dich, gib mir richtige antwort, o Ahura:
Wer war der Erzeuger und der Urvater der Weltordnung?
Wer zeigte der Sonne und den Sternen ihre Bahn?
Wer schuf es, dass der Mond zunimmt und abnimmt, wenn nicht du?
Dies alles, o Mazda, und noch anderes möchte ich erfahren.

Darnach frage ich dich, gib mir richtige antwort, o Ahura:
Wer hielt fest die Erde und den Luftraum darüber,
Dass er nicht herabfällt? Wer schuf Wasser und Pflanzen?
Wer schirrte Winden und Wolken ihre Schnelligkeit?
Wer schuf, o Mazda, die fromme Gesinnung?

Darnach frage ich dich, gib mir richtige Antwort, o Ahura:
Wer schuf kunstvoll das Licht und die Dunkelheit?
Wer schuf kunstvoll den Schlaf und die Thätigkeit?
Wer schuf die Morgenröten, die Mittage und die Abende,
Welche den Achtsamen an seine Pflichten erinnern?

Darnach frage ich dich, gib mir richtige Antwort, o Ahura:
Wer hat die gesegnete Erde samt dem Himmel geschaffen?
Wer machte durch seine Weisheit den Sohn zum Ebenbilde
    des Vaters?
Ich will dich, o Mazda, dem Verständigen nennen
Als den Schöpfer des Alls, du segens reichster Geist!"

Die Übereinstimmung der Gedanken geht in beiden Hymnen in der That bis ins einzelne. Es ist das Gesetzmässige in der Natur, so der Lauf der Gestirne, der Wechsel des Mondes, die Aufeinanderfolge der Tageszeiten, durch welche die Thätigkeit der Menschen bestimmt wird, was die Aufmerksamkeit beider Sänger anregt. *Hier ist Ahura Mazda, dort Jehovah der Schöpfer der Weltordnung.* Als solcher wird übrigens Mazda mehrfach in den Gāthā's geradezu bezeichnet. Er ist *haithyô ashahyā dāmish* (Ys. 31, 8), eine Benennung, die wir fest halten müssen, da sie in der Folge von Wichtigkeit ist für das Verhältnis des Ahura Mazda zu den Ameshaspenta's.

Wenn Ahura Mazda der Schöpfer der Welt ist, so kommen ihm auch alle die Attribute zu, die das alte Testament Jehovah zuschreibt. Ahura Mazda ist, wie wir früher schon sahen, der *heilige und allgerechte*, der das Böse hasst und, sei es im Diesseits oder im Jenseits ; nach Gebühr bestraft ; den Frommen aber nimmt er in seinen Schutz und verleiht ihm das ewige Leben. Er ist der *unwandelbare*, welcher "auch jetzt noch der gleiche ist" (Ys. 31, 7), wie er von Ewigkeit her gewesen; er ist der *allmächtige*, welcher thut was er will (*vasē-khshnyās*, Ys. 43, 1); er ist der *allwissende*, welcher vom Himmel herabschaut auf die Menschen (vergl. Psalms 14, oben S. 178) und alle ihre Anschläge sieht, die öffentlichen, wie die geheimen (Ys. 31, 13). Ahura Mazda ist *ein Geist*, er ist ein Wesen, das nicht mit menschlichen Zügen ausgestaltet werden kann, er ist "der segensreichste Geist" (*spenishtā mainyū*[1], Ys. 43, 2), der absolut gute. In der That sind anthropomorphistische Vorstellungen in den Gāthā's sehr selten. Wo sie vorkommen, da erklären sie sich einfach aus dem dichterischen Sprachgebrauche. Dem Zarathushtra war Ahura Mazda zweifellos ebenso sehr ein geistiges, übersinnliches, unfassbares und unbeschreibbares Wesen, wie Jehovah den Psalmendichtern.

Allerdings wird Ahura Mazda der Vater des Vohu-manô, des Asha, der Armaiti genannt (Ys. 31, 8; 45, 4; 47, 2) ; allein man vergegenwärtige sich, dass *vohu-manô, asha, ārmaiti* nur abstrakte Begriffe " fromme Gesinnung, Heiligkeit, Demut und Ergebenheit" sind. Daraus ergibt sich unzweifelhaft, dass wir es hier nicht etwa mit menschlichen Vostellungen zu thun haben, wie sie den Mythen der Griechen und Römer geläufig sind, sondern einfach mit dichterischer Ausdrucksweise. Es bedeutet das nichts anderes als wenn wir sagen : Gott ist der Vater alles Guten—ja er ist " Unser Vater."

Auch von den "Händen" des Ahura Mazda ist die Rede (Ys. 43, 4). Es wäre lächerlich, wollte man darin irgend welchen Anthropomorphismus sehen. Solche sprechweise konnte Zarathushtra natürlich ebenso gut anwenden, wie noch jetzt der betende Christ alle seine Sorgen und Wünsche in die Vaterhände Gottes legt. Das ist eben weder heidnische noch muhammedanische, weder zoroastrische noch christliche sondern allgemein menschliche Redeweise.

Irgend welche Züge aber, welche darauf schliessen lassen, dass man sich in der ältesten Zeit des Zoroastrianismus Ahura Mazda in irgend einer bestimmten sinnlichen Gestalt vorstellte, sind aus den

---

[1] In anderen Gāthāstellen scheint übrigens *spenta mainyu* von Ahura Mazda verschieden zu sein ; es ist eben vermutlich eine besondere Seite seines Wesens, vermöge dessen er der Geber des Guten in der Schöpfung ist (Ys. 45,6; 47,1, u. öfters).

Gāthā's sicher nicht zu entnehmen. Wenn wir aber in späterer Zeit, z. B. auf den Denkmälern der Achämenidenkönige eine bildliche Darstellung Ahura Mazda's finden, so dürfen wir daraus, denke ich nicht zu viel schliessen. Erstlich ist zu beachten, dass die Perser der Achämenidenzeit den Zoroastrismus als etwas Fremdes von aussen her bekommen hatten, also manche Vorstellung hinzugefügt oder geändert haben mögen; und dann — hat nicht auch Michel Angelo ein Bild Gott Vaters gezeichnet und damit der kirchlichen Kunst des Abendlandes einen Typus für die Darstellung der Gottheit gegeben?

Wir haben gesehen, dass Zarathushtra zu der Idee eines allmächtigen, allweisen, allgerechten Gottes, eines Schöpfers und Erhalters der Welt gelangt ist und damit seinem Volke an Stelle eines polytheistischen Naturdienstes den Monotheismus geschenkt hat. Wir haben ferner gesehen, dass die Art, wie diese einige Gottheit aufgefasst wird, lebhaft an die Vorstellungen des alten Testamentes von Jehovah erinnern, und zwar sowohl im allgemeinen wie auch in vielen bezeichnenden Einzelzügen. Allein ich halte es nichts desto weniger für durchaus irrig anzunehmen, Zarathushtra habe die Jehovah-Idee direkt oder indirekt von den Israeliten entlehnt. Wir haben nirgends sonst im ganzen Awestā Spuren, welche auf wirkliche Beziehungen zwischen den Irāniern und den Semiten schliessen lassen und dadurch auch eine Entlehnung der religiösen Vorstellungen rechtfertigen würden. Auch hat der Kultus des Ahura Mazda, trotz aller Ähnlichkeiten mit dem Jehovahdienste, doch sein echtes nationales Gepräge; man denke nur an die enge Verbindung des religiösen und des bäuerlichen Lebens, die schon in den Gāthā's hervortritt und einen charakteristischen Zug des ganzen Awestā bildet. Ich halte es überhaupt für höchst bedenklich, aus blossen Ähnlichkeiten der religiösen Vorstellungen auf Entlehnung schliessen zu wollen. Wenn Ahura Mazda und Jehovah eine gewisse Verwandtschaft der Auffassung und des Begriffes zeigen, so liegt das eben einfach darin, weil wir es hier bei den Irāniern wie dort bei den Juden mit einem Monotheismus zu thun haben. Wo aber einmal der Monotheismus zum Durchbruch kommt, da werden auch immer gewisse gleiche Vorstellungen sich geltend machen, welche eben dem Monotheismus eigentümlich sind und gewissermassen dessen Wesen ausmachen. Wenn man also nicht schlechthin leugnet, dass ein Volk oder ein hervorragender Geist irgend eines Volkes selbständig auf die Idee der Einheit Gottes kommen kann, — wenn man nicht dogmatisch den Juden das Monopol des Monotheismus zuerkennt, so wird man mir zustimmen in dem Satze, dass die Iränier selbständig, in sehr alter Zeit, ohne Einfluss von aussen, durch die zoroastrische Reform in den Besitz einer Monotheistischen Religion gelangten.

IV.
DIE THEOLOGIE DER GÂTHÂS.

Wir kommen nun auf einen Einwand, welcher möglicherweise gegen unsere Auffassung der Lehre Zarathushtra's gemacht werden könnte. Ist denn überhaupt, so könnte man fragen, der Zoroastrianismus ein wirklicher Monotheismus? Preist und bekennt nicht das Awestā eine ganze Anzahl von Genien, die Amesha-spenta, Mithra, Sraosha, Verethraghna, Haoma, Ardvi-sūra und andere? Sind nicht mehrere dieser Genien, wie z. B. Mithra, Gestalten, welche aus der vorzoroastrischen Zeit herstammen, welche sich auch in den vedischen Hymnen der Inder vorfinden und somit ohne Zweifel in den arischen Naturdienst gehören?

Wir wollen das Gewicht dieses Einwandes nicht verkennen; wir wollen demselben sogar eine gewisse Berechtigung und Wahrheit zugestehen. *Aber hier ist der Punkt, wo wir wohl zu unterscheiden haben zwischen den Gâthâ's und dem übrigen Awestā, zwischen der Lehre, wie sie unmittelbar von Zarathushtra selbst herrührt, und wie sie später im Laufe der Zeit volkstümlich sich ausgestaltete.* Betrachten wir nämlich die Gāthā's allein, so tritt uns aus denselben weit mehr ein reiner Monotheismus entgegen; im späteren Awestā erscheint er mehrfach getrübt und beschränkt. Auf die Gāthā's wird somit auch jetzt noch der Parse den Blick richten müssen, will er seine Religion nicht bloss in der ältesten sondern auch in der reinsten Gestalt kennen lernen.

Wie scharf und bestimmt tritt im späteren Awestā, namentlich in dem ihm gewidmeten 10 Yasht, die Geniengestalt des *Mithra* hervor. Er ist der Genius der Morgensonne, der das Licht herbeiführt. Als solcher ist er der Feind und Überwinder der Dämonen der Nacht. Er ist aber auch der Gott der Wahrheit, des Rechtes und der Verträge. Seine Machtsphäre erstreckt sich noch weiter: er ist Fürst und König der Erde, der Helfer in den Schlachten, den die Krieger anrufen bei Beginn des Kampfes, und der ihnen zum Siege verhilft. Endlich ist er der Rächer des Bösen, namentlich straft er Lüge und Vertragsbruch.[1]

Ähnlich können wir den *Tishtrya* aus dem jüngeren Awestā schildern. Er ist Gestirnsgottheit, speziell gebietet er über den Stern Sirius. Ihm wird die Macht zugeschrieben, den lechzenden Fluren Regen zu spenden. Er bekämpft den Dämon der Dürre und Trockenheit. Dass er die Herrschaft der Gestirne überhaupt in Händen hat kann nicht befremden. Auch die *Fravashi's*, die Manen, verteilen das befruchtende Wasser über die Erde; sie spenden überhaupt alles Gute, lassen Bäume und Pflanzen gedeihen und sind, wie Mithra Helfer in Kampf und Krieg. Kurz, wir haben es hier mit Genien zu thun, die lebhaft an die Gottheiten des Rigveda erinnern, an Varuna, Indra, Mitra und andere.

Wenden wir uns nun aber zu den Gāthā's zurück, so erscheint uns da die Sache in einem ganz anderen Lichte. Hier werden nicht einmal die Namen eines Mithra oder Tischtrya genannt. Auch die Fravashi's kommen nicht vor, ebenso wenig wird Haoma erwähnt oder Verethraghna, der Genius siegreichen Kampfes, oder Anāhita, die Genie der Gewässer. Es fehlen in den Gāthās gerade die Namen derjenigen Genien, welche im späteren Awestā am meisten zu plastischen Gestalten ausgebildet, am meisten mit individuellen Attributen ausgestaltet erscheinen.

Sollen wir das als blossen Zufall erklären? Ich hielte dies in der That für einen Fehler, so sehr ich mir auf der anderen Seite bewusst bin, wie bedenklich jedes, "documentum e silentio" ist. Es gibt eben doch zuweilen Umstände, unter denen man mit der Annahme eines Zufalls nichts erreicht und vieles unverstanden und unerklärt lässt. Wenn sich in den Gāthās niemals eine passende Gelegenheit fände, den Mithra oder den Tischtrya oder die Fravashi's überhaupt zu erwähnen, so würde es sich ja als Zufall erklären lassen, wenn ihre Namen nicht vorkommen. Solche Gelegenheiten aber gibt es oft genug. Warum wird z. B. Mithra nie genannt, wo von Kämpfen gegen die Ungläubigen die Rede ist? Es heisst ja doch von ihm Yt. 10, 36:

" Mithra eröffnet den Kampf,
Er nimmt Stellung in der Schlacht;
Im Streite stehend
Zerschmettert er die Schlachtreihe."

Oder auch die Fravaschi's würden passend angerufen werden; denn.

---

[1] Vgl. hierüber und zum ff. *Spiegel*, Eranische Alterthumskunde, II. S. 77 ff., 70 ff., 91 ff.

"Sie bringen in gewaltigen Schlachten am meisten Beistand" (Yt. 13, 37).

Oft genug ist ferner in den Gāthās von Feldern und Herden die Rede. Aber nie wird bei einer solchen Gelegenheit Tischtrya gerufen, obwohl dieser die Fluren segnet und die Herden gedeihen lässt.

Ähnlich steht es auch bei den anderen Genien, welche wir in den Gāthā's nicht erwähnt finden. Man kann nicht sagen, dass sich überhaupt kein Anlass findet, ihre Namen zu nennen; sondern *ihre Nichterwähnung ist offenbar beabsichtigt.*

Der ganze Charakter der Gāthā's ist in solchem Maasse ein philosophischer, auf das Abstrakte und Übersinnliche gerichteter, dass in ihre Theologie solche Gestalten, wie die erwähnten überhaupt nicht passen. Ich sage nicht, dass Zarathushtra und die übrigen Hymnendichter von Mithra oder Tischtrya oder Anāhita gar nichts wussten. Dieselben waren ohne Zweifel beim Volke viel verehrt; aber der Prophet billigte solche Kulte nicht; er wollte an die Stelle dieser Genien welche ihrem ganze Wesen nach allzu sehr an die Gottheiten des altarischen Naturdienstes erinnerten, höhere, philsophischere Begriffe setzen. Sämtliche Genien, die in den Gāthā's neben Ahura Mazda genannt werden, sind in der That solche abstrakte Begriffe; wie sich dieselben aber zu der von mir angenommenen monotheistischen Lehre der Gāthās verhalten, davon weiter unten.

Mithra, Tischtrya und die übrigen in den Gāthā's nicht genannten Genien werden im jüngeren Awestā ziemlich stark anthropomorphisiert. Sie werden gedacht und geschildert ganz ähnlich wie die Gottheiten des Rigveda. Man stellt sie sich vor in Menschengestalt, als Mann oder Weib (wie Anāhita), mit Rüstung und Gewand angethan, Waffen tragend, zu Wagen fahrend, in Palästen wohnend. Zuweilen erscheinen in sie sogar in Tiergestalt. Anthropomorphische Vorstellungen sind den Gāthā's, wie wir sahen, überhaupt Fremd.

Diejenigen Genien dagegen, welche in den Gāthā's neben Ahura Mazda sich erwähnt finden, in erster Linie die Amesha-spenta, sind auch im jüngeren Awestā am allerwenigsten, ja eigentlich gar nicht anthropomorphisiert. Eine Ausnahme bildet nur etwa Sraoscha, der in den Gāthā's noch eine ganz abstrakte Gestalt ist, später aber zu einem Genius ausgebildet wird, dessen Attribute manche Ähnlichkeiten mit denen des Mithra aufweisen.

Somit können wir einen durchgreifenden Unterschied zwischen der Theologie der Gāthās und jener des jüngeren Awestā konstatieren. In jener haben neben Gott nur solche Genien ihren Platz, welche zunächst weiter nichts sind als abstrakte Begriffe, in dieser dagegen auch solche, welche plastischer ausgebildet erscheinen und sich den Gottheiten der stammverwandten Inder vergleichen lassen. Würde von den Geniennamen, welche der letzteren Kategorie angehören, nur der eine oder der andere in den Gāthā's nicht vorkommen, so würde man das vielleicht wieder einen Zufall zu nennen geneigt sein; wo aber die Scheidung eine so konsequente, nahezu ausnahmslose ist, da wird man wohl System und Absicht in ihr erkennen müssen.

Wie aber kamen nun jene mehr anthropomorphen Genien, wie Mithra u.s.w., in späterer Zeit in das zoroastrische System hinein? Ich glaube, dass dies nicht allzu schwer zu erklären ist. Die zoroastrische Reform ist eine energische Opposition gegen den arischen Naturkultus. In den Gāthā's kommt auch nicht ein einziger von den Genien vor, welcher diesem Kultus angehört. Jede Opposition geht naturgemäss in das Extrem und sucht ihren Erfolg in der absoluten Verneinung des Bestehenden. Wird ja doch in einer Gāthāstelle der Kultus des Haoma, wenigstens in der Gestalt, wie er zu der damaligen Zeit geübt wurde als etwas Verwerfliches und Abscheuliches hingestellt (Ys. 48, 10)! Auf eine solche Aktion muss aber dann mit der Zeit die Reaktion folgen. Die Resultate aber, zu denen diese Reaktion führte, liegen in dem theologischen System des jüngeren Awestā vor. Hier ist ein Kompromiss getroffen mit dem Volksglauben. Die Götter, welche in diesem verehrt wurden, werden, freilich in veränderter und vergeistigter Gestalt, wieder hereingenommen in das neue System, um gewissermassen das Gefolge und den Hofstaat Ahura Mazda's zu bilden. Aber, wie gesagt, die Vorstellungen erleiden manche Umgestaltungen; sie werden den neuen Verhältnissen angepasst und dies geschickt namentlich dadurch dass die sittliche Seite an dem Wesen der einzelnen Geniengestalt mehr in den Vordergrund gestellt wird gegenüber dem physikalischen. Es entspricht dies dem Wesen des zoroastrischen Systems überhaupt, das sich in erster Linie auf ethischer Grundlage aufbaut.

Der heutige Parsismus wird, entsprechend dem ganzen Zuge unserer Zeit, wieder mehr an die Form seiner Lehre anknüpfen, wie sie in der Gāthā's vorliegt. Er wird das philosophische Element seines Glaubens in den Vordergrund stellen, in ähnlicher Weise, wie der Christ die sittliche Kraft seiner Religion mehr betonen wird al deren dogmatische Lehren. Gerade durch die Hervorhebung des den verschiedenen Religionen Gemeinsamen ist aber die verbindende Brücke zwischen ihnen gefunden.

Zu der Entwickelung der zoroastrischen Lehre, wie ich sie eben geschildert habe, finden sich auch bei uns im Abendlande Analogien. Auch in Deutschland gingen die ersten Verkündiger des Christentums darauf aus, den heidnischen Glauben von Grund aus zu vernichten. Nichts desto weniger gibt heutzutage jeder einsichtige und unbefangene Forscher zu, dass gar manches heidnische Element noch jetzt in unseren Volksvorstellungen und Volksgebräuchen versteckt ist. Es ist bekannt, dass in den Heiligen, wie sie in manchen Gegenden Deutschlands namentlich vom Landvolke verehrt werden, altheidnische Götter wieder aufgelebt oder vielmehr in veränderter Gestalt und mit veränderten Namen erhalten geblieben sind. So ist Thor, der Gewittergott, der ständige Begleiter des Wotan, zum heiligen Petrus geworden, und es darf uns nicht mehr Wunder nehmen, wenn Petrus nach dem Volksglauben auch andere Funktionen übernommen hat, die sonst seinem Vorgänger aus der Heidenzeit zukamen, wie z. B. die Verursachung von Regenwetter. Man hat eben die alte Vorstellung von dem Regen bringenden Gotte beibehalten, sie aber mit der Person des Petrus verbunden, da Thor's Name in der neuen Kirche keinen Raum mehr hatte.[1] Es ist also zwischen Christentum und Hiedentum ein Kompromiss geschlossen worden, indem jenes von diesem manche im Volke tief eingewurzelte Vorstellungen aufnahm, sie aber mit dem eigenen Geiste erfüllte.

Die Genien nun, welche die Gāthās neben Ahura Mazda erwähnen, sind, wie schon erwähnt, zunächst die sechs Amesha-spenta's: Asha, Vohu-mano, Khshathra, Armaiti, Haurvatāt und Ameretat, und dazu nenne ich noch Sraosha und Ashi. Es liegt mir ferne hier die Vorstellungen, welche sich an diese Genien knüpfen, im einzelnen aus einander zu setzen. Das wäre müssige Wiederholung.[2] Zur Orientierung sei nur kurz gesagt, dass *Ascha* Genius der kosmischen und der sittlichen Ordnung sowie Heiter des Feuers ist; sein Name bedeutet "Heiligkeit." *Vohu-manô* ist die "gute und fromme Gesinnung"; er beschützt die Herden, mit deren Zucht sich eben auch die Pflege frommen Sinnes verbindet. *Khshathra* ist das "Reich," das Reich der frommen und Gläubigen hier auf Erden, das Himmelreich im Jenseits. *Armaiti* ist

---

[1] Das war im Parsismus anders. Hier kam mit der Vorstellung auch der alte Name wieder zur Geltung. Wir müssen uns eben erinnern, dass derselbe doch immerhin aus der iranischen Naturreligion hervorgegangen ist, während der germanische Volksglaube dem Christentume etwas Fremdes war.

[2] Vgl. Civilization of the Eastern Iranians in Ancient Times, Vol. I., pp. XXXII. ff.

die "Demut" und "Andacht," die Behüterin der Erde. *Haurvatât* und *Ameretât* bedeuten "Wohlfahrt" und "Unsterblichkeit"; sie herrschen über Wasser und Pflanzen. *Sraosha* ist der "Gehorsam," und zwar gegen Gottes Willen und gegen die Vorschriften der heiligen Religion, und ähnliche Bedeutung scheint im jüngeren Awestâ auch *Ashi* zu haben.

Uns interessiert hier nur die Frage, wie sich diese Genien zu Ahura Mazda verhalten, ob durch sie nicht der von uns angenommene Monotheismus in der Theologie der Gâthâs beeinträchtigt und beschränkt, vielleicht sogar aufgehoben wird. Betrachten wir die Sache äusserlich, so muss man zugeben, dass die Amesha-spenta kaum eine geringere Rolle zu spielen scheinen als Mazda. Das Wort *Asha* z. B. kommt in den Gâthâs rund 180 mal vor, der Name *Mazda* 190-200 mal; *Vohu-manô* (auch *vahishtem-manô*) vielleicht 130 mal; die übrigen Namen allerdings nicht so häufig. Das sind keine Zahlen, die äusserlich auf eine verschiedene Geltung der verschiedenen Begriffe schliessen lassen, und doch besteht ein so durchgreifender Unterschied, dass es geradezu zur Unmöglichkeit wird, etwa Mazda und Asha auf eine Stufe zu stellen, ja überhaupt nur mit einander zu vergleichen.

Mazda ist wirklich zum Eigennamen geworden, zur Bezeichnung des höchsten einigen Gottes, nicht weniger als Jehovah im alten Testamente oder Allah bei den Muhammedanern. Asha dagegen —und ebenso die übrigen oben genannten Genien—*kann* nur gelegentlich zu einer Art Personifikation gelangen; die ursprüngliche abstrakte Bedeutung wird immer noch deutlich empfunden, an zahlreichen Stellen ist sie die allein richtige, an anderen kann man schwanken, welche Bedeutung die passende sein könnte, ja oft genug mag von den Verfassern der Hymnen der Doppelsinn sogar beabsichtigt sein.[1] Streng genommen sind also Asha und Vohu-manô, Khshathra, und Armaiti zunächst keine eigentlichen Genien, die neben Mazda stehen sondern sie repräsentieren gewisse Kräfte und Eigenschaften der Gottheit die *in* Mazda und in dessen Wesen eingeschlossen und

---

[1] Ähnliche Personifikationen abstrakter Begriffe, wie sie in den Gâthâ's ständig sind finden sich *gelegentlich* auch in den Psalmen. Man vergl. namentlich, Ps. 85, 11-14: "Nahe ist Jehovah's Hilfe seinen Verehrern, so dass Herrlichkeit wohnen wird im Lande. Güte und Treue begegnen sich Gerechtigkeit und Friede küssen sich. Treue sprosst aus der Erde, Gerechtigkeit blickt vom Himmel herab. Auch wird Jehovah Glück verleihen, und unser Land wird seinen Ertrag geben. Gerechtigkeit wandelt vor seinem Angesicht und schreitet vorwärts auf ihrem Pfade."

einbegriffen sind. Dies ist jedenfalls die ursprüngliche Idee ; doch soll damit nicht gesagt werden, dass jene Genien nie und nirgends zu einer gewissen Selbständigkeit gelangten. Es ist das namentlich an solchen Stellen der fall, wo die Amesha-spenta zusammen mit Mazda genannt werden und vollkommen parallel zu ihm stehen. Ich möchte sie dann etwa mit den Engeln des alten Testamentes vergleichen. Auch diese sind ursprünglich nur Erscheinungsformen Jehovahs selber, um später gewissermassen dessen Gefolge und Begleitung, seinen Hofstaat, zu bilden.

So erscheint z. B. Mazda's name mitten unter denen der ersten Amesha-spenta's Ys. 28, 3 :—

> Euch, o Ascha, will ich preisen und den Vohu-manô, den unvergleichlichen,
>
> Und den Mazda Ahura, mit welchen der ewige Khshathra vereinigt ist
>
> Und die Segen spendende Armaiti: kommt herbei auf mein Rufen, mich zu unterstützen!

Und ganz ähnlich Ys. 33, 11 (vgl. auch 12 u. 13):

> Der du der segensreichste bist, Ahura Mazda, und Armaiti
> Und Ascha, der die Niederlassungen mehrt, und Vohu-manô und Khshathra,
> Höret mich, erbarmet euch meiner, achtet immerdar auf mich!

Dass indessen nichts desto weniger Ascha und die anderen Genien nur ein Ausfluss des Wesens des Mazda sind, das wird dichterisch dadurch ausgedrückt, dass dieser als ihr Vater und Erzeuger, als ihr Schöpfer bezeichnet wird (s. oben S. 50 und 51). Wo aber Gott als Schöpfer der neben und ausser ihm existierenden Geister gilt, da kann doch von keinem Polytheismus mehr die Rede sein. Die Frage, ob es ausser Gott noch irgendwelche geistige Wesen gibt, welche gewissermassen zwischen ihm und den menschen stehen, hat mit der Definition des Begriffes des Monotheismus nichts zu schaffen. Nun ist aber in Bezug auf die Theologie der Gāthās noch vollends festzuhalten, dass die Namen der Amesha-spenta's zunächst abstrakte Begriffe sind. Wenn also Mazda der Vater des Asha genannt wird, so bedeutet das nur, dass er die sittliche und die kosmische Ordnung erschaffen hat.[1] Oder wenn er Vater des Vohu-manô und der Armaiti

---

[1] Daher ist er auch *asha hazaosha* " eines Willens mit Asha ;" was er thut stimmt überein mit der von ihm gesetzten Welt.

heisst, so besagt das, dass alle gute Gesinnung und alle demutsvolle Andacht, d. h. alles Gott wohlgefällige Leben auf ihm beruht und von ihm ausgeht.

Durch den Glauben an die Amesha-spenta's wird der Monotheismus der Gāthā-Theologie somit keineswegs beeinträchtigt. Ahura Mazda ist trotzdem der allein allmächtige (Ys. 29, 3), er ist derjenige welcher über alles die Entscheidung hat; wie er will, so geschieht (Ys. 29, 4). Er ist eines Wesens mit ihnen allen, oder wie der Dichter sich ausdrückt, er wohnt zusammen mit Ascha und Vohu-manô (Ys. 32, 2; 44, 9), d. h. er hat diese Kräfte zur Verfügung, sie stehen ihm zu Gebote, sie gehen von ihm aus und kehren zu ihm zurück. Ahura Mazda war zuerst und zu ihm gesellen sich Armaiti und Khschathra und Vohu-manô und Ascha (Ys. 30, 7), als naturgemässe Entfallungen seines Wesens. Diese Kräfte gehen von ihm aus, er teilt sie dem Menschen mit (Ys. 31, 21); er steht weit über ihnen:—

Darnach frage ich dich, gib mir richtige Antwort, o Ahura!
Wer hat die gesegnete Armaiti samt dem Khschathra geschaffen?
Wer machte durch seine Weisheit den Sohn zum Ebenbilde des Vaters?
Ich will dich, o Mazda! dem Verständigen nennen
Als den Schöpfer des Alls, du segensreichster Geist! (Ys. 44, 7).

Zum Schluss habe ich noch einige Worte über *Ashi* und *Sraosha* beizufügen. Bei ihnen zeigt sich deutlich, wie sehr sich die Theologie der Gāthā's von der des jüngeren Awestā unterscheidet. Dort kann *Ashi* überhaupt noch kaum als Name einer Genie gelten wie hier; das Wort hat vielmehr noch seine ursprünglich abstrakte Bedeutung: Lohn, Vergeltung; dann Segen, Erfolg (Ys. 28, 4; 43, 1; 43, 5, u. s. w). Eine Stelle, wo man es mit einiger Wahrscheinlichkeit als *nomen proprium* auffassen könnte, weiss ich nicht anzugeben. Der Prozess der Erhebung eines Abstraktums zu einem Geniennamen vollzieht sich bei *ashi* offenbar in der Zeit, welche zwischen der Periode der Gāthā's und der des späteren Awestā liegt.

Ähnlich steht es mit *Sraosha*. Im jüngeren Awestā ist daraus ein Genius von ziemlich fester und greifbarer Gestalt geworden mit ausgeprägten individuellen Zügen; in noch späterer Zeit wird er zum Boten Gottes, der dessen Befehle den Menschen zu überbringen hat. Hievon findet sich in den Gāthā's keine Spur. Wir beobachten hier nur die ersten Anfänge zu der Personifikation des Wortes in Stellen wie Ys. 33, 5, wo der Dichter den " machtvollen Sraoscha " anruft, und Ys. 44, 16. Hier erbittet sich der Verfasser einen Gebieter zum Schutz gegen die Feinde und wünscht, dass zu diesem sich gesellen möge "Sraoscha in Verbindung mit Vohu-manō," d. h. Gehorsam gegen die heilige Religion und fromme Gesinnung. In dieser Stelle liegt, wie ich glaube, ein beabsichtigter Doppelsinn ; wo aber *sraosha* sonst vorkommt, da hat es die ursprüngliche abstrakte Bedeutung " Gehorsam, Ergebenheit"—Gegensatz ist *asrushti* " der Ungehorsam" Ys. 33, 4 ; 44, 13—oder die konkrete Bedeutung "die Gehorsamen, die Ergebenen, die Frommen."

Wir können die Ergebnisse dieses Abschnittes in eine Reihe von Sätzen zusammenfassen :—

1. Die Theologie der Gāthā's ist eine abstraktere, philosophischere als die des späteren Awestā. Sie repräsentiert die älteste und ursprünglichste Form der mazdayasnischen Glaubenslehre.

2. Die Verehrung der mehr volkstümlichen Gottheiten, wie Mithra oder Tischtrya, ist den Verfassern der Gāthā's fremd. Die Kulte dieser Genien werden erst in einer späteren Epoche adoptiert durch eine Art von Kompromiss mit dem Volksglauben.

3. Die Theologie der Gāthā's ist eine Monotheistische: Mazda Ahura ist die Gottheit schlechthin.

4. Dieser Monotheismus wird durch die sonst in den Gāthās genannten Genien keineswegs beeinträchtigt, da diese Genien lediglich Hypostasen abstrakter Begriffe sind, in ihrer ursprünglichen Bedeutung noch überall gefühlt werden, überdies dem Wesen nach unter Mazda stehen, als dessen Schöpfungen sie gelten.

V.
IST DIE ZOROASTRISCHE RELIGION EINE DUALISTISCHE?

Man hat die zoroastrische Religion vielfach eine dualistische genannt. Diese Bezeichnung ist indessen nur dann berechtigt, wenn man unter Dualismus ein System versteht, in welchem neben der das Gute schaffenden und wollenden Gottheit Existenz einer ihr entgegenwirkenden Kraft angenommen wird. In diesem Sinne wäre die alttestamentliche Religion auch eine dualistische. Strenge genommen dürfen wir aber doch nur dann von Dualismus reden, wenn beide Prinzipien gleichberechtigt und gleichmächtig neben einander stehen, beide in gleichem Masse auf die Welt einwirken und der Mensch von beiden in gleicher Weise sich abhängig und beeinflusst fühlt. Wo aber der Mensch Kraft seiner sittlichen Wahlfreiheit sich für das Gute entscheiden und vom Bösen sich abwenden kann, wie dies in den

Gāthā's oft genug hervorgehoben wird, da ist die Bezeichnung Dualismus meines Erachtens nicht mehr gerechtfertigt. Die Existenz eines solchen würde, wie ich meine, unter anderem es erheischen, dass der Mensch dem bösen Geiste die nämliche Verehrung zu erweisen angehalten wird wie dem guten, dass er jenem Opfer und Gebete darbringt, um ihn zu versöhnen und alles Unheil abzuwenden, diesem dagegen, um seiner Segnungen teilhaftig zu werden. Dass aber von solchen Vorstellungen sich im Awestā keine Spur findet, das brauche ich doch gar nicht zu betonen.

Das Awestā, und zwar schon in seinen ältesten Teilen kennt allerdings einen bösen Geist, der in allen Stücken der Gegensatz zu dem guten Geiste ist. Die Annahme seiner Existenz sollte die Lösung der Frage sein, die naturgemäss jeder Denkende sich vorlegen wird, wie denn überhaupt das Böse in die Welt kommt, wenn doch die Gottheit ihrem Wesen nach gut ist und demnach auch nur Gutes aus sich hervorbringen kann. Woher stammen Schuld und Sünde, woher alles das Elend und die Unvollkommenheiten, die dem Menschen wie überhaupt der ganzen Schöpfung doch anhaften? Zarathushtra und die übrigen Verfasser der Gāthā's versuchten es, diese Frage auf philosophischem Wege zu lösen und ich will versuchen, im folgenden ihr System kurz darzulegen, wie es aus den Gāthā's sich zu ergeben scheint. Ich sage: scheint; denn die Gāthā's haben ja nicht den Zweck, ein philosophisches System zu entwickeln. Ihre Verfasser reden nicht zu einzelnen aus dem Volke, sondern zu dessen Gesamtheit; für sie kommt nicht der philosophische Gehalt ihrer Lehre, sondern deren praktische Seite, die Ethik, in erster Linie in Betracht. Wir müssen also aus kurzen Andeutungen und einzelnen Stellen der Hymnen die Vorstellungen uns zu konstruieren versuchen, welche den Verfassern über die in Rede stehenden Frage vorgeschwebt haben mögen. Naturgemäss sind das speziell solche Stellen, wo der Prophet durch den Zusammenhang sich veranlasst sah, von dem Wesen des Bösen zu sprechen. Darauf, dass wir über alte Einzelheiten des philosophischen Systems, das Zarathushtra sich gebildet haben mag, ins Klare kommen könnten, müssen wir von vornherein verzichten. Aber auch in Bezug auf die Hauptmomente, wie ich sie zu schildern versuchen werde, kann man vielfach verschiedener Meinung sein; man kann wohl leicht Stellen finden, welche von mir nicht genügend berücksichtigt zu sein, oder welche zu meinen Ansichten nicht völlig zu passen scheinen.

Im späteren Awestā ist der Gegensatz zwischen der guten und der bösen Geisterwelt auch formell aufs genaueste durchgeführt. Wie Ahura Mazda an der Spitze der ersteren, so steht Agra Mainyu an der Spitze der letzteren. Den sechs Amesha-spenta's sind je sechs Erzdaemonen gegenüber gestellt: Akem-manō dem Vohu-manō, Indra oder Andra dem Ascha, Sauru dem Khschathra, der Dämon des Übermutes Nāoghaithya der Spenta Armaiti, Tauru und Zairica dem Haurvatāt und Ameretāt. Weiterhin folgt dann das Heer der guten und lichten Genien gegenüber der Schar der Daeva und der Druj.

In den Gāthā's ist das System, wie mir scheint, nicht so konsequent durchgebildet. *Agra-mainyu* als Name des bösen Geistes kommt nur einmal vor, und zwar an einer Stelle (Ys. 45, 2), wo ihm nicht etwa Ahura Mazda, sondern *spanyāo mainyush* gegenüber gestellt wird. Auch *akō mainyush* kommt nur an einer Stelle (Ys. 32, 5) vor; zweimal findet sich *akem-manō* (Ys. 47, 5 und 32, 3), welches sonst die ursprüngliche abstrakte Bedeutung "böse Gesinnung" hat, und zweimal *acishtem manō* (Ys. 30, 6 ; 32, 13,) als Bezeichnung des bösen Prinzips verwendet.

Auf den ersten Blick möchte es nun scheinen, dass *agra mainyush* und *akō mainyush* formell das Gegenstück zu *spenta mainyush* bilden; *akem manō* und *acishtem manō* dagegen zu *vohu manō* und *vahishtem manō*. Dies ist nun aber in den Gāthās nicht der Fall. Alle diese Namen bezeichnen unterschiedslos den bösen Geist schlechthin, d. h. den, der im jüngeren Awestā nur Agra Mainyu genannt wird. So werden z. B. Ys. 32, 3, die Daevas als Brut (*cithra*) des Akem-manō bezeichnet, der in solchem Zusammenhange doch offenbar der höchste und das Haupt der bösen Geisterwelt sein muss. Das gleiche gilt wohl auch von Acishtem-manō, wenn es Ys. 30, 6 heisst, dass um ihn die Daemonen sich scharen, während die guten Geister zu Spentamainyu (Ys. 30, 7, und vgl. 5) sich gesellen. Ja es scheint so gar, dass in der nämlichen Stelle auch Aeshma, das sonst Name eines besonderen Daemons ist, nur zur Bezeichnung des Agra mainyu dient.

Es ist nun für die Erklärung des Verhältnisses des bösen Geistes zu dem guten von Wichtigkeit, dass es zu dem Namen Ahura Mazda formell überhaupt kein Gegenstück gibt. Die zur Benennung des bösen Geistes dienenden Namen stehen vielmehr den Namen Spentamainyu oder Vohu-manō gegenüber. Wo aber (Ys. 45, 2 ; 30, 4-7) beide Geister zusammen genannt werden, heisst der gute Geist nicht etwa Mazda, sondern *spenta (spanyāo, spenishta) mainyu*. Die Rolle des Spenta-mainyu selbst erscheint in den Gāthās nicht völlig klar. Derselbe wird bald mit Ahura Mazda identifiziert (z. B. Ys. 43, 2), bald ist er von ihm verschieden (Ys. 45, 6; 47, 1, u. a.); er muss somit ein göttliches Wesen sein, welches bald in der höchsten Gottheit aufgeht, bald von ihr losgelöst, eine gesonderte Existenz führt.

Halten wir dies alles zusammen, so lässt sich die Philosophie Zarathushtra's etwa folgendermassen charakterisieren. Das höchste Wesen est, die Gottheit schlechthin ist Ahura Mazda. Er ist natürlich gut und von ihm geht nur Gutes aus. Das Böse ist die Negation des Guten; es besteht nur im Verhältnisse zu diesem, wie Finsternis nur die Negation des Lichtes ist. Soferne nun Ahura Mazda das Positive ist, zu welchem das Böse die Negation bildet, heisst er Spentamainyu, das Böse oder dessen Personifikation ist Agra-mainyu oder Akō-mainyu. Beide Spenta-mainyu und Akō-mainyu werden daher als Zwillinge bezeichnet (Ys. 30, 3), weil sie allein für sich nicht existieren sondern jeder im Verhältnis zum anderen; beide gehen auf in der höheren Einheit Ahura Mazda. Sie existieren vor Anfang der Welt, ihre Opposition kommt aber gerade in der sichtbaren Welt zum Ausdruck. Ahura Mazda ist Schöpfer des Alls; wie er aber als Spenta-mainyu irgend ein Ding erschafft, so ist damit von selbst das negative Gegenstück gegeben, oder, wie der Dichter sich in populärer Form ausdrückt: Agra-mainyu, der böse Geist erschafft das Übel im Gegensatz zum Guten (Ys. 30, 4 ff.). Das erste, was die Zwillingsgeister erschaffen, ist Leben oder Tod, oder, wie man vielleicht philosophisch sich ausdrücken darf: Sein und Nichtsein, worin eben die Doppelseite ihres Wesens gekennzeichnet ist. Erschafft also Spenta-mainyu das Licht, so ist die Finsternis oder das Nichtsein, die Abwesenheit des Lichtes die Gegenschöpfung des Agra-mainyu; gibt jener die Wärme, so rührt von diesem die negation der Wärme, d. h. die Kälte. Alles Übel ist dem Zoroastrier somit nicht eigentlich etwas Reales, an und für sich Bestehendes, sondern eben nur das Fehlen des Guten. Es versteht sich damit aber auch von selber, dass Gut und Böse durchaus nicht gleichwertige parallele Begriffe sind, sondern letzteres lediglich relative Existenz besitzt. Geben wir dies aber zu, so wird man auch zugestehen müssen, dass der Zoroastrianismus ein Dualismus im eigentlichen Sinne des Wortes nicht genannt werden darf.

Sobald wir nun fragen, wie der Mensch sich zu diesen beiden Gegensätzen verhält, so berühren wir damit das Gebiet der *Ethik*; fragen wir aber endlich, wie zuletzt dieser Gegensatz zwischen Gut und Böse zum Austrag gelangt, so kommen wir damit auf die *Eschatologie*, die Lehre von den letzten Dingen, dem Weltende und Weltgericht. Beide, Ethik und Eschatologie, sind besonders wichtige Punkte der zoroastrischen Lehre, beide stehen naturgemäss in enger Wechselbeziehung, über beide enthalten auch schon die Gāthā's zahlreiche und wichtige Andeutungen.

Es ist bekannt, dass die ganze zoroastrische Ethik sich gründet auf den Dreiklang der "guten Gedanken, guten Worte und guten Thaten," dem *hūmatem, hūkhtem, huvarshtem*. Dies setzt schon ein hohes Mass sittlicher Bildung voraus, wenn die gedachte Sünde auf eine Stufe gestellt wird mit der Thatsünde und somit in der Gesinnung die Wurzel alles Handelns, zugleich aber auch der Massstab jeder sittlichen Beurteilung erkannt wird. Man wird zugeben müssen, dass die Stifter der Awestālehre damit doch zum mindesten die sittliche Stufe erreicht haben, auf welcher die besten Teile des alten Testamentes stehen, ja dass sie Neigung zu jener Vertiefung der sittlichen Anschauung zeigen, wie sie im Christentume zum Ausdrucke kommt.

Wir müssen nun aber hervorheben, dass bereits die Gāthās diesen Dreiklang kennen, der auch das ganze jüngere Awestā beherrscht. Es besteht somit kein Zweifel, dass die Begründung dieser Ethik auf Zarathushtra unmittelbar zurückgeht. Der Charakter dieser Ethik ist auch in der That ein so persönlicher und individueller, dass wir unwillkürlich zu der Annahme gedrängt werden: sie ist das Produkt eines einzelnen hervorragenden Geistes, der mit besonderer sittlicher Beanlagung ausgestaltet zu einer solchen Schärfe und Bestimmtheit in der Erfassung der ethischen Gesetze gelangte; dass diese Lehre aus einem ganzen Volke herausgewachsen, dass sie gewissermassen Eigentum einer Gesamtheit sei und nach und nach zu der Form sich entwickelt habe, in welcher sie im Awestā vorliegt, erscheint mir ganz unglaubwürdig.

Ys. 30,3, sagt der Dichter, dass die beiden Geister, die von Anbeginn waren, die Zwillinge, ihm im Traume verkündig hätten, was das Gute ist und was das Böse in Gedanken, Worten und Werken. Ebenso wird die Frömmigkeit, Ys. 51, 21, bezeichnet als Frucht der Gedanken, Worte und Werke einer demütigen Gesinnung. Andrerseits gehen böse Gesinnung, böse Reden und böse Handlungsweise von dem bösen Geiste aus (Ys. 32, 5). Beim Gottesdienste äussert sich die Dreiteilung in dem andächtigen Sinne, welchen der Betende hegen soll, in den guten Sprüchen, die er spricht, und in den Opferhandlungen, die er verrichtet (Ys. 30, 1); allein jene drei Begriffe ausschliesslich als rituelle Ausdrücke aufzufassen, das wäre eine Beschränkung, welche durch die Texte nicht gerechtfertigt wird. Dass die Gesinnung den Grundton des Dreiklanges ausmacht, dass Reden und Handlungen auf ihr beruhen und nach ihr beurteilt werden müssen, das drückt der Prophet deutlich genug aus, wenn er von den Worten und Thaten einer guten Gesinnung spricht (Ys. 45, 8).

Was nun die Stellung des Menschen zu gut und böse betrifft, so ist der hervorstechendste Punkt in der Ethik der Gāthā's die *vollkommen freie Wahl*, welche jedem einzelnen zusteht. Der Mensch steht nach zoroastrischer Auffassung nicht etwa unter dem Banne irgend eines Verhängnisses, einer von Ewigkeit her geltenden Bestimmung, die ihn bindet und seinen Willen unterdrückt. Da gibt es keine Erbsünde, die er als Folge der Verschuldungen seiner Eltern zu tragen hat und die seine Kraft zum Kampfe gegen das Böse lähmt. Das Böse liegt nicht in ihm, sondern ausser ihm; er kann es an sich heran kommen lassen und in sich aufnehmen, aber er kann es auch von sich weisen und bekämpfen.

Das ist gewiss ein gesunder Standpunkt, der alle Verantwortung auf den Menschen selber lädt und ihm die Möglichkeit benimmt, seine Lässigkeit zu entschuldigen mit irgend etwas, das nicht in seiner Hand liegt.

Dass die Entscheidung für gut oder böse Sache der freien Wahl ist, dies wird schon vorbildlich damit angedeutet, dass auch die Daemonen sich aus eigenem Antrieb auf die Seite des bösen Geistes stellen. Sie sind also nicht schlechthin böse, sie werden es erst, indem sie thörichter Weise gegen Ahura sich entscheiden (Ys. 30, 6). Ja es ist sogar ein freier Willensakt des bösen Geistes selber, dass er die Sünde zu seiner Domäne erwählte, während Spenta-mainyu die Frömmigkeit und Wahrheit für sich erwählte (Ys. 30, 5). Und ebenso sind es die Frommen und Gläubigen welche die richtige Wahl treffen der guten Gesinnung, Worte und Werke, nicht aber die Unfrommen (Ys. 30, 3).

Mit dieser Lehre von der freien Wahl des Menschen steht die schon oben von mir besprochne (S. 177-178) Anschauung, dass die Religion Sache des Verstandes ist, dass Frömmigkeit und Wahrheit einerseits und Unfrömmigkeit und Lüge andrerseits begrifflich sich decken, in engstem Zusammenhang. Der Mensch ist eben nach zoroastrischer Auffassung nicht an ein blindes Geschick gefesselt noch auch durch angeerbte Fehler in seinen Urteil beeinträchtigt. Gott hat ihm seinen Verstand gegeben — und wer Ohren hat, der höre, wer Urteil besitzt, der entscheide sich für das Richtige und Wahre! Der Sünder ist ein Thor und der Thor ein Sünder.

Wie gross die Gefahr für jeden einzelnen ist, in wie mannigfaltiger Gestalt das Böse in der sichtbaren Welt sich zeigt und den Frommen zu Fall zu bringen droht, dessen ist der Zoroastrier sich wohl bewusst. Sein Leben ist daher ein steter unermüdlicher Kampf gegen da Böse. Es wäre überflüssig, für diese ernste Auffassung vom Leben als einem ewigen Kampfe in getreuer Pflichterfüllung, in Arbeit und Mühe Beweisstellen aus den Gāthās zu bringen. Die Ermahnung auszuharren in der Frömmigkeit und Gottergebenheit und nicht müde zu werden, bildet so recht eigentlich den Grundton der meisten Lieder.

Förmmigkeit ist des Dichters sehnlichster Wunsch (Ys. 32, 9); er fleht zu Armaiti, sie möge ihn festhalten lassen am Glauben (asha) vund ihm den Segen einer frommen Gesinnung verleihen (Ys. 43, 1). Der Glaube ist das höchste Gut (vahishtem), das er von Gott erlangen kann. Um dieses höchste Gut fleht er für sich und für seinen Anhänger Frashaoshtra (Ys. 28, 9). Dem Mazda ist es eigen; von ihm aus gelangt es zu den Menschen, wenn diesen das heilige Wort verkündigt wird (Ys 31, 6; 45, 4). Um wie viel höher stehen in dieser Beziehung die Gāthā-Hymnen, als die des Rigveda. Dort sind es fast ausschliesslich geistige und sittliche Güter, welche der Dichter sich wünscht; nur in vereinzelten Fällen (Ys. 44, 10) bilden materielle den Gegenstand seines Verlangens. Die vedischen Sänger flehen um Rosse und Rinder und glänzenden Reichtum.

Ein hervorstechendes Merkmal der Gāthā's gegenüber dem jüngeren Awestā bildet das Zurücktreten des Kultus und der Zeremonien. Regelmässig wiederkehrende Gebete, Opferhandlungen, Rezitationen und täglich oder bei bestimmten Veranlassungen vorzunehmende Reinigungen spielen im jüngeren Awestā eine bedeutsame Rolle; sie bilden den eigentlichen Inhalt des Vendidād, des religiösen Gesetzbuches der Zoroastrier. Die Hüter dieser zahlreichen Vorschriften sind die Priester; sie haben deren Ausführung zu überwachen und dem Nachlässigen und Säumigen, welcher sie übertrat, die gebührende Busse aufzuerlegen. Das ganze Leben der

Zoroastrier wird von diesen Reinigungsvorschriften mit ihrem minutiösen Zeremoniell beherrscht. Werfen wir aber einen Blick in die Gāthā's, so finden wir keine Spur von allen diesen Bestimmungen und Bräuchen. Hiefür ist eine doppelte Erklärung möglich Entweder nehmen wir an, dass der Zusammenhang in den Gāthā's, die Tendenz und Absicht, welche ihre Verfasser verfolgten, überhaupt keine Veranlassung boten, von Ritual und Zeremoniell zu sprechen; oder wir erklären die Erscheinung damit, dass zu jener Zeit, wo die Gāthā's verfasst wurden, überhaupt noch keine solchen Einzelbestimmungen getroffen waren, sondern das ganze System erst nachmals, als die Gemeinde mehr gefestigt war und die neue Lehre weitere Verbreitung gefunden hatte, sich ausbilden konnte. Ich glaube, dass wir kein Bedenken tragen dürfen, letzterer Annahme zu folgen. Die Gāthā's schweigen ja nicht ganz von den äusseren Formen des Gottesdienstes. Sie sprechen von den Preisliedern, durch welche man die Gottheit verehrt (Ys. 34, 6 ; 45, 6 und 8; 50, 4) ; durch Opfer erhöht man Ahura Mazda (Ys. 45, 10); sie sind die Thaten der guten Gesinnung, mittels deren man Gott nahe kommt (Ys. 50, 9) und die heiligen Genien sich günstig stimmt (Ys. 34, 1). Allein das sind ganz allgemeine Vorstellungen. Die Ethik der Gāthā's ist in so hohem Masse eine innerliche, sie erkennt so entschieden die Frömmigkeit in einem heiligen Lebenswandel und in energischer Bekämpfung des Bösen, dass sich damit die Vorstellung, als könne durch das gewissenhafte Befolgen äusserlicher Zeremonien irgend ein Verdienst erworben werden, kaum zu vertragen scheint. Der Ausdruck, mit welchem im späteren Awestā die Ausübung der Reinigungsvorschriften bezeichnet wird, *yaozhdāo*, kommt in den Gāthā's überhaupt nur ein einzigesmal vor (Ys. 48, 5). Die Gāthā's kennen ja nicht einmal einen gemeinsamen Namen für den Priesterstand. Sie bezeichnen zwar die gesamte Gemeinde der Gläubigen und im besondern, wie es scheint, die Lehrer und Verkündiger der neuen Religion mit einem bestimmten Worte (*saoshyantō*); aber dieses Wort bekommt im jüngeren Awestā eine ganz andere Bedeutung, und der Ausdruck *āthravan*, womit hier die Priester bezeichnet werden, fehlt in den Gāthā's vollständig. Ohne die Existenz eines geschlossenen Priesterstandes ist aber die Ausbildung und Handhabung eines so in die Einzelheiten gehenden Rituals, wie der Vendidād es lehrt, undenkbar. Das Fehlen eines Priesterstandes aber wie auch das Fehlen eines ausgebildeten Rituals und Zeremoniells erklärt sich ganz ungezwungen aus den allgemeinen Kulturverhältnissen, wie die Gāthā's sie schildern. Damals war die zoroastrische Gemeinde erst im Entstehen begriffen, die Lehre noch eine neue, nicht seit langer Zeit im Volke bekannte und verbreitete; jene beiden Erscheinungen aber, ein nach aussen abgeschlossener Priesterstand und ein entwickeltes System von religiösen Bräuchen und Vorschriften begegnen uns nur unter gefestigten Verhältnissen. Sie setzen eine gewisse Tradition voraus, eine längere Entwickelungsperiode, in der es möglich geworden, das System nicht bloss in den allgemeinen Grundzügen festzustellen sondern auch im einzelnen auszubauen. Die allgemeinen Grundzüge des Zoroastrianismus aber liegen in den Gāthā's vor, der Ausbau im einzelnen im jüngeren Awestā. Ob freilich dieser Ausbau in allen Punkten dem Geiste entspricht, welcher die Gāthā's durchweht, das scheint nicht zweifellos zu sein.

Die Gāthā's sind entstanden, wie wir sahen, in einer Zeit heftiger Kämpfe. Oft genug befinden sich die Gläubigen in Not und Bedrängnis, die Gottlosen und Ungläubigen frohlocken und scheinen den Sieg davon zu tragen. Da musste sich von selbst der Gedanke aufdrängen: wie werden die Frommen entschädigt werden für alles Unrecht, das sie hier auf Erden erleiden, und wie werden die Gottlosen, die von Glück und Erfolg begleitet erscheinen, für ihren Frevel entschädigt werden. So ist schon in der frühesten Zeit des Zoroastrianismus der Gedanke einer ausgleichenden Gerechtigkeit im Jenseits lebendig. Er bildet einen der Grundpfeiler des ganzen Systems, ohne diese Hoffnung würden auch die Gläubigen kaum alle Verfolgungen siegreich überwunden haben, die sie anfangs erdulden mussten. Über alle Leiden des Diesseits hinweg blickten sie, den christlichen Märtyrern der ersten Jahrhunderte vergleichbar, auf die Freuden, welche im Jenseits ihrer warten.

" Wenn sie empfangen werden den Lohn für ihr Thun,
  Die, welche jetzt leben, die gewesen sind, und die leben werden,
Dann wird des Frommen Seele in Ewigkeit wohlgemut sein,
  Aber nie wird enden die Qual des Ungläubigen:
So hat Mazda Ahura nach seiner Macht bestimmt." (Ys. 45, 7.)

Der Ausgleich zwischen Verdienst und Schicksal erfolgt durch ein göttliches Gericht. Dieses Gericht ist ein doppeltes, ein individuelles und ein generelles. Das individuelle Gericht trifft jede einzelne Seele nach ihrem Ausscheiden aus dem Körper, das generelle Gericht dagegen die Gesamtheit am Ende der Welt, am jüngsten Tage. Mit dem letzteren erfolgt, wie es scheint die vollkommene Loslösung des Bösen vom Guten, die Aufhebung der Negation, nach welcher das Positive und Reale, das Gute, allein bestehen bleibt.

So viel wir aus den Andeutungen in den Gāthā's über das Schicksal der Seelen nach ihrem Abscheiden entnehmen können, stimmen die Vorstellungen jener Zeitperiode mit denen des späteren Awestā überein. Das Gericht findet statt bei der Brücke Cinvat, welche das Diesseits mit dem Jenseits verbindet. Über diese Brücke geht die fromme Seele hinüber in Gemeinschaft mit den Seelen aller derer welche auf Erden dem guten nachgestrebt haben (Ys. 46, 10). Sie geht nun ein in die "geistige Welt," die in den Gāthā's oft (Ys. 28,3 u. s. w.) der sichtbaren, körperhaften Welt entgegen gesetzt ist. Dort wird ihm die höchste Seligkeit zu teil. Dieselbe besteht vor allem darin, dass er Mazda und die himlischen Geister von Angesicht zu Angesicht sieht und mit ihnen in ewigem Lichte zusammen wohnt. "O Asha, wann werde ich dich schauen," fragt daher Ys. 28, 6 der Dichter, "und den Vohu-manō mit Wissen und die Stätte, die dem Ahura zu eigen gehört?" In die Behausung des seligen Geistes werden den Bösen zum Trotze dereinst die Frommen geführt werden nach Ys. 32,15. Wer durch Wahrheit die Lüge überwunden hat, dem wird von Mazda das himmlische Reich samt der ewigen Seligkeit verliehen werden (Ys. 30,8), und ungehindert werden die, welche am guten Glauben festhalten, in die Wohnung des Vohu-manō, des Ascha und des Mazda eingehen (Ys. 30, 10). Allen denen wird Gott das ewige Leben geben, welche Zarathushtra sich anschliessen (Ys. 46, 13), und dieses Leben ist ein Leben der Wonne; denn *garō demāna*, Wohnstätte des Lobgesanges, wird Ys. 45, 8 das Paradies, in dem die Frommen weilen, genannt.

Wir sehen wieder, wie die Gāthā's ihrem ganzen Charakter entsprechend, die Seligkeit im Jenseits als eine im wesentlichen geistige auffassen. Wie in der christlichen Lehre beruht sie vornehmlich im "Schauen Gottes," in dem engen Zusammensein mit der Gottheit. Indische Züge finden wir kaum. Der Zoroastrianismus steht hier wieder in schroffem Gegensatze zu den Naturreligionen, welche das Leben nach dem Tode als eine Fortsetzung des diesseitigen Lebens auffassen mit allen seinen Freuden, Genüssen und Gewohnheiten, aber ohne dessen Leiden und Mühseligkeiten.

Während die Seele der Frommen fröhlich die Brücke Cinvat überschreitet, welche sie zum Himmelreich führt, wird die Seele des Sünders, im Vorgefühle der sie erwartenden Strafe, von Furcht und Entsetzen ergriffen (Ys. 51, 13). Der göttliche Richterspruch verweist sie in die Hölle. Wie das Reich des Mazda lauter Licht ist, so ist Finsternis die Behausung der Dämonen (Ys. 32,10)[1]. Hier wird sie von den bösen Geistern unter Hohnreden empfangen und mit ekelhaften Speisen bewirtet (Ys. 49, 11). Aber wie rein geistige Freuden das wesentliche des Paradieses aus machen, so sind es auch vornehmlich seelische Qualen, unter denen die Seele des Bösen nach ihrem Abscheiden zu leiden hat. Sie ist getrennt von Mazda und den seligen Geistern, sie wohnt in Ewigkeit zusammen mit den Dämonen, sie wird namentlich gefoltert durch das eigene Gewissen, das sie anklagt und verdammt (Ys. 46, 11). Also Ruhe und heitere Fröhlichkeit auf der einen Seite, bei den Seligen, Unruhe, Gewissensbisse, Reue auf der anderen Seite, bei den Verdammten : das ist der Ausgleich im Jenseits für das Missverhältnis zwischen Verdienst und Schicksal, das wir so oft im Leben der Menschen hier auf Erden wahrnehmen.

Dieser Ausgleich vollzieht sich unmittelbar nach dem Tode des Einzelindividuums. Allein die Welt ist nicht für die Ewigkeit bestimmt, sie wird dereinst zu grunde gehen, und mit dem Weltende verbindet sich ein Weltgericht. Wir finden diese Vorstellung bereits in den Gāthā's. Das generelle Gericht steht in keinem Widerspruch zum individuellen Gerichte Letzteres findet in ersterem seine feierliche Bestätigung und, wir dürfen wohl annehmen, dass im Weltgerichte das Böse an sich vernichtet und aufgehoben wird. Die Gāthā's äussern sich hierüber allerdings nicht bestimmt ; allein das spätere Awestā enthält diese Lehre, und wir können wohl sagen, dass ohne sie die Vorstellung von einem Gerichte am Ende der Welt überhaupt so ziemlich gegenstandslos wäre. In den Hymnen wird das Weltgericht anscheinend gar nicht vom individuellen Gerichte unterschieden. Mazda, der von Anbeginne der Welt her war, hat es in seiner Macht festgesetzt, das Böses die Vergeltung der Bösen nnd Gutes die Belohnung der Guten sein solle am Ende der Welt. Bei diesem Weltende wird der Fromme eingehen in Mazda's Himmelreich (Ys. 43, 5, 6 ; 51, 6) ; d. h. er wird die Vernichtung überdauern welche das Böse und die Bösen treffen wird.

---

[1] *Acishtahyā demānē manaŋhō* "in der Behausung des bösen Geistes" ist der Formelle wie sachliche Gegensatz zu dem in Strophe 15 stehenden *vaṅheush ā demānē manaŋhé*.

SCHLUSSFOLGE.

Ich stehe nun am Ende meines Überblickes. Es schien mir in der That zeitgemäss und lohnend, einmal die Gāthā's als den ältesten Teil des Awestā herauszuheben und den Inhalt ihrer Lehre gesondert zu betrachten. Die Arbeit selber mag den Beweis liefern, dass dies möglich ist. Sie mag gleichzeitig ein Beitrag sein zu dem Nachweise, dass eine tiefe Kluft die Gāthā's von den übrigen Büchern des Awestā trennt, und dass die Parsen recht hatten und durch triftige Gründe geleitet wurden, wenn sie schon frühzeitig den alten Hymnen eine besondere Heiligkeit zuschrieben.

Meine Aufgabe erschien um so lohnender, als aus den Gāthā's eine besonders ursprüngliche und altertümliche Form der zoroastrischen Lehre sich ergibt und diese Form zugleich die reinste und erhabenste ist, die wir kennen. Sie ist noch frei von mancher jüngeren Zuthat und lässt uns die Persönlichkeit Zarathushtra's, seine sittlich ernste und doch menschliche Gesinnung und seine philosophische Beanlagung, die sich an die höchsten und bedeutendsten Probleme wagt, in günstigstem Lichte erscheinen. Wir erkennen in ihm einen Mann, der, seiner Zeit weit voraneilend, schon in fernem Altertume eine monotheistische Religion dem Volke verkündigte, das Wesen der Gottheit, das Verhältnis der Menschen zu ihr und die Entstehung des Bösen von einem philosophischen Standpunkte auffasste, und den Schwerpunkt nicht in Opfern und äusserlichen Zeremonien sondern in einer frommen Gesinnung und in einem dieser Gesinnung entsprechenden Leben erkannte.

So wendet sich diese Arbeit einerseits an die Parsen Indiens andrerseits an diejenigen unter den Europäern, welche für Indien und dessen Bewohner warmes Interesse hegen. Sie will jenen die älteste und gewissermassen auch die ideale Form ihrer Lehre vorführen, wie sie vermutlich von ihrem Stifter und Begründer selbst gedacht und aufgefasst wurde; sie will aber damit zugleich auch dem Europäer, der nicht selbst in der Lage ist, die heiligen Schriften der Parsen im Urtexte zu lesen, eine richtige Würdigung und unbefangene Beurteilung der parsistischen Religion und ihres sittlichen Gehaltes ermöglicht. Möge sie ein Stein sein, herbeigetragen zum Bau der Brücke welche Morgenland und Abendland mit einander verbinden soll!

APPENDIX.

I.

THE ALLEGED PRACTICE OF CONSAN-GUINEOUS MARRIAGES IN ANCIENT IRAN.

THE ALLEGED PRACTICE
OF
CONSANGUINEOUS MARRIAGES IN ANCIENT IRÂN.[1]

INTRODUCTION.

In the history of primitive marriage there are few subjects which exceed in gravity and interest the much-discussed question of the existence of consanguineous marriages in ancient Irân—in other words, of marriages between blood-relations of a near or remote degree among the early Zoroastrians. Although the attention of Parsi students of Zoroastrianism has often been drawn to this delicate question by the labours of esteemed European Oriental scholars, still it is strange to find how few of us have endeavoured to throw any light upon it, merely contenting ourselves with a bare denial of the existence of any trace of such marriage practices in our Sacred Writings. The causes of this remarkable omission may be easily traced to the manifold difficulties attending an examination of the evidence on the subject, which is met with in Western classical history and in Irânian archives. These difficulties are attributable partly to want of acquaintance with the languages of the original works; partly to the obscurities of those Avesta and Pahlavi passages which are supposed by foreigners to refer to marriages between nearest kinsfolk; and partly to the discouragement arising from the way in which some of the best European authorities have acquiesced in accepting the accounts given by Greek historians.

GENERAL REMARKS.

In all the inquiries which have long engaged the attention of European Orientalists, their efforts have been directed almost exclusively to verifying the testimony of classical reports to the effect that marriage between the nearest blood-relations

[1] Papers read by me before the Bombay Branch of the Royal Asiatic Society. Second Edition.

was not an uncommon practice among the ancient Irânians in the times of the Achæmenidæ, the Arsacidæ, and the Sâsânidæ. Nay, it has even come to pass that several European *savants* have claimed to have discovered positive evidence of such marriages in the Sacred Writings and in the later Pahlavi works of the Irânians themselves. Guided solely by their opinions,[1] the Rev. J. van den Gheyn, S. J., in his well-known French Essay on "Comparative Mythology and Philology," has been led to remark with reference to the moral tenets of the Avestâ[2]:—

"If the Mazdian writers delighted in psychological analyses, they were still more fond of discussions relating to morals. The Mazdian religion can boast of having the soundest, the sublimest, and the most rational system of morals among all the non-Christian religions. The basis of these morals rests on the free volition of man . . . .

"But side by side with these doctrines, so perfect and so rational, one may well be astonished to see that Mazdism approved of a doctrine which strangely contrasts with our ideas of morality. We mean to refer to the well-known *khvêtukdas*, exalted

---

[1] Particularly the opinion of my learned friend, the Rev. Dr. L.C. Casartelli, Professor of History and Geography, St. Bede's College, Manchester. See his *La Philosophie religieuse du Mazdéisme sous les Sassanides*, s. v. *Khvêtûkdas*.

[2] Comp. *Essais de Mythologie et de Philologie Comparée*, per J. van den Gheyn, S. J.; VII.—*Études Érâniennes*, II, *Les Études Avestiques de M. Geldner*, § 4, *Morale*, pp. 231-234 :—.

"Si les écrivains mazdéens aimaient les distinctions psychologiques, ils étaient bien plus épris des discussions de morale. La religion madéenue peut, se vanter d'avoir, parmi tous les cultes non-chrétiens, la morale la plus saine la plus haute et la plus raisonnable. Les bases de la morale s'appuient sur la libre volonté de l'homme . . . .

"Mais à côté de ces doctrines si saines et si raisonnable, on peut s'étonner de voir approuver une doctrine qui contraste étrangement avec nos idées de moralité. Nous voulons parler du fameux Khvêtûk-das, exalté comme une des œuvres les plus méritoires et les plus saintes. Et cependant, ce terme désigne le mariage incestueux entre proches parents, voire même entre père et fille, fils et mère, frère et sœur ! Quoi de plus rebutant ? Comment une religion d'une nature si élevée que le mazdeisme, a-t-elle pu inculquer une telle pratique ? C'est là une question historique qui se rattache à l'Avesta. Nous devons donc la laisser de côté."

"Les Parsis modernes, on le comprend, n'ont pas gardé ces habitudes immorales. Même ils protestent énergiquement contre l'accusation d'avoir jamais enseigné pareille doctrine. Malheureusement, ils ne peuvent anéantir leurs anciens livres, implacables temoins qui déposent contre eux."

as one of the most meritorious and sacred acts. This term, however, designates the incestuous marriage between near relations, even between father and daughter, son and mother, brother and sister. What could be more repulsive? How could a religion of so sublime a nature as Mazdism have inculcated such a practice? That is an historical question relating to the Avestâ. We ought, therefore, to put it aside.

"The modern Parsis, it is true, have not preserved such immoral customs. They even protest with energy against the accusation of having ever taught any such doctrine. Unfortunately, they cannot burn their ancient books, the unimpeachable testimony borne against them."

Such is the observation of the Rev. Mr. Gheyn. It is not, however, the outcome of personal investigations in the field of Irânian literature, but is almost exclusively founded on the latest sources of Oriental knowledge in the series of the "Sacred Books of the East" planned by Prof. Max Müller. But far more important observations on the subject, which claim our earnest attention, have been put forth by some of those European *literati* who have delved deep in the mines of Oriental learning, and brought to light some of the most precious gems which will ever remain as monuments marking an important epoch in the history of Oriental literature. I beg to draw attention to the opinion of Dr. F. von Spiegel, a veteran Avesta scholar, which I have translated from the 3rd Vol. of his German work on "Irânian Antiquities" (*Eränische Alterthumskunde*, Vol. III, pp. 678-679). He says:—"Much offence has always been caused in Europe by the marriages between near relations, namely, between brothers and sisters, between fathers and daughters, between sons and mothers. They have their origin in the tribal relationship amongst the Irânians. They married in their own tribe, since no *mésalliance* could be contracted, and everybody regarded his own tribe and his own family as the most preferable one. So early as in the Avesta the marriage of near relations is recommended (*Yasna*, XIII., 28; *Visparad*, III., 8); and it is also to the present day a custom among the nomads, whose daughters very often decline the most favourable offers of marriage out of their family circle, because they think that such marriages might convey them into a town, and likewise into a different tribe. The extreme case of such marriages between relations is the marriage of brothers and sisters. According to Herodotus, Cambyses first introduced the custom of marriage between brothers and sisters; but this is probably an error. The custom certainly existed already before him. That the kings were accustomed to take in marriage only the spouses of their rank from the family of the Achæmenidæ is witnessed in two passages by Herodotus. For this reason the marriages between brothers and sisters were much in favour with the royal family. Cambyses married his sisters (Her. III, 31); Artaxerxes, his two daughters (Plutarch, Art. C. 27); Tertuchmes, his sister Roxana (Ktes. Pers. C. 54); the satrap Sysimithres, even his mother (Curtius 8, 2, 19); Qôbâd I., his daughter Sambyke. Agathias tells us that this custom also continued to later times."[1]

Such, gentlemen, is the position of the European view fortified by fragmentary references to ancient history, and frowning against the most glorious edifice of the old Irânian ethology universally acknowledged to be the sublimest among the oldest religions of the world. This position it is the solemn duty of every Zoroastrian student of Irânian antiquities to inspect with the light of evidence furnished abundantly by history, both Occidental as well as Oriental. It is as undesirable as it is unphilosophic to dwell with idle complacence on the high praise which European scholars have almost invariably bestowed on Zoroastrianism for its sublime ethical conceptions, and to ignore allegations as to the practices in question of the early

---

[1] Compare Dr. Wm. Geiger, *Ostirânische Kultur*, p. 246 :—" Auch den West-irâniern war die Heirat von Blutsverwandten nicht fremd. Schon die klassischen Autoren wissen davon zu berichten. Herodot is der irrigen Ansicht, dass Kambyses sie eingeführt habe, als er seine Schwester Atossa zum Weibe nahm. Gerade in der königlichen Familie kam sie häufig vor. Man hatte hier besonderes Interesse daran, den Stammbaum rein zu bewahren und das eigene Geschlecht möglichst von anderen Familien zu separieren. Ausser Kambyses wäre Artaxerxes anzuführen, der seine beiden Töchter heiratete, sowie Toritichmes, der mit seiner Schwester Roxano, und Kôbâd I, der mit seiner Schwester Sambyke sich vermählte."—Also *cf.* Windischmann, *Zoroastrische Studien*, p. 268, and *L'Muséon* (1885), *Les Noms Propres Perso-Arcstiques*, par Th. Keiper, pp. 212 *seq.*

followers of Zoroaster. One of the true criteria of the morality of a nation is its marriage institution. The moral life of society begins and is nurtured in the family. It is, therefore, scarcely possible to conceive how a nation, much less a religion, which has been generally extolled for its pure system of morals, and proverbial for its strictly moral habits, should have sanctioned or tolerated a custom which must naturally have demoralized the highly valued precept of "*pious mind, pious words, pious actions.*"[1]

But, here, I may be allowed to observe that the Greeks who charged the Persians with the crime of consanguineous marriages, and who were distinguished among the Western nations before the Christian era for the high stage of civilization they had reached, were not unfamiliar with incestuous enormities. (1) In the *Prefatio* of Cornelius Nepos, the contemporary of Cicero, it is said that "Cimon, the greatest of the Athenians, was not dishonoured for having espoused his sister on the father's side." (2) The celebrated comic poet Aristophanes, who flourished in the 5th century B. C., relates in verse 1371 of his comedy of "The Frogs":—"He began reciting some of the verses from Euripides, where one perceives a brother miserable, having married his uterine sister." (3) Demosthenes in his Appeal against Eubulides of Miletus, asserts: "My grand-father had espoused his sister not uterine."[2] According to the *Scholiast* the marriage with a half-sister was permitted by law among the ancient Greeks. The details which M'Lenan has gathered on this subject, go to prove that the old Spartans were also accustomed to marry even their uterine sisters. Again Mr. Robertson

---

[1] Comp. my "Civil'zation of the Eastern Irânians," vol. I, pp. 162-163:—"It affords indeed proof of a great ethical tendency and of a very sober and profound way of thinking, that the Avestâ people, or at least the priests of their religion, arrived at the truth that sins by thought must be ranked with sins by deed, and that, therefore, the actual root and source of everything good or bad must be sought in the mind. It would not be easy to find a people that attained under equal or similar historical conditions to such a height of ethical knowledge."—Also *cf.* "Christ and Other Masters," by the Rev. Mr. Hardwick, p. 541:—"In the measure of her moral sensibility, Persia may be fairly ranked among the brightest spots of ancient heathendom."

[2] For these references to Greek incest I am indebted to the kindness of the Honourable Sir Raymond West, President of the B. B. R. A. Society, and of M. James Darmesteter.

Smith remarks in his "Kinship and Marriage in Early Arabia" (p. 162) :—"At Athens we find marriage with a half-sister not uterine occurring in later times, and side by side with this we find an ancient tradition that before Cecrops there was a general practice of polyandry, and consequently kinship only through mothers." Mr. Wm. Adam points out that Xenophon's memoirs of Socrates refer to the intercourse of parents with children among the Greeks (*vide* his dissertation on "Consanguinity in Marriage," contributed to the *Fortnightly Review*, vol. II., p. 719).

These are some of the facts which plainly indicate that the custom of consanguineous marriages did actually exist in ancient Greece at a very remote period. These facts are preserved in its native archives, which it is difficult to controvert. But, hence, it is allowable to infer that the Greek historians of ancient Irân were not unfamiliar with next-of-kin marriages, before they wrote a word upon any Oriental history or religion, and that their sweeping assertion of the incestuous practices of civilized Arians was to a certain extent due to their knowledge of the existence of such practices amongst Semitic nations[1] as well as amongst themselves.

---

[1] In some of the sacred documents of the Jews, particularly in the Books of Genesis and Exodus, it is recorded that Abraham was married to his half-sister Sarai, Nahor to his niece Milcah, Amram to his aunt Jochebed, and Lot to his two daughters The Book of Genesis xix. 36-38 says :—"Thus were both the daughters of Lot with child by their father; and the first-born bare a son, and called his name Moab; . . . . and the younger, she also bare a son and called his name Benammi."—At a much later period, the granddaughter of King Herod the Great is said to have married her uncle Philip. Again, the Assyrians are charged by Lucian (*Lucian de Sacrificiis*, p. 183) with the guilt of close consanguineous marriages.—Also Orosius, a Spanish Presbyter who flourished in the 5th century after Christ, relates in his *Historiarum adversus Paganos Libri* VII., that Semiramis, the widow of Ninus, married her own son, and authorized such marriages among her people in order to wipe out the stain of her own abominable action (*cf.* Adam, *Fortnightly Review*). The old Egyptians seem to have legalized the marriage between brothers and sisters (*vide* Rawlinson's History of Herodotus, Vol. II., p. 429, note 1); and, according to Philo, the Alexandrian Jew, there was no restriction even as to marrying one's whole sister (*Philo de Specialibus Legibus*, p. 778).—The recently published work of Mr. Robertson Smith illustrated the existence of the practice of marriage between nearest blood-relations among the early Arabs.

But how far all these statements as regards those Oriental nations may be reliable, I leave it to the students of their histories and religions to prove with positive evidence

In reference to the reports of Greek historians on Oriental customs, what assertion could be more sweeping and loose than that of Ptolemy, who (relying upon the authority of the *Paraphrasis* of Proclus, who flourished in the 5th century B.C.), when treating of India, Ariana, Gedrosia, Parthia, Media, Persia, Babylonia, Mesopotamia and Assyria, relates that "very many or most of the inhabitants of those countries intermarry with their own mothers" (*vide* Adam, F. R., " Consanguinity in Marriage," p. 713). But can this vague statement support so grave a charge? In the absence of something definite to go upon, some well attested instances, must we not pause before believing that the Indô-Irânians, even as individual peoples, could ever be guilty of the heinousness they are charged with?

With these preliminary remarks I address myself to my task, and lay before you what I purpose to demonstrate in the following propositions :—

I. That the slight authority of some isolated passages gleaned from the pages of Greek and Roman literature, is wholly insufficient to support the odious charge made against the ancient Irânians of practising consanguineous marriages in their most objectionable forms.

II. That no trace, hint or suggestion of such a custom can be pointed out in the Avesta or in its Pahlavi Version.

III. That the Pahlavi passages translated by a distinguished English Pahlavi savant, and supposed to have references to such a custom, cannot be interpreted as upholding the view that next-of-kin marriages were expressly recommended therein. That a few of the Pahlavi passages, which are alleged to contain actual references to such marriages, do not allude to social realities but to supernatural conceptions relating to the reaction of the first progenitors of mankind.

IV. That the words of our Prophet Zarathushtra himself, which are preserved in one of the strophes of the Gâthic hymn LIII, express a highly moral ideal of the marriage relation.[1]

---

[1] Here let me draw attention to the opinion of Dr. L. H. Mills on the contents of the Gâthâs. In S. B. E., Vol. XXXI., p. 1, the translator observes:—

I. Classical Testimony on the Subject.

Without presuming to attack any particular European theory, I beg to put forward my humble impressions in confirmation of the first statement. Among the Western classical writers, who are concerned with Persian history or religion, there are about fifteen who have touched upon the subject of next-of-kin marriages in ancient Irân, and who belong to different periods, from the 7th century B. C. to the 6th century A. D. They are Xanthus (fl. about B. C. 650); Herodotus (B. C. 484-409); Ctesias (fl. about B. C. 440); Strabo (B. C. 54 to A. D. 24); Plutarch (b. A. D. 66); Curtius (b. A. D. 70); Tertullian (A. D. 160-240); Origen, Clemens Alexandrinus, Diogenes Laertius, and Tatian (who flourished in the 2nd century A. D.); Minutius Felix, and Athenæus (fl. in the 3rd century A. D.); and Agathias (about A. D. 536-538). Of these Tertullian, Clemens Alexandrinus, Origen, Diogenes Laertius, Athenæus, Curtius, and Minutius Felix ascribe incestuous marriages to the Persians generally, according to Mr. Adam, "without any distinction or qualification." The spurious works of Xanthus as well as the genuine books of Strabo and Tatian, impute such practices to the Magians alone, without drawing any line of separation between the different Magian orders among the Chaldæans or the Persians. Herodotus, Ctesias, Plutarch, and Agatias make special mention of names of persons of rank, whom they charge with the guilt of such incest. Now, if we were to inquire to what different sources these reports owe their origin, we should find that Tertullian, Clemens Alexandrinus, and his pupil Origen, as well as the true Plutarch, based their statements with regard to this question on the authority of

---

" So far as a claim to a high position among the curiosities of ancient moral lore is concerned, the reader may trust himself freely to the impression that he has before him an anthology which was probably composed with as fervent a desire to benefit the spiritual and moral nature of those to whom it was addressed as any which the world has yet seen. Nay, he may provisionally accept the opinion that nowhere else are such traces of intelligent religious earnestness to be found as existing at the period of the Gâthâs or before them, save in the Semitic Scriptures." Elsewhere he also remarks: " Nowhere, at their period, had there been a human voice, so far as we have any evidence, which uttered thoughts like these. They are now, some of them, the great common places of philosophical religion; but till then they were unheard (*agushtâ*).''

Ctesias (Adam, F. R., p. 715; Rawlinson, Herodotus, Vol. I, p. 78). Diogenes Laertius, Strabo, and Curtius seem to rely upon the spurious works of Xanthus (*vide* Windischmann, *Zoroastriche Studien*, p. 268 *seq.*; Adam, p. 717).[1] The works of Athenæus and Curtius are supposed to be collections of extracts from the writings of historians, dramatists, and philosophers, who preceded them (comp. Smith's "Classical Dictionary," *s. v.*). In the absence of any available information, it is difficult to trace the isolated reports of Tatian and Minutius Felix to Xanthus, Ctesias, or Herodotus. Consequently, the only independent sources of information more or less authentic, seem to issue from only four of the classical writers above-named:—Xanthus, Herodotus, Ctesias, and Agathias. Their reports may be considered to have modelled the tone of classical history relating to ancient Irân.

However, in an enquiry with regard to their evidence, the questions most important and most natural are: What is their authenticity? How far may their testimony be relied upon? Are there any conflicting statements in these historians which should deter us from trusting implicitly to their guidance?

It is admitted that no two nations have ever succeeded in thoroughly understanding the manners and customs of each other. If this is so in our own day, when the means of information are numerous and ready to hand, what can we expect in those remote ages when the sources of information were very few and very uncertain. Again, it is necessary to be on our guard against putting absolute faith in any particular Greek writer.—Regarding Xanthus, Windischmann, in his German essay on the classical testimony relating to Zoroaster, published in his posthumous work *Zoroastrische Studien*, states (p. 263)[1]:—" As to the authenticity of the works of Xanthus (B. C. 529), a later writer, Artemon of Cassandra, advanced some doubts, and believed that they were (substituted five centuries after) by Dionysius Skytobrachion" (a native of Alexandria, who flourished about B. C. 120). This view is supported, as the writer says, by his tutor, F.G. Welcker. Also it is the opinion of Dr. Smith, expressed in

---

[1] Comp. my English version, pp. 76 *seq.* in this volume.

his "Classical Dictionary" that "The genuineness of the Four Books of Lydian History, which the ancients possessed under the name of Xanthus, and of which some considerable fragments have come down to us, was questioned by some of the ancient grammarians themselves. There has been considerable controversy respecting the genuineness of this work among modern scholars. It is certain that much of the matter in the extant fragments is spurious."

"The Persian informants of Herodotus," says Mr. G. Rawlinson in his Introduction to the "History of Herodotus" (pp. 67, 69), "seem to have consisted of *the soldiers and officials of various ranks*,[1] with whom he necessarily came in contact at Sardis and other places, where strong bodies of the dominant people were maintained constantly. He was born and bred up a Persian subject; and though in his own city Persians might be rare visitants, everywhere beyond the limits of the Grecian states they formed the official class, and in the great towns they were even a considerable section of the population. There is no reason to believe that *Herodotus ever set foot in Persia Proper, or was in a country where the Arian element preponderated*. Hence his mistakes with regard to the Persian religion which he confounded with the Scythic worship of Susiania, Armenia, and Cappadocia. . . . Herodotus, too, was, by natural temperament, inclined to look with favour on the poetical and the marvellous, and where he had to choose between a number of conflicting stories would be disposed to reject the prosaic and commonplace for the romantic and extraordinary. . . . Thus his narrative, where it can be compared with the Persian monumental records, presents the curious contrast of minute and exact agreement in some parts with broad and striking diversity in others. Unfortunately, a direct comparison of this kind can but rarely be made, owing to the scantiness of the Persian records at present discovered; but we are justified in assuming, from the coincidences actually observable, that at least some of his authorities drew their histories from the monu-

---

[1] These and several other words in the following quotations are put in italics by me.

ments; and it even seems as if Herodotus had himself had access to certain of the most important of those documents which were preserved in the archives of the empire."

Whatever might be the opinion of Mr. Rawlinson, one thing is clear on its face, that the truthfulness of the Persian informants upon whom Herodotus had depended was not quite beyond suspicion, *viz.*, the utter silence of Herodotus upon the founder of the Persian religion. While Xanthus is believed to have made mention of Zoroaster and his laws, while Plato, who flourished 55 years after Herodotus and must have drawn his materials consequently from sources as old as those of the latter, freely alludes to Zoroaster, it is impossible to conceive how Herodotus, who has described Persian life and Persian religion so eleborately, should have been unfamiliar with the name of the prophet of the land and the founder of the religion. Should we not assume that Herodotus became acquainted with the Magian belief merely through oral tradition recounted by persons who were ill-disposed towards the Magi, and who, therefore, were loth to divulge the name of their renowned Prophet?

Mr. George Rawlinson remarks further on (p. 77 *seq.*):—
"Several ancient writers, among them two of considerable repute, Ctesias, the court physician to Artaxerxes Mnemon, and Plutarch, or rather an author who has made free with his name, have impeached the truthfulness of the historian Herodotus, and maintained that his narrative is entitled to little credit. Ctesias seems to have introduced his own work to the favourable notice of his countrymen by a formal attack on the veracity of his great predecessor, upon the ruins of whose reputation he hoped to establish his own. He designed his history to supersede that of Herodotus, and feeling it in vain to endeavour to cope with him in the charms of composition, he set himself to invalidate his authority, presuming upon his own claims to attention as a resident for seventeen years at the court of the great king. Professing to draw his relation of Oriental affairs from a laborious examination of the Persian archives, he proceeded to contradict, wherever he could do so without

fear of detection, the assertions of his rival; and he thus acquired to himself a degree of fame and of consideration to which his literary merits would certainly never have entitled him, and which the course of detraction he pursued could alone have enabled him to gain. By the most unblushing effrontery he succeeded in palming of his narrative upon the ancient world as the true and genuine account of the transactions, and his authority was commonly followed in preference to that of Herodotus, at least upon all points of purely Oriental history."

Now regarding Ctesias, the same writer observes:—"There were not wanting indeed in ancient time some more critical spirits, e. g., Aristotle and the true Plutarch, who refused to accept as indisputable the statements of the Cnidian physician, and retorted upon him the charge of untruthfulness which he had preferred against Herodotus. It was difficult, however, to convict Ctesias of systematic falsehood until Oriental materials of an authentic character were obtained by which to test the conflicting accounts of the two writers. A comparison with the Jewish Scriptures and with the native history of Berosus first raised a general suspicion of the bad faith of Ctesias, whose credit few moderns have been bold enough to maintain against the continually increasing evidence against him. At last the *coup de grâce* has been given to his small remaining reputation by the recent Cuneiform discoveries which convict him of having striven to rise into notice by a system of 'enormous lying,' to which the history of literature scarcely presents a parallel."

Hence it is that the historian Grote is perfectly justified in remarking :—" This is a proof of the prevalence of discordant, yet equally accredited, stories. So rare and late a plant is historical authenticity."

As for Agathias, the Byzantine writer who flourished in the middle of the sixth century after Christ, his works ought to be consulted with greater caution. Besides, Diogenes Laertius is very often called " an inaccurate and unphilosophical writer." Even the true Plutarch's testimony is frequently questioned by modern critics. The reference to consanguineous marriages amongst the Magi: τουτοις δε και μητρα συνερχεσθαι πατριον νενομισται; in Strabo's Geography, Bk. XV, is a very short and isolated sentence, which has not the least connection with the main subject of the passage wherein it occurs, *viz.*, the mode of disposing of the dead among the early Persians.[1] It might, therefore, be justly regarded as an interpolation by some unknown reader, similar to the interpolations noticed in the work of Xenophon, Bk. VIII, Ch. V, p. 26, and condemned as such by all his critics of authority, *viz.*, Bornemann, Schneider, and Dindorf.

It must also be remembered that the works of some of those Greek philosophers who were well-known for their somewhat authentic description of the Zoroastrian religion and customs, *viz.*, Democritus (fl. about B. C. 460), Deinon the contemporary of Ctesias, Plato, Eudoxus, Hermippos, Theopompos, and Aristotle, do not contain the slightest trace or hint as to the alleged practice of next-of-kin marriages in ancient Irân.

Thus a majority of opinions may be cited to prove that the reports of classical writers on the subject of consanguineous marriages in old Irân are not at all beyond question. Moreover, I do not mean to deny that some of those Greek writers who have ascribed the marriage practices in question in the case of individuals to the old Irânians, may have had some grounds for their averment. But who can reconcile their conflicting evidence? Who can decide between the two inconsistent statements upon this subject by Xanthus and Agathias, where the former charges the Magi with the crime of marrying their parents, while the latter puts into the mouth of King Artaxerxes II words which plainly denounce such practices as being inconsistent not only with the laws of the land, but with the commandment of Zoroastrianism (*vide* Agathias Lib. II., C. 24). The Achæmenian monuments do not allude to such practices, nor have we any indigenous historical record of the Achæmenidæ or the Arsacidæ, upon which we could

---

[1] *Géographie de Strabon* traduit du Grec en Français, tome cinquième,à Paris, de l'Imprimerie Royale, 1819, pp. 140-141.

place any reliance for comparison. Alas! for the dispersion and destruction of our ancient literature, which, had it been preserved, would not only have assisted us to know the exact history of the old Irânian civilization; but also to controvert with ease all such discreditable allegations.

Nevertheless, the question arises:—Granted that the classical statements are to some extent doubtful; still are we not justified in believing that such marriages were customary or regarded as lawful during the rule of the Achæmenian kings, since the Greek reports refer to certain Persian monarchs or men of authority who contracted marriages with their nearest blood-relations?

It is true, Herodotus and Plutarch ascribe them to Cambyses III. and Artaxerxes II. Herodotus states in his accounts respecting Cambyses (*vide* Bk. III, 31 *seq.*):—"The second (outrage which Cambyses committed) was the slaying of his sister, who had accompanied him into Egypt, and lived with him as his wife, though she was his full sister, the daughter both of his father and his mother. The way wherein he had made her his wife was the following:—It was not the custom of the Persians, before his time, to marry their sisters; but Cambyses, happening to fall in love with one of his, and wishing to take her to wife, as he knew that it was an *uncommon thing*, called together the royal judges, and put it to them, 'whether there was any law which allowed a brother, if he wished, to marry his sister?' Now the royal judges are certain picked men among the Persians, who hold their office for life, or until they are found guilty of some misconduct. By them justice is administered in Persia and they are the interpreters of the old laws, all disputes being referred to their decision. When Cambyses, therefore, put his question to these judges, they gave him an answer which was at once true and *safe*:—'They did not find any law,' they said, 'allowing a brother to take his sister to wife, but they found a law that the king of the Persians might do whatever he pleased.' And so they neither warped the law through fear of Cambyses, nor ruined themselves by overstiffly maintaining the law; but they brought another quite distinct law to the king's help, which allowed him to have his wish. Cambyses, therefore, married the object of his love, and no longer time afterwards he took to wife another sister. It was the younger of these who went with him into Egypt, and there suffered death at his hands." ...... " The story," concerning the manner of her death, " which the Greeks tell, is, that Cambyses had set a young dog to fight the cub of a lioness—his wife looking on at the time. Now the dog was getting the worse, when a pup of the same litter broke his chain and came to his brother's aid ; then the two dogs together fought the lion, and conquered him. The thing greatly pleased Cambyses, but his sister, who was sitting by, shed tears. When Cambyses saw this he asked her why she wept : whereon she told him that seeing the young dog come to his brother's aid made her think of Smerdis (her brother), whom there was none to help. For this speech, the Greeks say, Cambyses put her to death."

But from these statements of the historian of Halicarnassus, is it not plain enough that the marriage of Cambyses with his sister—if we may rely upon the Greek evidence alone—was nothing more than the individual act of one of the most wicked tyrants that ever reigned in Persia, and that it was owing to the cruel and ferocious character of their ruler that this most irreligious marriage from the stand-point of the Magi was acquiesced in by the priests as well as the people? And is this action of a vicious and wicked king sufficient to justify us in affixing the stigma of such a custom to the whole Irânian nation, or in tracing it to their religious writings? Further, it should be remembered that Cambyses utterly disregarded his priesthood, defied the old sanitary ordinances of his people, and set small store by his religion.[1] He gave proof of this by

---

[1] Compare S. B. E., Vol. IV., "The Zend-Avestâ," by James Darmesteter, Part I, 1st edition, p. XLV. :—" If we pass now from dogma to practice, we find that the most important practice of the Avesta law was either disregarded by the Achœmenian kings, or unknown to them. According to the Avesta, burying corpses in the earth is one of the most heinous sins that can be committed. We know that under the Sâsânians a prime minister, Ceoses, paid with his life for an infraction of that law. Corpses were to be laid down on the summits of mountains, there to be devoured by bird and dogs ; the exposure of corpses was the most striking practice of Mazdian profession, and its adoption was the sign of conversion. Now under the Achœmenian rule, not only the burial of the dead was not forbidden, but it was the general practice."

attempting to encourage in his kingdom the practice of interring the dead amongst a people by whom it was detested. It is not, therefore, unreasonable to assume that the alleged marriage of Cambyses with his sister was suggested by his familiarity with such marriages among the Egyptians and the Greeks conquered by the Persians, and that it was carried into effect by a man of such violent passions as would brook no contradiction, and would not be balked of their gratification.

Here I may be allowed to observe, in passing, that it is difficult to agree with those European scholars[1] who doubt the accuracy of the assertion of Herodotus, that Cambyses was the first Persian to intermarry with his sister. I believe that their hypothesis, that the institution of such marriages had existed long before Cambyses reigned, is much more open to question than the statement of the Greek historian; and this will be demonstrated further on when I come to prove my second statement.

There is another Achæmenian monarch who is alluded to by Plutarch, on the authority of Ctesias and his followers, as having married his sister. According to Langhorn's translation of Plutarch's Life of Artaxerxes II, the Greek biographer relates:—" Artaxerxes in some measure atoned for the causes of sorrow he gave the Greeks, by doing one thing that afforded them great pleasure: he put Tissaphernes, their most implacable enemy, to death. This he did, partly at the instigation of Parysatis, who added other charges to those alleged against him......From this time Parysatis made it a rule to please the king in all her measures, and not to oppose any of his inclinations, by which she gained an absolute ascendant over him. She perceived that he had a strong

---

[1] Cf. Keiper, *L'Muséon*, 1885, pp. 212-213 : —" Hérodote tâchait d'expliquer le mieux possible cette habitude qu'il savait être de la plus haute antiquité, parce qu'elle semblait étrange aux Grecs. Il rattacha donc cette innovation prétendue au nom de Cambyse, parce qu'un fait de ce genre lui parut être, conforme au caractère despotique et capricieux de ce prince. Peut-être aussi a-t-il tiré cette information de ceux à qui il devait ses autres renseignements sur Cambyse. Nous reconnaissons ici un procédé pareil, à celui dont Xénophon use régulièrement dans la Cyropédie, quand il vent expliquer l'origine d'une habitude ou d'une institution des Perses qui était réellement ancienne ou qu'il croyait ancienne."—*Cf.* Spiegel's remarks which are herein quoted by me (p. 208).

passion for one of his own daughters named Atossa. He endeavoured, indeed, to conceal it on his mother's account and restrained it in public. Parysatis no sooner suspected the intrigue, than she caressed her grand-daughter more than ever, and was continually praising to Artaxerxes, both her beauty and her behaviour, in which she assured him there was something great and worthy of a crown. At last she persuaded him to make her his wife, without regarding the laws and opinions of the Greeks : ' God,' said she, ' has made you law to the Persians, and a rule of right and wrong.' "

Now, what do we gather from this passage ? Nothing more than that Artaxerxes regarded his passion for his daughter as being in every way hurtful to his reputation, in every way unacceptable to his people or unjustified by law, and, therefore, endeavoured to hide it from his mother as well as the public. Hence we may, likewise, infer that the statements of Herodotus as well as Plutarch harmonize with each other in showing that the marriage of an absolute monarch with a sister or a daughter was an act in which neither the Persian law nor people was acquiescent. If, according to a few scholars, it was a deed not unauthorized by the Avesta,—if it was a practice quite familiar to the Persian people of by-gone ages,—what earthly reasons could have persuaded Cambyses, the most passionate of monarchs, to ask for the decision of the judges on the question, or Artaxerxes to conceal his love for his daughter from the knowledge of his people ? Besides, we have the evidence of Agathias, that Artaxerxes contemptuously declined every offer to contract marriage with his nearest-of-kin relation, on the ground that it was quite inconsistent with the faith of a true Iránian. If we believe this, it is impossible to conceive that such a king could ever have taken his own daughter to wife. On the basis of this very evidence from Agathias, Mr. Wm. Adam observes (F. R., p. 718) :—" But if this could be alleged by Artaxerxes belonging to the royal race, what becomes of the worst charges brought against, not only the

Persian people, but even against the Magians or the ruling class?"[1]

Although Ctesias' books were generally acknowledged by his own countrymen to be teeming with incredible and extravagant fables and fictions—according to Plutarch, with great absurdities and palpable falsity—still we must admit that for the Greek writers who flourished after him no other historian would have been more reliable as regards the family life of Artaxerxes Mnemon than one who lived at the Court of Persia for seventeen years in the quality of physician to that king. Hence it is that most of the Greek historians who followed him, seem to generalize the practice of consanguineous marriage in ancient Irân, probably from Ctesias' coloured narrative of the alleged marriage of Artaxerxes with his daughter. Whatever may be the degree of truthfulness and honesty so far as Ctesias is concerned, it is not impossible to argue, from the character and intrigues of Parysatis, the mother of Artaxerxes, that a slanderous story of the nature described by Ctesias might have been set afloat in the king's harem to

---

[1] The question regarding the alleged marriage of Artaxerxes Mnemon with his daughter, reminds me of a statement of Firdausi, in his well known Persian Epic, the *Shâh-nâmah*, that Behman (Pahl. *Vohûman*), son of Isfandyâr (Av. *Spentô-dâta*, Pahl. *Spend-dâd*), who is also called the Artakhshatar of the Kayânians—hence his identification with Artaxerxes Longimanus and his successors down to Artaxerxes Mnemon—was married to Hûmâî, his daughter. This is a statement which is unique in the *Shâh-nâmah*, nevertheless it is based, however erroneously, on a reference contained in the *Bundahishn*, Chap. XXXIV. 8, which admits of two different ideas on account of the occurrence therein of a word ꜥꜥꜥ *yûkht* or *dûkht*, which is employed in Pahlavi in two different meanings. The Pahlavi passage upon which Firdusi must have relied runs — ꜥꜥꜥ ꜥꜥꜥ ꜥꜥꜥ ꜥꜥꜥ *Hûmâî î Vohûman yûkh*^{t} 30 *shant*. Here the word ꜥꜥꜥ may be read *dûkht* or *yûkht* and it may respectively mean (1) a daughter, (2) one who is coupled or joined in wedlock with another. Thus the passage may be rendered (1) Hûmâî, the daughter of Vohuman, (reigned) thirty years; or (2) Hûmâî, who was coupled with (*i.e.*, married to) Vohûman, (reigned) thirty years. The latter rendering is the more correct interpretation, and also in harmony with the elaborate biography of Behman, written in the reign of سلطان محمود ملکشاه سلجوق Sultân Mahmud Malikshâh Saljûk (Hijra 537-551), and known as the *Bahman nâmah*, which relates that the Hûmâî, whom Vohûman married, was not his own daughter, but the daughter of an Egyptian king named نصرجارث Nasrjârs. The words of the poet run as follows:—

gratify the rancour and most wicked vengeance of the queen-mother against the children of Statira, the innocent victim of her revenge for the murder of her own daughter Amistris, the wife of Terituchmes and sister of Artaxerxes. It is also not improbable that Ctesias' narrative of the marriage of Atossa with her father owed its origin to the vindictive Parysatis alone, and was adopted by a writer who preferred to relate astounding inventions instead of sober truths. Oriental history is not unfamiliar with the malignant accusations of the crime of incest by step-mothers or even by mothers-in-law against their daughters or daughters-in-law. It might, therefore, be inferred that if the Greek writer did not invent any fiction as to the domestic life of the Persian ruler, there was another and a more powerful cause which would have given rise to such an abominable story and established it as sober truth in the mind of the original biographer of Artaxerxes.

Besides this, a few European scholars seem to point to another such instance in the history of Artaxerxes Mnemon. They discover in Ctesias that Terituchmes, the brother-in-law of the king, and husband of Amestris, was married to his sister Roxana. However, with all deference to their scholarship, I may be permitted to draw attention to the original words of the Greek writer, wherein, as far as I am able to comprehend, the notion of marriage is by no means involved.

وزین در فراوان سخنها براند	فرستاد بر زین یل را بخواند
همی پشت من کرد خوارہ تباہ	کہ پدری بنزدیک من یافت راہ
نیامد کس از گور من پدید	چندین روزگارم بپایان رسید
کہ آرام گیرد جہان بر همای	دل من چنان کرد یکبارہ رای
جز آنکی کند کس تو بیند سپاہ	چہ گویی سپارم بدو تخت گاہ
....	....
فراہش مکن بنہ آن و نمای	نگہدار تاج کیان دو همای
از او شہریاری نباید برید	زمین بار دارد چو آید پدید
بنہ بر زمان بر سرش تاج زر	اگر دختر آرد گر آرد پسر
بدندان آن اژدہا کش بگفت	زمانہ سخن در دانش شگفت

According to a passage occurring in the English translation of Plutarch's Lives, by Langhorne (III, p. 451), Ctesias relates:—"Terituchmes, the brother of Statira (the wife of king Artaxerxes II), who had been guilty of the complicated crimes of adultery, incest, and murder, . . . married Hamestris, one of the daughters of Darius, and sister to Arsaces; by reason of which marriage he had interest enough, on his father's demise, to get himself appointed to his Government. But in the meantime he conceived a passion for his own sister Roxana, and resolved to despatch his wife Hamestris." It is said further on, that "Darius, being apprised of this design, engaged Udiates, an intimate friend of Terituchmes, to kill him, and was rewarded by the king with the government of his province." Such is the plain evidence of Ctesias; but it does not assert that Terituchmes was ever married to Roxana. Here is evidently the case of a passion conceived by a licentious brother for his sister. It must, however, be remembered we have again to deal with a story of Ctesias, a story which may naturally be regarded as the outcome of a general hatred at court against Terituchmes, and also as the invention of a motive for his most cruel murder of his wife, the daughter of Parysatis — a queen who had contrived the most wicked means of gratifying her vengeance against her son-in-law and all other unfortunate victims who were suspected of abetting him. Whatever may be the source to which we may trace this story, it is still difficult to determine whether Terituchmes married again at all after having murdered his wife Amestris.

As regards Sysimithres, a single isolated reference in a writer like Curtius is hardly sufficient to claim our attention.

Next we turn to the name that belongs to the period of the Sâsânidæ, a single positive illustration, indeed, of incestuous marriage, according to the Greeks, during the long period of more than 450 years. That name is Kôbâd I., father of the famous king Noshiravân. He is reported by Agathias to have married his daughter Sambyke. However, it is remarkable that neither Professor Rawlinson nor Firdûsi seem to notice this occurrence. Nevertheless, trusting implicitly to the account of Agathias, a writer who was contemporaneous with Kôbâd's son, we must here consider the influences under which the king might have been persuaded to yield to such an act. Let us refer to the history of that part of his reign which described the imposture of Mazdak and the effect which the latter produced upon that weak-minded king by preaching his abominable creed. "All men," Mazdak said, "were, by God's providence, born equal—none brought into the world any property, or any natural right to possess more than another. Property and marriage were mere human inventions, contrary to the will of God, which required an equal division of the good things of this world among all, and forbade the appropriation of particular women by individual men. In communities based upon property and marriage, men might lawfully vindicate their natural rights by taking their fair share of the good things wrongfully appropriated by their fellows. Adultery, incest, theft, were not really crimes, but necessary steps towards re-establishing the laws of nature in such societies." (*Vide* Rawlinson, "The Seventh Great Oriental Monarchy," pp. 342, *seq.*)

Such being the teaching of Mazdak, it is easy to see what attractions it would have for a licentious prince who would willingly substitute it for the moral restraints of his purer faith. Be this as it may, Kôbâd's apostacy was followed by a civil commotion, which ended in the deposition of the king and his imprisonment in the "Castle of Oblivion." Now, does not this successful popular resistance to royal incest and adultery prove that the minds of the Irânians were averse to any violation of the moral law as to the relation between the sexes? There is one important point to be observed in the accounts of Agathias bearing on the doctrines which the Mazdakian heretics professed, *viz.*, his assertion that consanguineous marriages were enormities recently introduced in Irân. If we accept this remark of a contemporary writer, does it not give a death-blow to all preceding authorities? Hence Mr. Adam rightly asserts (F. R., p. 716):—"But if 'those enormities were recent,' this contradicts all the preceding more ancient authorities, which affirm their earlier prevalence from Ctesias downwards."

Now, discarding all the fanciful hypotheses indulged in by speculative thinkers upon early human ideas and practices, I shall make a few assumptions that naturally strike me, while examining the evidences above-mentioned. The first point to be remarked upon is that great care is required to avoid the confusion arising from the indiscriminate use of the words "sister," "daughter," "mother." Among some Oriental people the designation "sister" is not merely applied to a sister proper or daughter of one's own parents, but, as an affectionate term, also to cousins, near or distant, to sisters-in-law, to female friends, &c. Likewise, the word for daughter is used to denote not only one's own daughter but also the daughter of one's own brother or sister, and generally the daughter of a relative, &c. Similarly, the term "mother" does not signify the female parent alone, but it is employed as a respectful form of address to an elderly lady who enjoys the honour of being the materfamilias of a household. It is, likewise, necessary to observe that in Old-Persian or Pahlavi there are rarely any distinct expressions to distinguish sisters from sisters-in-law or female cousins. It is not, therefore, too strained an interpretation to believe that what Herodotus, Ctesias and others supposed to be sisters and daughters, should have been perhaps next-cousins or relations. In the same manner, it might be surmised that a mistake would be made owing to the same name being borne by several female members of a family. Thus the wife and a daughter, or the wife and a sister, or the wife and the mother, having the same name, what was asserted of one might be wrougly applied to the other. Innumerable instances may be found in Parsi families where the name of the mistress of the house coincides with that of one of her daughters-in-law, nieces, &c.

But, one can scarcely infer from the particular illustrations of classical testimony on the subject, which are met with in Herodotus, Ctesias, and Agathias, and are open to many objections, that incestuous marriages were common and legal among the old Irânians as a people, and especially among the Magi. The very statement of the Greeks, that the Achæmenian monarch was supposed to be above the law of the land and of religion, indicates that his adultery or incest was not in accordance with the established institutions of his realm. Nor did the people in the time of Kôbâd I. allow such incest to pass without vehement opposition. Even if we accept the evidence of the Western historians who charge Cambyses, Artaxerxes, Mnemon, Kôbâd, and Terituchmes with incest, it must be noted that these few are the only instances they have been able to gather in the long period of upwards of a thousand years, and that they are insufficient to support so sweeping a generalization as that incestuous marriages were recognized by law, and commonly practised among the old Irânians. It is just as unreasonable as to ascribe the custom of marriage between brother and sister to the civilized Grecians, because we discover references to it in Cornelius Nepos, Demosthenes, and Aristophanes. If the *Mahâbhârata* tells us that the five Pandava princes who had received a strictly Brâhmanic education, were married to one wife, should we, therefore, ignore the existence of the Brâhmanic law,[1] which clearly lays down (Max Müller, " History of Ancient Sanskrit Literature", p. 53; M'Lennan, p. 215) "they are many wives of one man, not many husbands, of one wife," and charge with the custom of polyandry all the ancient Brâhmanic Indians who constituted one of the most eminent and highly intellectual nations of the early Oriental world.

From what I have said above, it is not difficult to see that the doubtful evidences of the Greeks neutralize themselves, and that it is absurd to form, with any reliance upon them, a definite opinion as regards the marriage customs of the old Irânians. I, therefore, repeat my conviction which I have set forth in my first statement—*That the slight authority of some*

---

[1] Compare "Tagore Law Lectures" (1883), by Dr. J. Jolly, p. 155:—" But I have been led recently to consider my views," remarks Dr. Jolly, " by the investigations of Professor Bühler, who has pointed out to me that a certain sort of Polyandry is referred to in two different Smritis. Apastamba (II. 10, 27, 2-4) speaks of the forbidden practice of delivering a bride to a whole family (*kula*). brihaspati refers to the same custom in the same terms." Further on he says :—" The text of Apastamba refers to the custom as to an ancient one, which was enjoined by the early sages, but is now obsolete."

isolated passages gleaned from the pages of Greek and Roman literature, is wholly insufficient to support the odious charge made against the old Iránians of practising consanguineous marriages in their most objectionable forms!

The Meaning of the Avesta word *Hvaêtvadatha*.

II. In proof of the second statement—*That no trace, hint or suggestion of such a custom can be pointed out in the Avesta, or in its Pahlavi Version*—it is first of all necessary to enquire what is the opinion of the Avesta on the subject; whether we are able to trace to any Avestâ precept the alleged custom of next-of-kin marriage in old Irán. According to European scholars, the term that expresses such a marriage is ⟨⟨avestan⟩⟩ *hvaêtvadatha* or *khaêtvadatha* in the Avesta, and ⟨⟨pahlavi⟩⟩ *khvêtúk-dât* (originally *hvêtúkdâd*) or ⟨⟨pahlavi⟩⟩ *khvêtúk-dasíh* in Pahlavi. It has, therefore, been our object to examine the evidence put forward in favour of the European standpoint of *Yasna* XII, 9, (Spiegel's edition, *Ys.*, XIII, 28), which, it is assumed, contain under the word *hvaêtvadatha* an allusion to next-of-kin marriages in question.

In the Avesta the term *hvaêtvadatha* occurs in five passages only, each of which belongs to five different parts of the text, excepting the *Gâthâs*, namely, *Yasna* XII, 9; *Visparad* III, 3; *Vendidâd* VIII, 13; *Yasht* XXIV, 17; and *Gâh* IV, 8 (Westergaard's edition). Of these, the idea expressed in *Gâh* IV is repeated or almost quoted in *Visparad* III, 3, and in *Yasht* XXIV. So we have only to consider three references in the *Yasna*, the *Gâh* and the *Vendidâd* respectively, and to see to what extent they can be used to throw light on the meaning of *hvaêtvadatha*. The word, as it stands in the Avesta, is employed as an epithet or a qualifying word. In one place it forms an epithet of the Avesta religion, in the second an attribute of a pious youth, in the third a qualification for a pious male or female.

Etymologically *hvaêtvadatha* may be regarded as a compound word composed of *hvaêtu* and *datha*, of which the first part may be compared with Skr. *svayam*, Lat. *suus*, Pahlavi *khvísh* and Mod. Pers. *kh'ish*, which are derived from Av. *hva*, Skr. *sva*, Lat. *sibi*, and Eng. *self*. Hence it may originally mean "self," "one's self," "one's own," "a relation," or "a kindred." The second part *datha*, which is equivalent to the Pahl. *das*, comes from the Av. root *dá* "to give," "to make," "to create;" *dath* being properly a reduplication peculiar to the Irânian dialect, from the Indô-Irânian root *dâ* "to give," &c. Thus the derivation of the whole word itself might suggest for it a number of definitions. It may mean "a gift of one's self, or to one's self, or from one's self," "a gift of one's own, or to one's own," "a gift of relationship or alliance," "a making of one's self," or "self-association," "self-dedication," "self-devotion," "self-sacrifice," &c.[1] These are some of the significations which may be indicated on the ground of etymology; however, it is hazardous to choose from them any particular notion without the authority of the native meaning. On applying to the Pahlavi translation of the Avesta to know the meaning attached to the word by early commentators, I am disappointed to find that it affords no more light than can be obtained from a mere Pahlavi transliteration, *khvetûk-dât* or *khvetûk-dasîh*, of the original Avesta expression *hvaêtvadatha*. The reason for this striking omission of any definite interpretation in the Pahlavi version, may perhaps be that the technical meaning of the word was, even centuries after the compilation of the Avesta, a thing too

---

[1] Compare Prof. Darmesteter's remarks on the derivation of the word suggested by Dr. Geldner in his *Ueber des Metrik des jüngeren Avesta (Etudes Irâniennes*, Vol. II., p. 37):—"Parfois les étymologies de l'auteur sont si ingénieuses qu'on est peiné d'être forcé de les repousser ou du moins de les ajourner : le *hraêtradathô*, le marriage entre parents, devient par la simple application d'une loi d'écriture, *hraêtu-radatha*, c'est-à-dire que le mot signifierait étymologiquement la chose qu'il désigne en fait : mais, si tentante que soit l'étymologie pour un sanscritiste, comme *rad* existe en zend, et que par suite, s'il était là, tradition qui connaissait le sens du mot entier n'avait aucune raison de le méconnaître, la forme pehlvie du mot *hraêtûk-daçth* nous prouvera que le mot doit se deviser comme le divisent les manuscrits, en *hraêtva-datha*; ceci rend très douteuse l'étymologie de M. Geldner, qui a d'ailleurs l'inconvénient d'être trop logique et trop conforme au sens : les mots sont rarement des définitions."

familiar to the native Zoroastrians to require any interpretation ; or that the nature of the good work implied by *hvaêtvadatha* was too doubtful in the minds of the old Irânian priests to be definitely and lucidly explained.

Consequently, very little help can be obtained from the indigenous authority of the Pahlavi translation of those Avestâ passages wherein the term *hvaêtvadatha* occurs. Fortunately, however, there is no lack of passages in Pahlavi, which, though sometimes very obscure and difficult, give us a meaning for the first member of the compound, *viz.*, *hvaêtu*, and which is *kh'ish* or *kh'ishih*, meaning "self," "himself," 'one's own" or "kindred," "relation," "individuality," &c. The Pahlavi meaning of "self" or "relation" is still preserved in the Mod. Pers. word *kh'ish*, and accords best with the etymology and the context. Dr. F. Von Spiegel translates *hvaêtu* by "*der Verwandte*" (*Yasna* XXXII. 1, &c.) "the allied or relation," and remarks in note 7, page 125, of his German translation of the Avesta, that it denotes "the spiritual relation to Ahura Mazda, as though one feels himself almost in communion with Him.[1]" It is characteristic that in the Gâthâs the word *hvaêtu* very often stands in connection with the terms *verezenya*[2] and *airyamna*, signifying "an active labourer" fulfilling the desires of Mazda, and "joyful devotion" towards Him (XXXII, 1; XXXIII, 3, 4; XLIX, 7; XLVI, 1; LIII, 4). The Gâthâ XXXII, 1 says:—" Unto Him may the allied[3] aspire, his deeds coupled with devotion." In XXXIII, 3 and 4 Zarathushtra speaks:— (3) " He is the best for the Righteous Lord, O Ahura! who having knowledge, becomes Thy ally, Thy active labourer and Thy true devotee, and who arduously fosters the cow ; it is he who thinks himself to be in the service-field of *Asha* (Righteousness) and *Vohu-manô* (Good Mind)."— (4) " O Mazda!

---

[1] Comp. Zeitschrift der deutschen morgenländischen Gesellschaft, Vol. XVII. (1863 . " Bemerkungen über einige Stellen des Avesta," by F. von Spiegel. pp. 58-69.

[2] According to Pahlavi, *verezenya* may mean "an active neighbour" of the Almighty.

[3] The Rev. Dr. L. H. Mills, " A Study of the Gâthâs," p. 87.:—" (his) Lord kinsman."

I hate whosoever is disobedient and evil-minded towards Thee, disregardful of Thy *ally*, a demon in close conflict with Thy *active labourer*, and the scorner of Thy *devoted one*, the most evil-minded against the nourishment of Thy cow?"

These and several other like passages enable us to understand that *hvaêtu* denotes one of the three spiritual qualifications which are requisite for human sanctity, *viz.*, a communion with the Almighty, the practical fulfilment of His will, and the free mental devotion to Him. Likewise *khetshih i Yazdân*, "relationship or communion with the Deity", is the frequent desire and motive of the pious *Mazdayasna* while discharging his moral or religious duties. It is a gift to which he aspires every moment.

Relying upon this meaning of *hvaêtu*, it is not difficult to assign an idea to *hvaêtva-datha*, which will harmonize with the context and be reconciled with the results of comparative philology. According to the Gâthâs, it can only be "the gift of communion" with the Deity; etymologically, it may also mean "self-association," "self-dedication," &c.[1] In Gâh IV, 8, the term is used as an appellation of piety, where the passage runs—

"I commend the youth of good thoughts, of good words, of good deeds, of good faith, who is pious and a preceptor (lord) of piety; I praise the youth truth-speaking, virtuous

---

[1] Should we attach importance to the meaning in which the word is sometimes found employed in the later Irânian writings, still *khrêtâk dasîh* could hardly denote "next-of-kin marriage." Only marriages between relations, whether near or distant, are therein referred to.

and a preceptor of virtue; I praise the *hvaêtvadatha* youth, who is righteous and a preceptor of righteousness." Here *hvaêtvadatha* can very appropriately bear the idea of a most desirable attribute with which a pious youth might be gifted in the moments of devotion, *viz.*, " a communion with Ahura Mazda," or "self-dedication."—Of the two remaining passages in Avesta, that in *Vendidâd* VIII is so difficult and obscure that almost all the European translators have failed to discern any definite sense in it. Even the Pahlavi does not help us here, because of the mere transliteration of the Avesta words. What is most important to be considered is *Yasna* XII. 9 (Sp. Ys. XIII, 28), a passage in which Prof. F. von Spiegel and several German *savants* who follow his opinion, seem to discover traces of the precept of consanguineous marriage, (*vide* Geiger, *Ostirânische Kultur*, p. 246 ; Justi, *Altbaktrisch*, *s. v.*; Noeldeke, *Encyclopædia Britannica*, Vol. XVIII., *s. v.* Persia ; Geldner, *Metrick*, *s. v.*). I have already remarked upon this passage in the first volume of my English translation of Prof. Wm. Geiger's *Ostirânische Kultur im Alterthum* (p. 66, note), and I beg to repeat that there is not the slightest indication that the passage in question has any reference to conjugal union of any kind ; but, on the contrary, the term *hvaêtvadatha* agreeing with the noun *daêna* " religion" in number, gender, and case, is evidently one of the epithets applied to the *Mazdayasnân* religion, and implies the virtue of that religion to offer the sacred medium of alliance with Ahura Mazda, or self-devotion towards Him. The Pahlavi Commentary plainly tells us that the manifestation of this gift of communion with the Deity on earth was due to Zoroastrism, while every stanza of the Gâthâs extols this highest and noblest ideal of the human spirit in the pious sentiments of Zarathushtra himself (*cfr.* Ys. XXVIII, 3, 4, 6, 7, etc.)

I quote and translate the passage (*Yasna* XII, 9) literally as follows :—

"I extol the Mazda-worshipping religion, that is far from all doubt, that levels all disputes,[1] the sacred one, the *gift of communion* (with God); the greatest, the best, and the purest of all religions that have existed and will exist, which is (a manifestation) of Ahura and of Zarathushtra."

Here it is impossible to conceive the idea of marriage between nearest relations in a passage which glorifies the virtues of a religion. Happily, my own humble conviction has been supported, with reference to the Avesta, by Dr. E. W. West, a scholar whose high and unrivalled attainments in Pahlavi in the European world of letters, will ever be a matter of pride to every English Orientalist. In his essay on the "Meaning of Khvetûk-das," appended to Vol. XVIII of Prof. Max Müller's edition of the "Sacred Books of the East" (pp. 389-430), the learned writer summarizes the result of his examination of all the passages referring to *hvaêtvadatha* in the Avesta in the following manner (*vide* p. 427):—

"The term does not occur at all in the oldest part of the Avesta, and when it is mentioned in the later portion it is noticed merely as a good work which is highly meritorious, without any allusion to its nature; only one passage (*Vendidâd*, VIII, 13) indicating that both men and women can participate in it. So far, therefore, as can be ascertained from the extant fragments of the Avesta—the only internal authority regarding the ancient practices of Mazda-worship—the Parsis are perfectly justified in believing that their religion did not originally sanction marriages between those who are next-of-kin."

---

[1] Comp. S. B. E. Vol. XXXI., Dr. Mill's translation :—"The Faith which has no faltering utterances the Faith that wields the felling halbert" (p. 250).

The References to *Khvêtûk-dât* or *Khvêtûk-dasîh* in Pahlavi.

III. In reference to the third proposition:—*That the Pahlavi passages translated by a distinguished English Pahlavi savant, and supposed to refer to such a custom, cannot be interpreted as upholding the view that next-of-kin marriages were expressly recommended therein; and that a few of the Pahlavi passages which are alleged to contain actual references to such marriages, do not allude to social realities, but only to supernatural conceptions relating to the creation of the first progenitors of mankind*—I beg to call your attention again to the exhaustive essay on this subject by the English Pahlaviist, Dr. E. W. West, who seems to have raked the extensive field of Pahlavi literature, and collected with laborious industry all the Pahlavi passages bearing on the term *khvê'ûk-dasîh*. This learned scholar expresses the result of his patient and useful research in the following words:—

"Unless the Parsis determine to reject the evidence of such Pahlavi works as the *Pahlavi Yama*, the book of *Ardâ-Virâf*, the *Dinkard*, and the *Dâdistân-i-Dinik*, or to attribute those books to heretical writers, they must admit that their priests in the later years of the Sâsânian dynasty, and for some centuries subsequently, strongly advocated such next-of-kin marriages, though probably with little success." (*Vide* S. B. E., Vol. XVIII, p. 428.)

Thus, while Dr. West serves us as a useful champion to guard from any adverse stigma the sublime tenets of the Avesta regarding marriage, while he seems to doubt the authenticity of Greek historians as regards Persian matters (p. 389), we are deprived of his powerful support the moment we enter the field to defend ourselves against the obscure and detached evidences brought from Pahlavi *tomes*. Here I refer to the proofs which are put forward by the Pahlavi savant in support of his personal view that next-of-kin marriages were advocated by Persian priests in the later years of the Sâsânian monarchy.

It must be noticed here that this latter opinion of Dr. West differs completely, as regards the age in which the alleged custom might have prevailed, from what was previously asserted in the first part of his " Pahlavi Texts" (S. B. E., Vol. V, p. 389, note 3), where the learned author observes:—"But it is quite conceivable that the Parsi priesthood, about the time of the Mahomedan conquest, were anxious to prevent marriages with strangers, in order to hinder conversions to the foreign faith, and that they may, therefore, have extended the range of marriage among near relations beyond the limits now approved by their descendants." Again, in a note to the fourth chapter of his English translation of the " Dinâ î Mainû î Khrat," Pahlavi Texts, Part III (S. B. E., Vol. XXIV, p. 26), he says that some centuries before the composition of that book, *i. e.*, long before the reign of Noshiravân, the term *khvêtûk-dasih* was only confined to marriages between first cousins.

But all these remarks, gentlemen, go to show that Dr. West does not agree with other scholars in tracing in the Sacred Writings of the Irânians the existence of such a custom in the times of the Avesta, the Achæmenidæ, the Arsacidæ, or the Sâsânidæ generally; but he gives as his opinion, that it may perhaps have been advocated by some priests in Irân in the sixth century A. D. or later. Thus the speculation of several European savants, from Kleuker downwards, that the custom in question prevailed among the Avesta-people, has been dissipated by the inquiry of one of their own learned body.

However, in his discourse on the "Meaning of Khvêtûk-das," Dr. West attempts to translate about thirty Pahlavi passages to show how far *khvêtûk-dasih* may denote next-of-kin marriage in Pahlavi. Five of these references are contained in the Pahlavi Translation of the Avesta, and two in the Pahlavi Commentary (*Yasna* XII, 9; *Visparad* III, 3; *Gâh* IV, 8; *Vishtâsp Yt.*, § 17; *Vendidâd* VIII. 13; Pahl. gloss to *Ys.* XLIV, 4; and *Bahman Yt.*, Chap. II., 57, 61); eight of them belong to the *Dinkard*, Bk. III, Chapters 80, 193, and 285, Bks. VI, VII, and IX : *Varshtmânsar Nask, Fargard* XVIII, § 27 ; *Bayân*

Nask; Fd. XIV, § 2, XXI, § 9); eight to the *Dádistán-i-Dinik* (Chaps. XXXVII, 82; LXIV, 6; LXV, 2; LXXVI, 4, 5; LXXVII, 6, 7; LXXVIII, 19); three to the *Mainú i Khrat* (Chaps. IV, 4; XXXVI, 7; XXXVII, 12); and one to the Pahlavi *Ravâyet.*

It is needless to point out that of these thirty references more than twenty-two may be excluded from our inquiry, since, according to the result of Dr. West's own survey of them, it is admitted that "there is nothing in those passages to indicate the nature of the good work" meant by the word *khvêtúk-dasíh* (namely, *Ys.* XII. 9; *Vsp.* III, 3; *Gáh.* IV, 8; *Vend.* VIII, 13; *Vishtásp, Yt.*§ 17; *Dk.*, Bk., III, Chaps. 193, 285; *Dk.*, Bk. VI; *Mainú-i-Khrat*, Chaps. IV, 4; XXXVI, 7; XXXVII, 12; and *Bahman Yasht*, II, 57, 61). Besides, the first five passages above-mentioned of the *Dádistán-i-Dinik* contain, according to him, mere "allusions to the brother and sister," who were the first progenitors of mankind. As for the remaining three of the same book, he says, it is not certain that "the term is applied in them to the marriages between the nearest relatives." Consequently, we have to examine only nine passages out of thirty, viz., two of the *Bagán Nask*, one of the *Varshtmânsar Nask*, three of the *Dinkard*, one of the Pahlavi gloss to *Yasna* XLIV, 4, one of the Pahlavi *Ardâ-Virâf*, and one of the Pahlavi *Ravâyet*, which, from the standpoint of Dr. West, contain direct or indirect traces of the practice of marriage between the next-of-kin.

Before we set out to consider these nine references, it will be useful to know the extent to which the work of *khvêtúk-dasíh*—whatever may be its nature or meaning— is extolled or regarded as a righteous or meritorious action in the Pahlavi writings:—

In Chap. IV. of the Pahlavi *Diná i Mâinú i Khrat,* the reply to the question: "Which particular meritorious action is great and good?" is as follows:—"The greatest meritorious action is liberality, and the second is truth and *khvêtúk-dasíh,* the third is the *Gásânbâr,* the fourth is celebrating all the religious rites, the fifth is the worship of the sacred beings, and the providing of lodging for traders." Here *khvêtûk-dasîh*, in connection with liberality and truth, might imply some moral habit almost equal to them in degree of excellence.

The *Shâyast Lâ-shâyast*, Chap. VIII, 18, says: "*Khvêtûk-dâd* extirpates sins which deserve capital punishments." Also it is said by Ahura Mazda elsewhere:—"O Zaratûsht! of all those thoughts, words, and deeds, which I would proclaim, the practice of *khvêtûk-dasîh* is the best to be thought, performed, and uttered."

The *Bahman Yasht*, which may be regarded as one of the oldest Pahlavi works written on the *exegesis* of the Avesta, gives us a clear idea of the term. This idea best harmonizes with our notion regarding the meaning of Ys. XII, 9. It says in Chap. II, 57:—"O Creator! in that time of confusion" (*i. e.*, after the conquest of Persia by the Arabs), "will there remain any people righteous? Will there be religious persons who will preserve the *kûstî* on their waist, and who will perform the *Yazishnê* rites by holding the *Barsams*? And will the religion that is *khvêtûk-das*, continue in their family?" A little further on it says:—"The most perfectly righteous of the righteous will that person be who adheres or remains faithful to the good *Mazdayasnân* religion, whereby the religion that is *khvêtûk-dasîh* will continue in his family." These two passages are supposed by Dr. West to be translations from the original Avesta text of the *Yasht* devoted to the archangel *Vôhu-manô* (S. B. E., Vol. V, Part I, p. 212, note).

In a passage in the *Shâyast Lâ-shâyast* (chap. XVIII, 4), it is declared:—" Whosoever approximates four times to the practice of *khvêtûk-dâd*, will never be parted from Ahura Mazda and the Ameshaspends.

I leave it to you, gentlemen, to say what signification ought to be attached to the word *khvêtûk-dasîh* from its connection with the moral and spiritual conceptions mentioned in the above citations. I need only assert that the moral excellence of *khvêtûk-dasîh* is parallel to truth and sanctity; that its attainment, according to the *Yasna* and *Bahman Yasht*, is by the intermediary of the Zoroastrian religion of Ahura Mazda; and that the approximation to the condition of *khvêtûk-dasîh* is well nigh a participation in spiritual conference with the Almighty and the Ameshaspends or archangels. Consequently, it is a pious and noble gift of which the Zoroastrian conception must be purely moral, and not abominable as is the idea of marriage between the next-of-kin.

Referring to the eight Pahlavi passages under inquiry, it is with some hesitation that I find myself differing from the literal English translation of two of them, *viz.*, the 80th chapter in the third book of the *Dînkard*, and the twenty-first Fargard of the *Bagân Nask*.

The difficulties of interpreting the often highly enigmatic and ambiguous Pahlavi are multifarious[1], and one is often astonished at the totally different versions of one and the same obscure passage, suggested by scholars of known ability, so much so that they appear to be versions of two quite distinct passages having no connection whatever with each other.

---

[1] Comp. S. B. E., Vol. V., Introduction, pp. XVI—XVII.

" The alphabet used in Pahlavi books contains only fourteen distinct letters, so that some letters represent several different sounds; and this ambiguity is increased by the letters being joined together, when a compound of two letters is sometimes exactly like some other single letter. The complication arising from these ambiguities may be understood from the number of sounds, simple and compound, represented by each of the fourteen letters of the Pahlavi alphabet respectively :—

a, â, ha, kha. ba. pa, fa, va. ta, da. cha, ja, za, va. ra, la. za. sa, yī, yad, yag, yaj, dī, dad, dag, daj, gī, gad, gag, gaj, jī, jad, jag, jaj (17 sounds). sha, *sha*, yâ, yah, yakh, ih, īkh, dā, dah, dakh, gā, gah, gakh, jā, jah, jakh (16 sounds). gha. ka, ga, i. m. na, va, wa, ū, ō, ra, la. ya, ī, ē, da, ga, ja.

. . . . There are, in fact, some compounds of two letters which have from ten to fifteen sounds in common use, besides others which might possibly occur. If it be further considered that there are only three letters (which are also consonants as in most Semitic languages) to represent five long vowels, and that there are probably five short vowels to be understood, the difficulty of reading Pahlavi correctly may be readily imagined."

Accordingly, it is permissible to assume that the ambiguous passages adduced by Dr. West, as seeming to allude directly or indirectly to consanguineous marriage, will bear quite another meaning from a still closer research than the first efforts of the learned translator seem to have benefited by. I think, therefore, it is as reasonable as appropriate to defer for the present any attempt on my part to give a definite translation of any of these extensive passages which are acknowledged by Dr. West himself to be obscure and difficult (S. B. E., Vol. V., p. 389), contenting myself with giving briefly what remarks I have to make upon them.

One of these obscure passages constitutes the eightieth chapter in the third book of the *Dinkard*. It is very extensive, and contains a long controversy between a Zoroastrian and a Jew,[1] concerning the propriety or impropriety of the doctrine of the Avesta as regards the creation of mankind, the different uses of the term *khvêtûk-dasih*, &c. Herein it is difficult, owing to the confusion of different ideas as well as to the obscurity of the text, to distinguish the words of the Jew from those of the Zoroastrian. Any sentence that would seem to be a point in favour of the European view, may naturally be ascribed to the Zoroastrian as well as to the Jew. It is not, therefore, easy to determine whether it is the Zoroastrian or the Jew who advocates or condemns a particular position or custom. However the portions wherein both the Translators (Dastur Dr. Peshôtanji and Dr. E. W. West) agree, show that the term *khvêtûkdasih* is technically applied in this passage to supernatural

---

[1] The antagonism between the religious beliefs of the early Jews and those of the Mazdayasnians is well known to the *Dinkard*, the *Mainu î Khrat*, the *Shâyast La-shâyast*, and the *Shikand Gûmânîk Vizâr*. The Mainû î Khrat records the destruction of Jerusalem by Kai Lohrasp and the predominence of the Zoroastrian faith therein. The Shikand Gûmânîk Vizâr points to, some inconsistencies in the Jewish belief regarding the birth of Messiah. Its Chapter, XV, 31, states : "And there are some even" (according to Dr. West's translation) "who say that the Messiah is the sacred being himself. Now this is strange, when the mighty sacred Being, the maintainer and cherisher of the two existences, became of human nature and went into the womb of a woman who was a Jew. To leave the lordly throne, the sky and the earth, the celestial sphere and other similar objects of his management and protection, *he fell for concealment into a polluted and straitened place.*"

unions, what are called the *khvêtûk-dasîh* between the father and the daughter, the son and the mother, the brother and the sister. We know that in the Avestâ, *Spentâ Armaiti* (Pahl. *Spendârmat*) is the female archangel, and as Ahura Mazda is called the Creator and Father of all archangels, *Spendârmat* is, therefore, called His daughter. Now, *Spendârmat* is believed to be the angel of the earth; and since from the earth God has created the first human being, *Spendârmat*, in the later Pahlavi writings, is alleged to have been spiritually associated with the Creator for such a mighty procreation as that of Gayômard, the first man according to Irânian cosmogony. Thus this supposed supernatural union passed into an ideal conception, and technically denoted what is called "the *khvêtûk-dasîh* between the Father and the daughter." Again, it is said that the seed of Gayômard fell into the mother-earth by whom he was begotten. So Mashiah and Mashiâneh were called the offspring of that union between Gayômard and Spendârmat, or of "the *khvêtûk-dasîh* between the son and the mother"; and since the first human pair was formed of brother and sister, *viz.*, Mashiah and Mashiâneh, their union, which was an act in consonance with the Divine Will, came to denote "the *khvêtûkdasîh* between the brother and the sister." This idea of *khvêtûkdasîh*, it must be remembered, is a later development of the abstract and religious notion of a direct spiritual alliance with the Deity, or of self-devotion. The term was afterwards applied to the unions of the first progenitors of mankind, which were believed to have been brought about by the operation of the Creator Himself. In creating man endowed with the knowledge of His Will, it was the Creator's design to raise up an opposition against the morally evil influence of Ahriman on earth. Accordingly, wherever the *khvêtûk-dasîh* between the father and the daughter, the son and the mother, the brother and the sister, are referred to in the later Pahlavi writings, they do not imply any commendation of such unions among ordinary men, but only among the first human beings to whom they were naturally confined, to produce a uniform and pure race of mankind without any promiscuous blending with irrational creatures or animals. What are called the *khvêtûk-dasîh* between the father and the daughter, the son and the mother, the brother and the sister, are, therefore, expressly the supernatural association between *Ahura Mazda* and *Spendármat*, between *Gayômard* and *Spendármat*, and the union between *Mashiah* and *Mashiáneh*.

Now, as to the signification of the word *khvêtûk-das*, the transition from meaning the gift of communion with the Almighty and with the supernatural powers, to meaning the gift of moral union between the human sexes or among mankind generally, is an easy and a natural step. Such an idea of a bond of union in a tribe, race, or family, is suggested by the writer of this eightieth chapter of the Dînkard in question. Notwithstanding, it is in the first passage and in the thirteenth that the English translator seems to have discovered a definite reference to consanguineous marriages. I may, therefore, be allowed to put forward in this place my own interpretation of these paras., to show that it is not next-of-kin marriages that they in any way recommend, but only moral or social union in a tribe, race, family, or near relations; and that the thirteenth passage explicitly condemns incestuous marriages as unlawful practices indulged in by lewd people. My version of the passages is as follows:—

"*Khvêtûk-dasîh* means a gift of communion. Thus honour is obtained, and the union of power acquired by adherents, relatives, or fellow-creatures, through prayers to the Holy Self-existent One. In the treatise on human relationship, it is the (moral) union between the sexes in preparation for, and in continuity to the time of the resurrection. In order that this union might proceed more completely for ever, it should subsist between the innumerable kindred tribes, between adherents or co-religionists, between those who are nearly or closely connected." What follows describes the application of the term to the three kinds of supernatural unions which were necessary for the procreation of a kindred human pair in this world. The passage says: "There were three kinds of *hampatvandîh* 'co-relation,' for example, between the Father (the Deity) and the daughter

(Spendârmat); between the son (Gayômard) and the mother (Spendârmat); between the brother (Mashiah) and the sister (Mashyâneh). These I regard as the most primitive on the basis of an obscure exposition by a high-priest of the good religion."

The succeeding statement gives again a clear explanation regarding the propriety of such unions in the creation of mankind.

The thirteenth passage of the same chapter of the *Dinkard* says:—

"If a son be born of a son and a mother, he (the begetter) would be reckoned the brother as well as the father; that would be illegal and incestuous (‍ *jêh*). If so, such a person has no part in the prayers (of the Deity) and in the joys (of Paradise); he produces harm, and does thereby no benefit; he is extremely vicious and is not of a good aspect." (*Cf.* Dastur Peshotanji's Translation of the Dinkard, Vol. II, p. 97.)

It must also be observed that the allusion in this same passage to an *Arumân* or an inhabitant of Asia Minor, somewhat strengthens the opinion of the translator of the Dinkard as to the advocacy of the Jew himself for the marriage with a daughter, sister, &c. Dr. West admits that, in the portion where anything like "conjugal love" is meant, "marriages between first cousins appear to be referred to" (p. 410). The passage runs as follows:—"There are three kinds of affection between the offspring of brothers and sisters" (see Dr. West's rendering, p. 404) "one is this, where it is the offspring of brother and brother; one is this, where the offspring is that of brothers and their sisters; and one is this, where it is the offspring of sisters."

It is only to this passage, or to the period when it may have been composed, that we can ascribe the development of the idea of marriage relationship between cousins attached to the term *khvêtûk-dasîh* under the erroneous interpretation of its ambiguous paraphrase *khvîsh-dehêshnih*, which occurs in it. Here the term implies the different degrees of union—first, between supernatural powers and the Deity; next, between supernatural

powers and mankind; then, between the first man and woman,
—hence the bond of moral or social union in a tribe, race, or
family. The later interpretation, however, confines, as is
expressly indicated in the Persian *Raváyets*, love or marriage
union among mankind only to such of the cousins as are
described in the quotation mentioned in the precedig para.
The idea of *khvêtûk-dâd*, denoting an act of forming relationship between cousins, has rarely been expressed again in the
subsequent Pahlavi writings, nevertheless it has been preserved
in the later Persian *Raváyets* by *Kámah Behreh, Káus Kámah*,
and *Narimân Húshang*.

Now, regarding the passage in the earlier part of the
fourteenth *Fargard* of the *Bagān Nask*, it may well be remarked that the *khvêtûk-dasîh* of *Spendārmat* and *Ahura Mazda*
here referred to is again, according to Dr. West's translation,
an allusion to the communion of two spiritual powers for the
creation of man, and not an indication of marriage between a
father and a daughter. Dr. West, likewise, observes (p. 196):
—" This quotation merely shows that *khvêtûk-das* referred to
connection between near relations, but whether the subsequent
allusions to the daughterhood of *Spendârmat* had reference to
the *khvêtûk-das* of father and daughter is less certain than in
the case of the Pahlavi *Yasna*, XLIV, 4." The same might
also be said concerning the passage from the seventh book of
the *Dînkard*, mentioned at page 412, [1] where we are informed,
as Dr. West remarks only about the *khvêtûk-dasîh* of Mashiah
and Mashiâneh.

Likewise, concerning the passage inserted irrelevantly in the
Pahlavi Commentary to stanza 4, Yasna, Chapter XLIV, which
refers to the *fatherhood of Ahura Mazda* and to the *daughterhood
of Spendârmat*. The passage is rendered by Dr. West (p. 393)
thus:—

" Thus I proclaim in the word that [which he who is Aûharmazd made his own] best [*Khvêtûk-das*]. By the aid of righteousness Aûharmazd is aware who created this one [to perform

---

[1] *Vide* S. B. E. Vol. XVIII.

Khvêtûk-das]. And through fatherhood (of *Aûharmazd*) Vôhuman (referring to Gayômard) *was* cultivated by him, [that is, for the sake of the proper nurture of the creatures, *Khvêtûk-das was* performed by him]. So she who is his (Aûharmazd's) daughter is acting well, [who is the fully-minded] Spendârmat, [that is, she did not shrink from the act of *Khvêtûk-das*]. She was not deceived, [that is, she did not shrink from the act of *Khvêtûk-das*, because she is] an observer of every thing [as regards that which is Aûharmazd's, [that is, through the religion of Aûharmazd *she* attains to all duty and law]."

From this quotation it is easy to see that here the reference is plainly to the particular supernatural *khvêtûk-dasîh* of *Ahura Mazda* and *Spendârmat,* and not to any practice of consanguineous marriage among the old Irânians.

The passage in the latter part of the eighteenth Fargard of the *Varsht-mânsar Nask,* evidently describes, as the heading,

ارم امرامل امشاضرفاشن شه *madam stâêishnô frashôkartô ziman,* actually indicates, the nature of the resurrection of the first parents of mankind, *viz.,* Mashîah and Mashiâneh, their birth and union after the entire annihilation of evil, and the renovation and the reformation of the human world.

In reference to the passage in the Pahlavi *Ravâyet,* however, it may be suggested that the Pahlavi expression *khvêtûk-dasîh levatman bordâr va bentman vabîdûntan,* as used in a couple of sentences, might well denote the exercise of the gift of communion with the Almighty, or self-devotion, in association with one's mother, daughter, or sister ; in a word, it must have been considered as highly commendable and meritorious that a whole Zoroastrian household should be given to devotion or pious resignation to the Will of the Supreme Lord of the Zoroastrian religion.

There now remain two passages which claim our particular attention. One of these belongs to the book of the *Ardâ Virâf,* another to the *Dinkard* in the twenty-first Fargard of the

Bagân Nask. The passage in Virâf in which European scholars discover the alleged practice of marriage between brothers and sisters, runs as follows :—" Virâf had seven sisters, and all these seven sisters were like a wife unto Virâf"—They spoke thus : " Do not this thing, ye *Mazdayasna*, for we are seven sisters and he is an only brother, and we are all seven sisters like a wife unto that brother." Here arises an important question, whether it is possible to conclude hence that those seven sisters were actually married to Virâf, or that they were merely dependent upon him for their sustenance, just as a wife is dependent upon her husband. It is, indeed, characteristic that the sisters do not call Virâf their husband, but their brother, and they further regret that the disappearance of their brother from this life should deprive them of their only support in this world. Again, the Pahlavi word ܘܩ *chigûn*, " like, " implies a condition similar to that of a wife and not the actual condition of a wife. Such an expression of similarity was quite unnecessary, if those sisters were actually the wives of Virâf. On the other hand, there is a difference in the words of the two oldest texts from which all subsequent copies were transcribed. A copy which is preserved in the collection of Dr. Haug's MSS., and dated *Samvat* 1466, has quite a different word, *zanán*, "wives" in the place of *akhtman*, "sister." If we should accept the former word, the meaning would be " Virâf had seven wives, who were all sisters." By-the-bye it is difficult to conceive how Virâf, one of the most pious men of his day, should have been so luxurious or licentious as to take as his wives all his seven sisters, an instance altogether unparalleled in the whole history of Ancient Persia. The passage in question, I believe, expressly points to an instance of the dependent condition of women not unknown to the Zoroastrian community, of unmarried sisters or daughters being wholly supported in life by parents, a brother, or even a brother-in-law. It rather represents an extreme case of rigid seclusion on the part of Virâf and his austere exercise of acts of piety, devotion, and self-denial.

The next passage which is assumed by the English translator to be a reference to the marriage of a father and a daughter and "too clear," according to him, "to admit of mistake, though the term *khvêtûk-das* is not mentioned," is cited from the middle of the *Vahishtôk Yasht* Fargard of the *Bagân Nask*. The contents of this Fargard are summarized in a Pahlavi version of it, and found about the end of the *Dinkard*. Regarding this ambiguous citation, it may be observed that it admits of more than two significations, the choice between which is made to suit the particular construction and interpretation adopted by the translator. Generally speaking, this twenty-first Fargard of the *Bagân Nask* seems to esteem, among other acts of religious credit, the exaltedness of a modest attitude of respect, which a woman observes towards her father or husband. "*Tarsgásih bên abitar va shôê*" is an expression which denotes, literally, "awful respect to one's father or husband," and is a special point of female morals frequently urged in the sayings of the ancient Irânian sages or high priests. The same idea appears to have been inculcated by this passage of the *Bagân Nask*, which, if rendered accordingly, would put forward a meaning quite different from the one expressed by Dr. West, whose version of the Pahlavi text runs as follows (p. 397):—

"And this, too, that a daughter is given in marriage to a father, even so as a woman to another man, by him who teaches the daughter and the other woman the reverence due unto father and husband."

According to my humble interpretation, the passage would convey quite a different idea. I translate the passage thus:—

"*And this, likewise (is a virtuous act), that a woman pays respect to another man (or stranger), just as it is paid by a daughter to her father, in her womanhood or married condition, through him who teaches his own daughter or any other woman respect towards one's father or husband.*"

Here we have a religious position ascribed to a person who inculcates on women a modest and respectful behaviour towards male strangers and nearest male relations. This passage does not expressly imply any notion of marriage; on the contrary, it points to modest reverence which in every Oriental community is due from a woman to a male stranger, from a wife to her husband, or from a daughter to her father, &c.

Even if we should accept the interpretation of Dr. West— as one might be constrained to do by the ambiguity, obscurity, or erroneous transcription of the original text of all the Pahlavi passages under inquiry—still it would be difficult to prove that next-of-kin marriages were actually practised in Irân even "in the later years of the Sâsânian monarchy." His statement only indicates that incestuous marriages were merely advocated[1] by one or more Pahlavi writers on account of their misapprehension of the Avestâ tenets, and also "with very little success."

Finally, in support of the view that even the genuine Pahlavi writings do not proclaim as meritorious a practice which in the eye of reason and culture is highly discreditable, I may be allowed to adduce a passage from the seventh book of the *Dinkard*, on the supernatural manifestations of Zoroaster's spiritual powers. This passage expressly ascribes to the Mazdakian followers the vicious practice of promiscuous intercourse between the sexes, denouncing those who indulged in it as of the nature of wolves or obnoxious creatures. In the divine revelation communicated to the prophet Zarathushtra by Ahura Mazda, and recorded as such in the *Dinkard*, about the changes and events which were to happen during the millenniums that followed the age of Zoroaster, there is one which predicts as a calamity to befall the religious welfare of the early Sâsânian period, the birth of Mazdak in this world, the abominable influence of his creed and the consequent beastly condition of his imbecile adherents. The passage in question may be rendered as follows:—

("Ahura Mazda spoke") : "And again of the adversaries of the *Mazdayasnân* religion, and of the disturbers of piety, the

---

[1] This may well be ascribed to the ignorance or erroneous notions of the subsequent Pahlavi copyists.

Aharmôg (Mazdak) and they who will be called also Mazdakians. . . . . .will declare one's offspring as fit for mutual intercourse, that is, they will announce intercourse with mothers, and they will be called wolves, since they will act like wolves, they will proceed according to their lustful desire just as one born of the wolf does with its daughter or mother, and they will also practice intercourse with their mothers, their women will live like sheep or goats."

This revelation plainly indicates how abhorrent the practice of promiscuous intercourse between the sexes, was to the idea of the early Zoroastrians, and that it was to be expressly the teaching of a heretic who was to rise for the annihilation of the social morality of the Sâsânian Irân, and to preach to the imbecile monarch Kôbâd I. what, according to the *Ahuramazdian* revelation, was believed to be the detestable doctrine of sexual intercourse between the next-of-kin. Such was not the creed of the primitive Zoroastrism, but of its opponents and enemies, of Mazdak and his immoral beastly followers.

THE NOBLE IDEA OF THE MARRIAGE RELATIONSHIP IN THE AVESTA.

IV.—Finally, in support of the theory that the Avesta comprehends a purer and nobler idea of the marriage-relationship, no better proof could be adduced than a stanza in the Gâthâs, wherein, according to Dr. Wm. Geiger, the bond of marriage is regarded "as an intimate union founded on love and piety." This stanza must have formed part of the marriage-formula which seems to have been recited by Zoroaster on the occasion of the celebration of the marriage between the Prophet's daughter *Pouruchishtâ* and *Jâmâspâ*[1]:—

---

[1] The Pahlavi Commentary to stanza 4 of the Yasna, chap. LIII., says:—
Avash valmanich aê abû rái rástryûshân kári [*aigh katê-khûdâêih rái*] *aêdûnich avô nafshman* [*ash tan pavan nishmanih bará yehabûnishnô*], *aharûbô* [*Pôrúchistô*] *avo valman i aharôbo* [*Jâmâspô*] *yehabûn*.

" Admonishing words I say unto the marrying maiden,

"And to you (the youth), I who know you. Listen to them,

" And learn to know through the laws of religion the life of a good mind ;

"In piety you shall both seek to win the love of each other, only thus will it lead you to joy ! " (*Yasna* LIII., 5 ;[1] *vide* my " Civilization of the Eastern Irânians, " Vol. I., p. 62.)

Although the Avestâ text, of which the larger portion is destroyed or lost, is a scanty collection of fragments in its present condition, still there is no lack of references which show us that the custom of contracting marriages amongst the Irânians in the age of the Avestâ, cannot at all be reconciled with any theory of incestuous wedlock. The expression *moshu-jaidhyamna*, "courting or solicitation," direct or indirect, for the hand of a maiden, and its root *vadh* or *vaz*, "to convey or take home the wife" (*ducere puellam in matrimonium*), presuppose that intermarriage between different families or citizens was not unknown to the Avesta-nation. The idea of conveying a bride to the house of the bridegroom, which is implied in the Av. root *vadh* (signifying in the Zend-Avesta " to marry"), implicitly contradicts the notion of several European scholars that the Avesta people were fond of marrying in their own family only, and with their nearest relations. Besides, the moral position of the wife in the Irânian household, was in no way inferior to that of an English *materfamilias*. Similar as she was in rank to her husband, her chastity was an ornament to the house, and her piety and participation in private and public ceremonies a blessing. Moreover, the prayer of an Irânian maiden imploring the *Yazata Vayu* for a husband, does not at all allude to any desire for marrying a next-of-kin relation, but simply an Irânian youth who may be valiant, wise, and learned :—

---

[1] The last verse is translated by Dr. Mills : "(And to you, bride and bridegroom), let each one the other in Righteousness cherish ; thus alone unto each shall the home-life be happy."—(*Vide* S. B. E., Vol. XXXI., p. 192.)

"Grant us this grace, that we may obtain a husband, a youthful one, one of surpassing beauty, who may procure us sustenance as long as we have to live with each other; and who will beget of us offspring; a wise, learned, and ready-tongued husband" (*vide* my C. E. Irânians, p. 61; Yt. XV, 40).

Further, there is no trace of consanguinity in *Vendidâd*, chap. XIV., where one of the meritorious acts of a Zoroastrian priest or layman, is to give his daughter in marriage to any pious *Mazdayasna*. It is characteristic that wherever the subject of marriage is alluded to in the Avestâ the word *hvaêtvadatha* is never mentioned. It is also to be remembered that Zarathushtra having six children born to him, three sons and three daughters, did not think of marrying his own son with his own daughter, nor did he ever take his own mother or one of his own daughters to wife. If it was actually the creed of the Prophet, Zoroaster ought to have realized it first of all in his own family and among his primitive supporters.

The question as regards the existence of the practice of consanguineous marriages in ancient Irân, will not, I hope, create a difficulty for any longer time. Not only has the meagre testimony upon it of Greek and Roman historians been shown to be unreliable and erroneous, but also the attempt to trace it to the old Irânian Sacred Books, *viz.*, the Zend-Avesta, has entirely failed.

So long as no cogent proofs are brought to bear on the question, sufficient to convince a student of Irânian antiquities or religion, I shall be content with the arguments or remarks I have been able to put forward on the other side, repeating at the conclusion of this paper the convictions with which I set out, *viz.* :—

I. That the *slight authority of some isolated passages* gleaned from the pages of Greek and Roman literature, is wholly insufficient to support the odious charge made against the old Irânians of practising consanguineous marriages in their most objectionable forms.

II. That no trace, hint, or suggestion of a custom of next-of-kin marriage can be pointed out in the Avestâ or in its Pahlavi Version.

III. That the Pahlavi passages translated by a distinguished English Pahlavi savant, and supposed to refer to such a custom, cannot be interpreted as upholding the view that consanguineous marriages were expressly recommended therein That a few of the Pahlavi passages, which are alleged to contain actual references to such marriages, do not allude to social realities but to supernatural conceptions relating to the creation, and to the first progenitors of mankind.

IV. That the words of our Prophet himself, which are preserved in one of the stanzas of the Gâthâ, chap. LIII., express a highly moral ideal of the marriage-relationship.

THE PRESIDENT'S OPINION.*

The Honourable Sir Raymond West,[1] in proposing a vote of thanks to the lecturer, said :—You will all agree with me that the paper that has been just read is a very important one, and we are very much indebted to Mr. Sanjana for reading it and adding so much to the treasures of the Society. I hope it will be ranked amongst the papers which deserve to be printed and enshrined in our records. There is a special appropriateness in a Parsee priest bringing forward the subject which affected the honour and credit of his race and religion, and I can scarcely imagine that the work could have been done with better spirit, greater clearness, and better appreciation of the historical and scientific evidentiary method in which to go to work upon a task of that particular kind.

---

* [*Extract from the Proceedings of the Bombay Branch Royal Asiatci Society for the month of April* 1887.] There were present on the occasion : Sir Jamshedji Jijibhai, Bart., C.S.I., Mr. Justice Jardine, Mr. C. E. Fox, Mr. Kharshedji Fardunji Parakh, Mr. Sorabji Shapurji Bengali, C.I.E., Sir Jehangir Kavasji Jehangir Readymoney, Dr. J. G. da Cunha, Mr. Kharshedji Rustomji Cama, Mr. Jamshedji Bahmanji Wadia, Surgeon Steele, Dr. Atmaram Pandurang, Dr de Monte, Mr. Jamshedji Kharshedji Jamshedji, Segnior O. S. Pedraza, Mr. Javerilal Umiashankar Yajnik, and others.

[1] He is now Vice-President of the Royal Asiatic Society of Great Britain and Ireland.

I cannot pretend to the knowledge of Zend and Pahlavi that would enable me to discuss with any profit the proper sense of the much-debated expression on which Mr. Sanjana has expended such close and searching criticism. I will but offer a few remarks on the general aspects of the question which he has handled with so much learning and zeal. It is evident, on a reference to Herodotus, who is the only one of the Greek writers quoted to whom I have been able to make a direct reference, but equally evident from the, no doubt, correct quotations from the other Greek authors, that they wrote rather from loose popular stories, and with a view to satisfy their reader's taste for the marvellous than from a thorough and critical examination of the subject of consanguineous marriages as one of momentous importance.

Herodotus has been confirmed in so many instances in which it seemed most unlikely that he has gained, and well deserves just confidence whenever he relates anything as within his personal knowledge; but of the subject of King Cambyses' marriage, he must needs have gathered his information at secondhand. The other Greek writers hardly profess to do more than retail their stories out of a stock gathered with industry no doubt, but entirely without the control of the critical spirit which in modern times we have learned to consider so indispensable. Ctesias, who must have known a great deal about Persia and its people, from original observation, has told so many undoubted falsehoods that his evidence is unworthy of credit on any contested point. The first sources of European information on the subject before us are thus remarkably unsatisfactory, yet it is to be feared that it is with impressions derived from these sources that the Western scholars have approached the Parsee literature. So influenced they may very naturally have construed the mysterious and rare phrases supposed to involve a sanction of incestuous unions, in a frame of mind which had led to illusions such as the Dastur has insisted on and striven to dispel.

One would gather from the narrative in Herodotus that the marriage of Cambyses was of a kind to startle and shock the sensibilities of his people—else why recount it? That would indicate very probably the survival in the popular legends, drawn from a pre-historic time, of some ancient tale of wrong which the popular fancy was pleased to annex to a king who had played so great a part and had so terrible a history as Cambyses. In almost every country one may observe a tendency, when some ruler or chief has taken a strong hold of the popular imagination, to tack on to his biography any floating legend that wants a personal centre that story-tellers and readers can clothe with a certain reality. In England the group of legends that gathers round the British hero, King Arthur, affords an illustration of this. Some scholars have assigned a similar origin to the stories of Achilles and Odysseus in the two great poems commonly ascribed to Homer. At a later time many stray legends went to add to the glory of Robin Hood, and in Ireland still unowned achievements of daring and ferocity are commonly assigned to Cromwell. In Eastern countries the sovereign and the royal family are looked on— and still more were looked on—as standing so entirely apart from the common people, that any tale of wonder or horror would almost inevitably be connected with them. They really do so many things exceeding ordinary experience, that listeners of uncritical character, not knowing where to draw the line, would accept without question statements of other things quite uncredible or even unnatural.

It must be admitted, too, that these Eastern monarchs and royal families might easily learn in ancient times, as they have in modern times, to think there was something sacred about their persons which made ordinary offences no sins in them. A course of adulation and superiority to legal coercion readily breed a contempt of moral restraints. It commonly produces an inordinate pride. We might thus have a Persian prince indulging in unions like the king of Egypt and the Incas of Peru, which would, after all, be only in them the practice, or the casual excesses, of tyrants besotted with despotic power. Germany in the last century was full of royal foulness, which yet stood quite apart from the general life of the people. Unbridled lust disturbs the reason almost more than any other passion. History abounds in instances of it, and if Persian despots and their children were sometimes incestuous in their moral delirium, we should not be justified in reasoning from such instances to any custom of the people. The stories rather imply that these excesses were startling, and probably revolting, as were the tales at one time current about James the Sixth of Scotland and First of England.

If one applies to the narratives of the Greek writers, the tests by which one would pronounce on the guilt or innocence of an accused, it may, I think, safely be said the evidence is insufficient.

It would then surely be *wrong to convict an otherwise highly moral nation*, endowed with fine sensibilities, of a revolting practice, *on the testimony on which one would not condemn a pick-pocket*.

It is very likely, indeed, that the ancient Persians, like other nations, before their emergence from the savage state, looked without disfavour on connexions that we now cannot think of without a shudder. The prevalence of family polyandry is as well authenticated as any fact in Anthropology. The ancient Britons had one or more wives for a group of brothers, so had the Spartans. A similar arrangement prevails among some of the Himalayan tribes, and traces of it are to be found in the Hindu law literature. The children in such cases are formally attributed to the eldest brother. A communal system, under which all the females were common to the tribe, seems in many cases to have preceded the family polyandry on the arrangements that we may see still amongst the Nairs. Where such a system prevailed it would very often be impossible to say whether a young woman about to be taken by a young man was or was not his sister. If she had been borne of a different mother, she could not be more than his half-sister, and as civilization advanced and the family was founded on the basis of single known paternity, the half-sister in Greece continued to be regarded as a proper spouse for her half-brothers.

A marriage of such persons furthered the policy of the Greek statesmen by keeping the family estates together. Amongst the Jews also, who, as we know, recognized the levirate which the Hindus first commanded and afterwards condemned, union with a half-sister by a different mother must have been recognized as allowable, at any rate by dispensation from the chief in David's time. This is evident from the story of Amnon and Tamar; and we may gather that the practice had once been common. In the Polynesian Islands there are tribes of which all the women are common to all the men of other particular tribes. When the children, as commonly, take their classification from the mother, it is obvious that consanguineous unions must be frequent. They seem even to be regarded in some cases as connected with religious needs, since at certain festivals all restraints on licentiousness are cast aside even amongst males and females of the same family who do not ordinarily even speak to each other.

There seems to be everywhere tendency to connect sexual anomalies with the mysteries of religion, and with persons of extraordinary national importance. The account given of the parentage of Moses, if taken literally, makes him the offspring of a nephew and an aunt. Beings who are so highly exalted are supposed to be quite beyond the ordinary standard.

Both these sources of legends may have been in operation in ancient Persia, as it was known, and but superficially known to the Greeks. There too, no doubt, as elsewhere, the transition from female to male gentileship was attended with a period of great confusion. A similar change took place, it seems, amongst the Hindus at a very early time; and in Greece Orostes is almost inclined to insist that he was not related to his own mother. As one set of relationships took the place of another, many apparently strange connections would be formed which yet would not really be incestuous when properly understood. Language would adapt itself, as we see in fact it did, but imperfectly, to the change of the family system. The Greeks probably knew Persian very imperfectly. In this country the young civilian is continually puzzled by finding words of relationship received in a much wider sense than their usual English equivalents, and the Greeks may well have found equal difficulty in catching the precise sense of Persian terms of relationship in the tales that were told to them. Their own system would make them take some narratives as quite rational, which to us are revolting; in other cases the strangeness of the story told of a king or prince would prevent a critical examination of the terms employed. It would be welcome just in proportion as it was outrageous.

It seems likely that such considerations as these may not have been allowed due weight by European scholars in their interpretation of the few passages in which an ambiguous phrase seems to countenance the notion that incest is recommended. I venture to suggest, as I have been able to do in my conversation with my learned friend, Mr. Sanjana, that a sense akin to that of *svyamdatha* in Sanskrit—an idea of self-devotion, varying according to the context in its precise intention—would satisfy the exigencies of all or nearly all the doubtful passages. This, however, is no more than a speculation: I cannot judge its worth. I can only thank Mr. Sanjana on behalf of the Society, and most sincerely, for the very valuable addition he has contributed to our transactions. I trust it will form a new starting-point in history and criticism by the view it presents to European scholars.

OPINIONS.

"I have examined your translation of Dr. Geiger's 'Zarathushtra in den Gâthâs' in the specimens sent me. In a few passages in order to attain an easier style you have given a free rendering of the original German; but so far as my examination has gone you have caught both the meaning and the spirit of the original throughout and have succeeded in reproducing in excellent readable English this learned German thesis on a subject of admitted difficulty. You deserve to be congratulated on the success with which you have accomplished your difficult task."—*The Rev. Dr. D. Mackichan.*

"Having been favoured with an inspection of the proof-sheets of your translation of Professor Geiger's Essay on "Zarathushtra in the Gâthâs," I have much pleasure in expressing the satisfaction I have felt in the perusal of so carefully written and so scholarly a work. It deals with a subject of greatest importance to the Parsi community, and one on which many Europeans in this country will be glad to obtain precise information in a well-arranged form. It will be evident that the Essay of Professor Geiger is of special excellence and displays much originality of thought, and it may indeed be called the first serious attempt to treat the theology of the Gâthâs with really scientific exactitude. Your rendering of the often difficult German text is a task of great merit. I have read the tanslation with great pleasure, and can cordially recommend it to the perusal of all Parsis desirous to get a deeper insight into the many excellent and lofty doctrines expounded in the most ancient of their sacred books."—*The Rev. Dr. Alois Führer.*

"I have already read over the greater part of your version, and find it remarkably well done. That a Parsi priest should succeed so well in rendering a German scientific work into idiomatic English, is truly a most creditable fact for the Mazdean Community of Bombay. I read with particular interest your own notes and additions, most of which are deserving of very careful consideration from European *savants*. I hope soon to see the continuation of your very important work, besides many other original productions which will be of value for the promotion of Avestic and Pehlevi studies in India and in England. Meanwhile let me sincerely congratulate you on what you have already so brilliantly achieved."—*The Rev. Dr. L. C. Casartelli.*

" I should have thanked you before now for the very handsome and interesting volume, the fruits of your meritorious industry, which you were kind enough to send me last week. * * * * * A full exhibition of the details and most characteristic developments of any one of the religious systems which have helped to form the character and shape the destinies of men possesses an abiding interest which is felt even by those who do not exactly regard the revival or purification of the existing historical religions as an indispensable condition of future progress. But undoubtedly whatever makes these religions more rational, and therefore more truly spiritual, is matter for congratulation This, I think, your labours will help to effect, and I greatly hope they may be appreciated by your countrymen."—*Dr. Wm. Wordsworth.*

To The Secretary to the SIR JAMSHETJI J. ZARTOSHTI MADRESSA.

SIR,—I have the honour to inform you that according to your request I examined Mr. Darab Dastur Peshotan Sanjana in the German language. The book which he had read for this purpose was "Goethe's *Wanderjahre.*" Goethe, as you are well aware of, is one of the most difficult of the German classical writers. But in spite of the difficulties presenting themselves to a beginner, Mr. Sanjana translated several passages with great skill and knowledge into idiomatic English. I then tried him in other passages out of the works of the same author *Prose* as well as *Poetry*, and to my astonishment he distinguished himself also there. After a short time of meditation about the passage proposed he gave a true and sensible translation.

Mr. Sanjana is certainly to be congratulated upon the remarkable progress he made in the course of three years by his great diligence joined with natural talent for languages.—*Yours, &c.,*

E. USTERI, S. J.

" We have to thank the translator for an excellent version of a most interesting book. Dr. Geiger has devoted much earnest labour to the investigation of the history and religion of the primitive Zoroastrians. Indeed, there are few more interesting histories than that which belongs to the development of the Zoroastrian faith among the early inhabitants of Eastern Iran. The translator has done his work admirably, expressing the German original in singularly clear, terse, and idiomatic English. He has also added some very valuable notes."—*Guardian.*

"A considerable contribution to Oriental study."—*Scotsman.*

"Dr. Wilhelm Geiger's extensive and careful researches into the religion and life of the primitive Zoroastrians have excited much interest throughout Europe, and his great work is well known to all who are occupied in kindred studies. Those who cannot read German easily will now be able to read a good English translation, which is doubly valuable from the fact of the writer being a Parsee, and therefore naturally understanding and sympathising with the subject and being able occasionally to correct errors of the author. The translation will be valuable even to those who possess the work in the original German."—*Westminster Review.*

"A German scientific work translated into English by a Parsi priest is a novelty in literature; and when to this is added the fact that the original work is the best and most complete that has been written on the subjects of which it treats, and that the translation is as good as can be expected from any Englishman, it may safely be recommended as a book well worth perusal by any one who wishes to learn all that can be really ascertained from the *Avesta* texts about the manners and customs of the ancient Zoroastrians. A short but comprehensive essay on the religion of the *Avesta*, its sacred beings and demonology, has been contributed by Dr. Geiger as an introduction to the English translation, and forms by no means the least interesting part of the work."—*Dr. E. W. West in the 'Academy.'*

"It is a pleasure, in passing, to refer to the debt of gratitude which Eranian scholars owe both to the High-Priest (Dastur Dr. Peshotan) himself for his various editions of hitherto inaccessible Pehlevi texts, and to his accomplished son Darab Dastur, for the really excellent English versions and editions of the German writings of Spiegel and Geiger, on Avestic subjects,—particularly his handsome translation of the latter's *Civilization of the Eastern Iránians in Ancient Times,* of which the second volume has just appeared."—*The Babylonian and Oriental Record.*

[*Extracted from the Journal of the Royal Asiatic Society of Great Britain and Ireland.*]

KÂRNÂME-I ARTAKHSHIR-I PÂPAKÂN; the Pahlavi Text, with transliteration, English and Gujarāti translations and introductions; also an appendix, including extracts from the Shāh-nāmeh. By DĀRĀB DASTUR PESHOTAN SANJANA. 8vo, pp. 269. (Bombay, 1896.)

This historical romance was first translated into Gujarāti by the learned father of its present editor; his translation was published at Bombay in 1853, and has now been so thoroughly revised as to be practically rewritten. The Pahlavi text was also translated into German by Professor Nöldeke, from copies of the same MSS., and this translation was published at Göttingen in 1878.[1] But the original text is now printed for the first time, with transliteration, translations, and corresponding passages from the Shāh-nāmeh, specially for the use of College students in Bombay, and also for Pahlavi scholars and readers in general. For the students it appears very suitable, as the simple narrative style of the text presents few difficulties to a competent reader, beyond the identification of some names of persons and places.

Before Pahlavi MSS. of the Kārnāmak had become known to scholars it was generally assumed when the work was mentioned by a Persian writer, that it must have been a chronicle of events written by Artakhshīr himself. Thus Richardson (in his Dissertation on the Literature of Eastern Nations, p. vi) states that Artakhshīr "wrote a Kār-nāmah, or journal of his achievements," which "was afterwards improved by Nōshirvān the Just." But all the three translators have come to the conclusion that this Pahlavi Kārnāmak can only be a narrative drawn up, from the original records of Artakhshīr (as the first words of the Pahlavi text actually assert), probably in the time of Khusrō Nōshirvān, or perhaps rather later. And the editor of this edition suggests that Buzurg-Mihir, Khusrō's chancellor, may have been the epitomizer of the older records.

The contents of this Pahlavi Kārnāmak are briefly as follows :—After the death of Alexander there were 240 rulers in Irān, of whom Ardavān, in Stākhar, was the chief. Pāpak was frontier governor of Pārs, and had no son ; while Sāsān, of the race of Dārā, descendant of Darius, was his shepherd ; but he did not know that Sāsān was of the race of Dārā. On three successive nights Pāpak was disturbed by different dreams about Sāsān, and sent for the interpreters of dreams, who explained that Sāsān, or his son, would rule the world. Pāpak then sent for Sāsān and asked him about his ancestors, promising him protection, and Sāsān told him the secret of his parentage. Pāpak was glad and told him to put himself into a bath (*avzano*), clothed him with royal garments, fed him well, and afterwards gave him his daughter in marriage, who bore a son, named Artakhshīr, whom Pāpak accepted as his own son.

[This adoption made Pāpak the lawful father of Artakhshīr, as stated in Sāsānian inscriptions ; but some writers about Nōshirvān's time were still aware that Sāsān was his real father.]

On account of his proficiency in learning and athletic exercises, Artakhshīr was summoned by Ardavān to court when fifteen years old, to be educated with other princes. He soon surpassed them all in riding and hunting, and in such games as polo (*càpigàn*), chess (*catrang*), and backgammon (*nev-Artakhshīr*). But, owing to a dispute with Ardavān's eldest son, while hunting a wild ass (*gôr*), he fell into disgrace, and was sent to work in the king's stables. Here a handmaid of Ardavān saw him and fell in love with him, often visting him in the stables.

One day the king consulted the astrologers, who told him that some servant, who should run away within three days, would soon unite the whole land under his absolute sway. The handmaid told this to Artakhshīr, who induced her to run away with him on horseback with many valuables, in the direction of Pārs. When Ardavān discovered their flight, he pursued them with his troops, and heard from some peasantry that they had passed by, hours before, followed by an eagle which, the astrologers told him, must be the kingly Glory, and, if it overtook them, they would be safe. The next day some travellers told him that the eagle was seated on one of the horsses when the fugitives passed them; and the high-priest said that further pursuit was useless. So Ardavān returned home and sent his son, with troops, to capture the fugitives in Pārs.

[In this episode, there is some doubt whether the animal which personates the kingly Glory is *luk*, "an eagle," or *varak*, "a ram"; the only difference between the two words, in Pahlavi characters, being the initial *va* in the second word, which, in some cases, may be an optional final *o* of the preceding word in the sentence. The doubtful word occurs five times, and in the oldest surviving MS. of the text, from which all other known copies have descended, the initial *va* is certainly absent in three cases, and it may be an optional final *o* of the preceding word in the other two cases. So far, the evidence is in favour of *luk* (=Persian *luh*), "an eagle"; and this reading is further supported by the Zamyād Yasht, 34-38, in the Avesta, which states that the kingly Glory departed from Yima in the shape of a bird, (*meregha*); the first time in the shape of a Vāreghna bird, and this is repeated for the second and third times. Nöldeke has preferred to consider the animal as a ramt, probably because the Shāhnamah uses the word *ghurm*, but some particulars of Firdausi's description of this animal are not quite consistent with the appearance of a ram, such as "a wing like the Sīmurgh and a tail like the peacock." The Zvārish verbs *rehatūn* and *sagītūn*, which are used in the Pahlavi text, appear to be applied to the motion of both birds and quadrupeds.]

The Kārnāmak next narrates how Artakhshīr went on towards the sea-coast, and many of the people of Pārs submitted themselves to him. At one place, afterwards called Rāmishn-i Artakhshīr, a magnanimous man, named Banāk (or Bōhak) of Ispāhān, who had fled from Ardavān, came and joined him, with his six sons and several warriors. Artakhshír ordered a town to be built, and left Banāk and his forces there, while he himself proceeded to the sea-coast, where he built the town of Būkht-Artakhshír and established a Vāhrām fire on the shore. He then returned to Banāk, to raise an army, and, after hard and continuous fighting, Ardavān was conquered and slain, and his daughter became the wife of Artakhshír, who, returning to Pārs, built other towns and constructed various public works.

Collecting a large army, he went to war with Mālīg, king of the Kúrds, in which he was first beaten, but after some wandering he conquered the Kūrds, obtaining much plunder, which was lost in a battle with the army of Haftān-bōkht, lord of the Dragon (*kirm*), who carried it off to Kūiār in the district of Kūzārān (?), where the Dragon dwelt.

Artakhshír had intended to go to Armenia and Ātūrpātakān, where Yazdānkard of Shahrzūr was ready to submit; but he was compelled to stay and fight with the sons of Haftān-bōkht, and was again defeated. Haftān-bōkht had seven sons (hence probably his name), one of whom now came from Arvāstān with reinforcements, Arabs and Mēzanigān, over the sea, and Artakhshír's forces were hemmed in. Mitrōk, son of Anōshakpād, of Pārs, took the opportunity to plunder Artakhshír's capital.

Then Artakhshír departed alone, and came to the house of two brothers, Būrjak and Būrj-ātūr, who comforted him and showed how he might kill the Dragon. But first he marched to Artakhshír-gadā, defeated Mitrōk, and slew him. Then, disguised and with the two brothers, he obtained admittance into the town of the Dragon, and when the creature was about to eat, he poured melted metal into its mouth; when, at a prearranged signal, his troops attacked the fortress and destroyed it. He then returned (home) the second time (*dô bâr*); and his troops came towards Kirmān for war with Pārcān.

Artakhshír had two sons of Ardavān with him, and two others had fled to the king of Kāpūl; these latter wrote to their sister, who was married to Artakhshír, sending her poison, and hinting at the death of her husband being necessary. Upon this hint she thought it her duty to act, and when her husband came in, thirsty from the chase, she handed him some poisoned meal-milk; but they say that the Farnbag fire flew in, like a red eagle, and struck the goblet out of the king's hand with its wing. Both king and matron (*zihânako*) stood confounded, while a cat and dog licked up the liquid and expired. The king sent for the high-priest, and ordered him to take the culprit to the executioner;

she pleaded pregnancy, but in vain. The high-priest, who had already protested, secretly intrusted her to his wife's care, until her son was born, who was named Shāhpūhar ("the king's son"), and he remained with them for seven years; but his mother's fate is doubtful.

One day, while hunting, Artakhshīr was reminded of the child he had wilfully lost, by the devotedness of a pair of wild asses to their foal; and he became so melancholy as to alarm his courtiers. The high-priest, princes and nobles, chieftains and secretaries, all anxiously inquired the reason of his despondency; when the king explained how he had been reminded of the lost child, and feared he had committed a grievous sin. The high-priest then confessed that he had disobeyed the king's orders, and a handsome and accomplished son had been born, who was then produced; the high-priest was richly rewarded, and a city was built on the spot, called Rāyō-i Shāhpūhar ("the splendour of Shâhpūhar").

Afterwards, Artakhshīr became weary of continual wars for consolidating his power, and determined to inquire of various wise Kaits who were soothsayers, whether he was destined to become the sole ruler of Irān. For this purpose he sent one of his faithful dependants to a Kait of the Hindus, to ask him the question to which he replied that the sole ruler of Irān must be a descendant of two families, that of Artakhshīr and that of Mitrōk, son of Anōshakpād. When the king heard this, he was angry, because Mitrōk had been his greatest enemy; so he went to the dwelling of Mitrōk and ordered that his children should all be killed. But one daughter, three years old, was saved alive by the village authorities, and intrusted to a farmer's care, by whom she was suitably brought up.

One day, Shāhpūhar came that way while hunting, with nine horsemen; and the girl, who was drawing water for the cattle, welcomed them to the shade and water. The horsemen tried to draw water, but the bucket was too heavy for them to raise when full of water. Shāhpūhar was annoyed at their want of strength, and went himself to the well and drew up a bucketful. The girl recognized him by his strength, of which she had often heard. Being asked who she was, she first said she was the daughter of the farmer; but, this being disbelieved, she begged protection, and then owned that she was the only survivor of Mitrōk's seven children. Shāhpūhar then married her, and they had a son named Aūharmazd: but all these circumstances were kept secret from Artakhshīr for seven years.

One day, Aūharmazd went to the racecourse with the princes, and was playing at polo (*cúpagán*) with them, when Artakhshīr and his courtiers were present. One of the youths drove the ball so near to Artakhshīr (who took no notice of it) that none of the princes dare approach it, till Aūharmazd advanced boldly and struck the ball back. Artakhshīr asked who the boy was, but no one knew. So Aûharmazd himself was asked, and said he was the son of Shāhpūhar, who was then called, and he stated the circumstances of the boy's birth, and the reasons for their concealment. Artakhshīr was satisfied, and exclaimed: This resembles what the Hindu Kait said."

Afterwards, when Aûharmazd came to the throne, he was able to bring the whole land of Irān back to a single monarchy, and the chief neighbouring rulers became submissive and tributaries. Likewise, the Kaiser, or Emperor of the Romans, the Tāb of Kāpūl, or King of the Hindus, the Khākān of Tūrān, and other chief rulers, from various quarters, came to his capital with courteous salutations.

This statement, which concludes the Kārnāmak, seems singularly inapplicable to the short reign of Aûharmazd I. It is true that his father, Shāhpūhar I, when he came to the throne, some thirty years before, made his son governor of Khurāsān, where he seems to have distinguished himself; but Aûharmazd I actually reigned very little more than one year, a period which could have given him little opportunity of gaining the respect of neighbouring sovereigns. The compiler of the Kārnāmak, in its present form, must either have imagined the congratulations of the sovereigns, or they may have been presented merely as a politic token of respect for the new dynasty, which had once more united the Persians under a single powerful ruler. The deference, which had been really extorted by the deeds of the father and grandfather, might have been readily paid to the son who had succeeded to their power, and might have been expected to live many years. Under such circumstances, the congratulations would have been mentioned in the original records; but that the later compiler of the Kārnāmak, writing some 280 years afterwards, should have attributed them solely to the personal achievements of Aûharmazd I, displays a lamentable ignorance of history.

The extracts from the Shāhnāmah, appended by the editor, correspond very closely with the tale told in the Kārnāmak. Though both the Pahlavi writer and the Persian poet supply some details omitted by the other, they agree in all matters of importance, as if the information of both had descended from the same original.

Regarding the MSS. of the Kārnāmak, it is certain that the oldest one, known to be still surviving, is in the library of Dastur Dr. Jāmāspji Minōcheherji Jāmāsp-Asānā in Bombay. When I copied it, twenty-one years ago, it was the 22nd Pahlavi text in an octavo volume of 142 folios, containing about thirty-three texts, and about one-fifth of the words were more or less worm-eaten. According to its colophon, this volume was written by Mitrō-āpān, son of Kāi-Khûsrôb, who completed it in *agiari* or small fire-temple, at Tānak or Tāmnak,[1] on 10th October, 1322. And at the end of the Kārnāmak text there is a note that it "was written from the copy of Rūstēm Mitrō-āpān." This Rūstēm was a great-uncle of Mitrō-āpān, who also copied the Ardā-Virāf-nāmak, completing it in Irān on 13th June, 1269, and a Vispērad, at Ankalesar, in India, on 28th December, 1278. We have, therefore, good reasons for believing that Rūstēm wrote his copy of the Kārnāmak in Irān, and brought it to India, some time between the last-mentioned two dates, or about 625 years ago. It is also worthy of notice that the Yā*d*kār-i Zarirān, the first Pahlavi text in this old manuscript volume, was likewise transcribed from a copy made by the same Rūstēm.

That all other old MSS. of the Kārnāmak are derived from Mitrō-āpān's copy is evident because they copy several of his blunders, and misread some of his uncouth letters.

Ervad Dūrāb could not obtain access to Dastūr Jāmāsp's old MS., but he probably collated an old copy of it, made in 1721 by Dastūr Jamshēd Jāmāsp Āsā, when the original was in much better condition than it was twenty years ago. His present edition is very carefully prepared, and its general accuracy and convenience will, no doubt, be thankfully appreciated by Parsi students and other readers. The translations will probably be more useful to beginners than a vocabulary would be, as they save time and stimulate thought, when the teacher requires the text to be properly construed.—E. W. WEST.

December, 1897.

www.ingramcontent.com/pod-product-compliance
Lightning Source LLC
Chambersburg PA
CBHW052212240426
43670CB00037B/426